LAWS OF COMMUNICATION

The Intersection Where Leadership Meets Employee Performance

Richard Schuttler, Ph.D.

with

Jake Burdick
and 21 Supplemental Authors

WILEY

JOHN WILEY & SONS, INC.

Book cover photography and graphic design by Sydney L. Rouse.

To order books or for customer service, please call 1(800)-CALL-WILEY (225-5945).

This book was typeset by Black Diamond Graphics, Charlottesville, Virginia.

Printed in the United States of America by Integrated Book Technologies, Inc.

ISBN 978- 0-470-50336-2

10 9 8 7 6 5 4 3 2 1

CONTENTS

FOREWORD

As a linguist, I have spent my life studying the ways in which human beings communicate. A key observation in my studies is that communication is not a send-and-receive process. People simultaneously send and receive messages constantly and filter the content through their own net of life experience. So speaking and talking are not separate events for human beings, and understanding is a matter of aligning the perspectives of those who are trying to communicate.

In short, it's a wonder that we ever communicate at all. Over a long professional relationship and personal friendship with Rich Schuttler, we have had the opportunity to communicate on many occasions, and I am convinced that we actually did communicate a few times. But, much of our bond comes from those times when we missed the mark and had to work to figure out how that happened and what it was the other was really saying. It's in such exchanges that communication really takes place.

And, that is the essence and the value of this book. Good communication is easy to recognize but difficult to replicate. What we learn about communication we learn in large part from bad communication—our mistakes. With any luck we take what we learn and apply it to our next attempts, and sometimes we even get better at it. The goal is to understand how others see the world and rationalize their perceptions in light of our own experiences. We can then establish a common base for interaction.

We employ a variety of tools to accomplish this baseline. A device such as the stoplight metaphor for the stages of communication development is a good example. Another tactic is to take a basic framework, like a set of communication "laws," and see how they apply in different contexts. We are often surprised to find out that communication in the corporate boardroom and the hospital emergency room are essentially the same at the core, but very different when viewed through the lens of experience. It's the ability to integrate and accommodate various perspectives that ultimately leads to communication.

In this book, the authors present communication in several dimensions. It's examined in a variety of professional contexts, for example those of business, healthcare, and education. It's also examined in light of its relationship to individual and organizational performance. In still another dimension, the interaction of words and behavior are examined as part of the human condition. What we learn in the end is that communication is somewhere in the intersection of content and context. The contributing authors demonstrate effectively that the whole that we recognize as communication is more than the sum of the parts. Much of the enterprise of communication is dedicated to the management of content and negotiation of worldviews. Yet, throughout this endeavor, communication has an integrity that pervades.

Bill Pepicello, Ph.D.
President, University of Phoenix

PREFACE

The premise of this book resides in a simple belief that employee and organizational performance correlates directly with how supervisors communicate with their workers. The fundamental outcome of this book suggests that to improve organizational communications, workplace relationships must be cultivated and groomed. This is a book for leaders at all levels, with or without the title, to understand how they can be better at what they do and how to improve performance.

This book in essence is a prescription to achieving full potential—individually or organizationally. I contend that the manner in how we collectively educate people about communicating is flawed. This book provides new insights to the essence of organizational communications that also parallels many aspects of how people communicate everywhere and with everyone in their lives.

Often it is falsely noted that technology has increased the ability to communicate. While it might be true that technology offers the opportunity to enhance an organization's ability to communicate, it rarely has, and has mostly provided new vehicles to abuse worker relationships and to send mixed messages. This book takes a practical view of what it takes to improve the manner in which people communicate and the effect of doing that well or not so well.

Purpose of the Book

The purpose of this book is to provide a simple, yet unique, *stoplight* metaphor (red, yellow, green) that illuminates how the *Laws of Communication* govern relationships between employee performance and a leader's approach. The stoplight model provides common qualities of performance based on how a supervisor communicates to subordinates. The stoplight colors of red, yellow, and green signify how best to understand and approach communications.

Red = Danger: Failure to stop could be hazardous for all.

Yellow = Caution: Concern is warranted; danger is looming. Be prepared to stop suddenly.

Green = Continue: All is fine; continue, but remain aware of potential hazards.

The Laws of Communication suggest:

1. A correlation between how a supervisor communicates with the subordinate (one-to-one) and the subordinate's resulting performance.

2. A correlation between how the organization communicates with all employees (the organization to all employees) and the organization's resulting performance.

Why This Book?

For all that has been written and spoken about communicating effectively, few ever do. The plethora of material has resulted in a lack of being able to communicate across a distributive workplace environment whether that is a one-to-one basis or collectively from the organization to its employees. Common statistics suggest that the number one reason employees quit their jobs is due to poor relationships with their supervisors. This book helps to serve a vital need—a better understanding of the performance results of employees based on the relationships they have with their organizational leaders.

This book serves an immediate need to provide insights to employees at all levels to better understand what they can do to affect change in a positive way. The concepts provided in the *Laws of Communication* and in the supplemental chapters suggest examples in three different zones (red, yellow, and green) that correlate performance based on how employees are communicated to.

In the *red zone*, team morale, communication, and performance is low, the team does not work well together, and turnover is high. In the *yellow zone*, communication is better than in the *red zone* and the team has some success but also has some failures and struggles with maintaining consistency on the team. In the *green zone*, team morale, communication, and performance are high, the team works well together, and employees want to work in this environment.

The Laws of Communication can be used to train senior leaders, mid-level leaders and managers, and all other employees. The Laws provide governing rules with clear cut lines between danger (*red zone*), risky leadership (*yellow zone*), and success (*green zone*). Given the exposure, the information in this book will provide immediate and long lasting improvements.

Features of This Book

This book is designed to provide a simple yet critical grounding in the realities of how workplace supervisors influence worker performance. This is provided in a variety of figures that highlight the types of worker performance one can expect based on how supervisors and organizations communicate their intentions and expectations.

This book contains a unique international collection of supplemental contributions from 21 authors who are subject matter experts in their professions. They represent a variety of industries, businesses, and countries. Each provides a perspective of how the Laws of Communication have manifested themselves and are found in different settings. Often the supplemental authors provide "best practices" for others to consider adapting.

Finally

The one perspective that holds true from the *Laws of Communication* and from the authors of the 21 supplemental chapters is that communicating effectively comes from well-developed relationships. For without trust and respect, no matter what is communicated, it will not be received well. The fundamental aspects of workplace communications have far less to do with grand mission statements, ideal market conditions, desires to serve a customer, or the need for one's professional advancement, but with how one person treats another as well as how an organization's culture is aligned.

Note: Stoplight Colors for Figures

In the black and white print copy of this book, the red, yellow, and green zone colors are not able to be seen. In the ebook, one will see each area colored accordingly. Color copies of all graphs are available at the author's web site **www.lawsofcomm.com** and at the publisher's provided web site for faculty and students at **www.wiley.com**.

ACKNOWLEDGEMENTS

I would like to acknowledge the 21 supplemental chapter authors from around the world who believed in this project and graciously found time in their busy schedules to relate their experiences to this project. Their expertise, individually and collectively, adds value and dimension to the *Laws of Communication.*

Several contributors have been friends for years; I hope all will be friends for life!

The Foreword is provided by Dr. Bill Pepicello, President of the University of Phoenix. I would like to acknowledge his insightful introduction to this book. His support and belief in my abilities has come through in humor and heartfelt jests over the years—mostly humor!

Thank you to Jake Burdick, co-author and editor. I always felt we made a great team despite the fact that we should both get an award for being patient with one another!

DEDICATION

I have been more than fortunate to have great people to look up to that unknowingly provided examples for me to learn from and emulate. My United States Navy shipmates of 23 years allowed me to succeed despite my own failings and short-sightedness at times. The Navy made a man out of a city boy—a gratitude I can never repay but I was gladly willing to give my time to them in exchange for what they gave me! The men and women in the military simply are the "best of the best."

My academic friends and colleagues always found more in me than I still find in myself. Perception is powerful when it works to one's own advantage! The University of Phoenix and Upper Iowa University provided a proving ground for me, a soapbox to learn and talk from. I hope I have done them as well as they have done for me. Those who can teach—do! And those who do it well make the world a better place than we found it…a task that is never easy, even if it looks like it is.

My friends from all walks of life, from Robby and Larry to Gary, Sandi, and Ruby, who have helped to keep me grounded yet at times, I realize they have no idea how I have been able to accomplish whatever measures of success that God has blessed me with. The reality is neither do I. The real blessing has always been them in my life—not me in their lives.

My family unknowingly created someone who grew to appreciate what they tried to instill in me. In the case of my father, who was not able to see me grow beyond my 11th birthday, we'll have a discussion one day—one that would have taken me a lifetime to experience. My biggest cheerleaders have always been my mother and sister—they really have been two constant sources of love and encouragement.

ABOUT THE 21 SUPPLEMENTAL AUTHORS

Dr. Kelly Preston Anderson is married and has three daughters. He teaches religion on the high school and collegiate levels, travels as a motivational speaker for Brigham Young University and provides leadership training for elementary and secondary schools. Dr. Anderson holds a Bachelor's degree in Mandarin Chinese, a Master's degree in Education, and a Doctorate degree in Management and Organizational Leadership. Dr. Anderson's doctoral dissertation was named the top-selling dissertation of 2005 and the third best-selling dissertation of 2006 according to ProQuest. He is also the author of *Excellence in Leadership: 8 Skills for Leaders of All Ages.*

Website: http://www.excellenceinleadershiponline.com

Dr. Tom Box is a Professor of Strategic Management at Pittsburgh State University. His Ph.D. is from Oklahoma State. From 1980 to 1984 he was Senior Vice President of Operations at Southwest Tube Manufacturing Co. From 1984 to 1990 Tom was on the faculty of the University of Tulsa. He joined the PSU faculty in 1990. He has more than 75 journal and proceedings publications and five books. He is a member of the Academy of Management, the Allied Academies and the Society for Advancement of Management. He is also President of his own consulting firm, TMB & Associates.

Website: http://www.pittstate.edu/mgmkt/box.htm

James J. Casey, Jr., Esq. is Director of Contracts and Industrial Agreements at The University of Texas at San Antonio. He has worked in university research administration since 1994, and past affiliations include Northwestern University and the University of Wisconsin-Madison. He has held significant positions within the National Council of University Research Administrators (NCURA), including membership on the Board of Directors and Editor of the *Research Management Review*. A licensed Wisconsin attorney since 1990, his academic credentials include: B.A., *cum laude*, University of Wisconsin-Whitewater; M.A., Marquette University; M.P.A., University of Dayton; and J.D., University of Dayton School of Law (member, *Dayton Law Review*). His contributing chapter was written when he served as a Visiting Professor of Leadership at Upper Iowa University, Hong Kong, China.

Dr. Carolyn M. DeLeon is the Vice-President of Human Resources in a regional acute care hospital employing more than 2000 healthcare workers. She is responsible for the operation and strategic development of the hospital's human resources functions. She is part of the senior leadership team and provides key leadership for organizational development, performance improvement and employee engagement. Dr. DeLeon holds an MA in Communication Sciences from San Jose State University and a Doctorate of Management in Organizational Leadership from the University of Phoenix. She is the author of *Dawning of a New Day: A Journey Out of Darkness: Life Lessons to Help You Through Grief.*

Website: http://www.dawningofanewday.com

Dr. Julia East is the President and CEO of the National Standard-compliant Southwest Florida Community Foundation (www.floridacommunity.com) with 315 endowed funds, $56 million in assets, and a five-county service area as well as two affiliate community foundations. Responsible for the overall operations of the foundations, she works with a Board of Trustees and two Advisory Boards comprised of over 80 community members. One of her primary roles is community liaison, requiring keen communications skills. Dr. East holds an M.S. in Communications from Clarion University of Pennsylvania and a Doctorate of Management in Organizational Leadership from the University of Phoenix.

Dr. Mark Esposito is an Organizational and Sustainability expert and focuses on sustainable change and leadership in all facets of organizational and human performance. He currently works as Professor of Management & Behavior for Grenoble Ecole de Management and as Professor of Management for the International University of Monaco. He currently also serves on the faculties of two world-ranked business schools, such as ESCP-EAP, European

School of Management and U21 Global in Singapore. He is co-author of the book, *Sustainable Future of Mankind*, with several other illustrious academicians and consults in the area of sustainability worldwide.

Website: http://www.mark-esposito.com

Karen Fong graduated from Loma Linda University with a BS in Medical Technology. She received her MBA from California State University, San Bernardino. Later she received ASQ Certification as a Certified Quality Auditor and a Certified Quality Manager/ Organizational Excellence. In 2004, Karen participated in the Hawaii Award of Excellence, a state level Malcolm Baldrige program. In 2006, Karen was selected as a National Malcolm Baldrige Examiner. In 2007, Karen was selected to be a Judge for the ASQ Team Excellence Program. She is a volunteer inspector for two lab accrediting agencies: AABB and College of American Pathologists.

Dr. Alice Gobeille has over 13 years experience working in manufacturing as a Quality Director and Six Sigma Master Blackbelt. Her specialty is global implementation of Quality Management and Six Sigma programs for Fortune 500 companies. Dr. Gobeille has a Doctorate of Management in Organizational Leadership from the University of Phoenix and two Master's of Science degrees in Quality Systems and Six Sigma Management from the National Graduate School in Falmouth, MA. Dr. Gobeille is a statistics and project management Professor at the University of Phoenix and The National Graduate School. She is President of Stratagems, LLC, where she assists business leaders with their strategic growth through executive coaching, Six Sigma training, and project launches.

Dr. Bernd Heesen, Professor of Management at the University of Applied Sciences Ansbach/Germany, is a leading expert in the field of Management Information Systems and Business Intelligence. His expertise is based upon a rich experience as an executive at SAP SI America and as an entrepreneur. Dr. Heesen has published his work in a variety of journals and has presented at conferences. He was selected by the SAP University Alliances as one of the international experts in the field of Business Intelligence. In this function he developed a curriculum and conducts faculty workshops for universities in Europe and the U.S.

Website: http://www.heesenonline.de

Gerald Huesch is one of the world's leading authorities on leadership. His specialty is to align and guide corporate management levels towards a global agile organization, mastering company critical endeavors like major restructurings, pre- and post-merger integrations, and spin-offs. Gerald's delivery is profoundly practical, empowering, joyful, and inspiring. He was nominated in 2007 for the German Speaker Hall of Fame. As the President and CEO of the Global Leadership School, he lectures at various business schools globally. His motto is: *"If you want the WHAT, see the Harvards, the McKinseys or the libraries; if you need the HOW, go to Gerald Huesch.*"

Websites: http://www.linkedin.com/in/geraldhuesch
http://www.Global-Leadership-School.com

Francisco J. Melero provides consulting, training, and coaching in organizational and personal performance excellence. Areas of expertise include leadership, management, facilitation, quality systems (Lean Six Sigma, Malcolm Baldrige, ISO 9000), and information technology. Mr. Melero's career includes domestic and international experiences with large organizations as well as entrepreneurial ventures, government, and non-profit agencies. Francisco believes in cultivating long-term relationships with clients, and that becoming a trusted advisor is not fostered through transactional activities but through transformational partnerships. Mr. Melero is a passionate student of many fields and is pursuing his Doctorate of Management in Organizational Leadership from the University of Phoenix.

Website: http://www.melero.com

Dr. Michael Nanna graduated from Wayne State University with a B.A. in Psychology, a Master's degree in Education, and a Ph.D. in Evaluation & Research. He later completed post-doctoral training in Educational Leadership & Policy Studies at Arizona State University before serving as a Policy Analyst in the Office of the Senior Vice President at ASU. He currently teaches at Wayne State University and the University of Phoenix, as well as working as an independent research consultant. He is a devout practitioner of martial arts and yoga and works part-time in law enforcement as a Reserve Police Officer.

P.S. Perkins is the Founder & CEO of the Human Communication Institute, LLC dedicated to Communication Management Training. A Professor of Speech Communication, she is a 20-year veteran of higher education. Her newest publication is *The Art & Science of Communication: Tools for Effective Communication in the Workplace*, Wiley Publishers, released May 2008. P.S. is a featured practitioner in the new motivational film, *Pass It On!*, as well as a featured writer for *Personal Development Magazine*. A graduate of UNC-Chapel Hill and New York University, she is currently pursuing her Doctorate in Organizational Leadership and Change with Walden University.

Website: http://www.hci-global.com

Dr. Chris Roberts is a Professor of Strategic Management in the Department of Hospitality and Tourism Management, Isenberg School of Management, University of Massachusetts, Amherst. He has eight years of hotel industry experience and has owned and/or operated a travel agency for another eight years. He also has eleven years of corporate marketing and sales experience with the Bell Telephone System. Dr. Roberts has published widely with more than 45 publications in academic journals and industry publications. He has given more than 50 presentations at conferences and seminars. His research focus is on the strategic decision-making process.

Email: Q@mgmt.umass.edu

Dr. Jack Roose is a Human Capital Consultant with Watson Wyatt Worldwide in their Honolulu Office. Jack specializes in the areas of designing total compensation strategies supporting the direction of an organization; variable pay programs including team-based and individual incentives; executive compensation; and performance appraisal. Jack also focuses on improving organizational effectiveness through organizational assessments, employee surveys, and action planning; strategic planning and organizational design; and the applications of service excellence / total quality management. Jack has been with Watson Wyatt for 23 years. Prior to joining Watson Wyatt, worked 12 years in the corporate functions of a large insurance company and a large financial services organization. He has been an active participant in the Baldrige-based Hawaii Award of Excellence, from serving on the original design team to training examiners and facilitating the judging process. He has a Ph.D. in Industrial/Organizational Psychology from Bowling Green State University.

Dr. Ruby A. Rouse has over 17 years experience working as a director of marketing for various organizations, including a million dollar dental practice in South Texas as well as a private investment firm in San Antonio. Her current research focuses on the Supervisor Communication Inventory (SCI), a diagnostic tool she developed based on the first *Law of Communication*. Having held a variety of leadership positions in business and higher education, Rouse is a lead faculty member at University of Phoenix's School of Advanced Studies where she facilitates doctoral level courses. Her publications specialize in marketing, research, communication, and healthcare, including articles in the *Journal of Behavioral Medicine*, *Journal of Leadership Studies*, *Health Marketing Quarterly*, *Health Communication*, and *Journal of Professional Services Marketing*. Rouse holds a Bachelor's degree in Journalism from Texas A&M University, a Master's degree in Speech from the University of Houston, and a Doctoral degree in Marketing Communication from the University of Connecticut. More information about Dr. Rouse and her research is available at the website below.

Website: http://drrubyrouse.googlepages.com/index

Paul Ryder has worked in the Telecommunications industry for 15 years. Paul is currently the operations lead for a product development organization launching a new wireless broadband technology. He is a recognized leader in the Program Management and Product Development disciplines. Paul has held director-level positions in program management, product development, strategy, and operations. Paul's access to executive leadership has provided him with valuable insights into how many of the largest Telecommunications firms develop, communicate, and implement strategic direction. Paul has a Bachelor of Science from the University of Maryland, an MBA from Loyola, and is currently pursuing his doctoral degree at the University of Phoenix.

Dr. Michael Stewart, formerly a trader/salesperson for JPMorgan Chase in New York, now oversees a middle office team that provides special services to institutional clients across the globe. Michael has more than fifteen years experience in investment banking in the bond markets. Michael recently accepted the position of youth director with a local church in Montclair, New Jersey to help shape the lives of children for the 21st century. Michael received his Bachelors Degree in Accounting and his MBA in Finance from Rutgers University. He earned a Doctorate of Management in Organizational Leadership from the University of Phoenix.

Dr. Warren St. James received a B.S. in Psychology from Morehouse College, Master's in Education from American Intercontinental University and his Doctorate of Management in Organizational Leadership from the University of Phoenix. While working on his doctorate, he became part of the management team at Delta Airlines, where he remained for almost 30 years. During that time, Warren received numerous nominations for the highest organizational award presented to an employee—Chairman's Club and the designation of Distinguished Toastmaster. Post Delta, Warren became part of the leadership team of Alumni Association Network with the role of "Director of Leadership and Organizational Culture" for postgraduate students. His management initiatives involve mentorship, coaching, and facilitator extraordinaire. Warren is heavily involved in management organizations such as The American Management Association; Worldwide Association of Business Coaches, Academy of Management, International Coach Federation and American Society of Training and Development.

Dr. Kelley M. Waugh has been a registered nurse in Las Vegas, Nevada for the last 20 years. Her experience includes neo-natal, pediatric, and adult care, in both critical and non-critical venues. Dr. Waugh has also been instrumental in the role as nurse manager for the VA Healthcare System, and has taught nursing leadership and communication classes in both the organizational and academic arena. Dr. Waugh holds a Masters in Nursing and a Doctorate of Management in Organizational Leadership from the University of Phoenix. Dr. Waugh is also a faculty member at University of Phoenix, where she continues to facilitate health sciences at both undergraduate and at the graduate level. Her professional memberships include: Sigma Theta Tau and the Cambridge Who's Who for Academic Excellence in Healthcare.

Dr. Karina A. F. Weil is a teacher, writer, researcher and consultant with over 18 years of experience in human resources in cross-borders South America and U.S.-Asia Pacific leading consulting organizations. In the 1990s, her awareness of the import of speech in business outcomes took her to Europe and Asia to educate herself on the concepts of intuition, intentionality and manifestation through the power of verbal communication. She later taught techniques for self-awareness and self-empowerment through sound to international audiences. She communicates in seven languages. Currently, Karina is one of the forerunners in the field of assisting executives and leaders to position themselves as personal development and spiritual leaders in the business world.

SECTION 1
Defining the Laws of Communication

CHAPTER 1
THE LAW OF COMMUNICATION: CORRELATING PERFORMANCE TO COMMUNICATION

Richard Schuttler

> ***Communicate, communicate, communicate, and then communicate just a bit more!***

Communicate, communicate, communicate, and then communicate just a bit more! This simple motto appears to be easy, yet it's difficult to do. Why don't we communicate effectively, especially when we've been communicating our entire lives? Some researchers even say that we were communicating before we were born as we were kicking and pushing in our mother's womb. But a quick review of any organization struggling to preserve a productive workforce that is both effective and efficient often reveals poor communication as a common element of despair.

The *Law of Attraction* suggests that we attract or get what we think about. And, the *Law of Cause and Effect* suggests that for each cause there is an effect that influences something else. The *Laws of Communication* provide that individual and organizational performance can be correlated to how supervisors and the organization as an entity communicate to workers and other stakeholders. If organizational leaders plan and purposely communicate effectively, they could easily cause performance to increase. What follows are two laws of communication and how they reveal themselves in organizations.

The role of every leader and supervisor in an organization is to communicate vision, mission, intent, and philosophy. In an ideal workplace, communication is regular, clear, effective, and active rather than missing or strained. Great communicators have common qualities that contribute to their strong communication styles.

Once we see these qualities, we can begin to copy them and incorporate them into our own skill set. We may have our own heroes who are or were great communicators. These heroes might be parents, grandparents, pastors, teachers, mentors, sport heroes, or coaches. Often, we admire popular political figures who capture our attention with their passion and their forthright conviction to their message.

Beyond politics, world leaders and business executives often referred to President Ronald Reagan as "The Great Communicator." His communication style was effective, and often he was able to encourage people to *see* his vision, which included a better reality than they were living, simply by suggesting "the best is yet to come." In fact, the eulogies provided for the former president consistently stressed his communication skills. Several of the statements made at his funeral are collected in the following table:

Table 1.1. Communication Characteristics of President Ronald Reagan

Made easy jokes with reassurances	Always maintained grace under pressure	Turned enemies into friends
Was candid, yet often had tough words	Exhibited gentlemanly conduct	Gave a clear invitation to a new beginning
Put humility before honor	Held straightforward convictions	Avoided bigotry and prejudice
Was politely-stated	Loved a good story	Conveyed strength and gentleness
Possessed steadiness and calm	Maintained cheerful confidence	Exhibited elegance and ease
Demonstrated inspirational conduct	Offered humor and laughter	Acted on behalf of values and ideals

These characteristics were credited to one person, yet they are common to many leaders and managers who create an atmosphere that allows people to work together for a common purpose by providing a vision that is practical and achievable. A great communicator has the ability to create a shared vision that attracts others to a cause. In part, a "cause-strategy" is designed to allow followers to realize there is more than the need to conduct business by creating working relationships based on mutual trust and respect.

Common communication characteristics can be learned and applied with an awareness and opportunity to practice. Newly promoted supervisors and seasoned organizational leaders can easily learn to communicate effectively when they gain confidence in their roles. Like any skill, practicing effective relationship building and communication skills will lead to great levels of success and increase confidence. This confidence can result in less conflict by the simple virtue of clarity of thought in both verbal and written dialogue.

What Happens When Leaders and Managers Fail to Communicate Effectively?

Survey results from the *2004 Economist Intelligence Unit* reported that out of 276 senior executives in the United States and Canada, only 43% rated their companies as successful or very successful at carrying out strategic initiatives over a 3-year period. The executives cited communication between senior management and frontline employees as the biggest challenge to ensuring proper execution—and, interestingly, they also noted that this part of the business was "the most important to get right." In 2005, Kaplan and Norton noted that, on average, 95% of employees are unaware of, or do not understand, their organization's strategy. This statistic should be concerning, as it's the frontline workers who communicate directly to an organization's customers.

According to a North American study of CEOs conducted in 2000 by Ipsos-Reid, 94% of Chief Executive Officers agreed that communication is a strategic management role that contributes to the success of their organizations (Moorcroft, 2003). Yet, many organizational assessments suggest that there is disparity between how senior leaders, midlevel managers, and frontline workers assess communication.

Collectively, these statistics are consistent with supporting literature that details the symptom of ineffective organizational communication throughout all industries and in organizations that are small, medium, and large in size. It is the role of an organization's senior leaders to ensure that effective communication is achieved and maintained.

Benchmarking High Performing or Best in Class Businesses

To make this point even more clearly, benchmarking *high performing* or *best in class* businesses hints at the qualities that reflect a successful organization's culture.

Table 1.2. Qualities of high performing organizations

Open and renewed communications	Feedback regular and constantly sought	Multiple vehicles of communication
Corporate citizenship	Shared strategic focus	Seamless influence
Continuous improvement	Vision and mission lived	High morale
Customer-focused	Low absenteeism	Entrepreneurial spirit
Trustful environment	Little confusion	Two-way communications
Visible leadership	Active customer participation	Clear focus on priorities

Organizational leaders have responsibility for and accountability to influencing employee performance. In fact, how well a leader or manager performs in two aspects of communication can determine the effectiveness of employee performance. These two aspects of communication can be found in the workplace:

1. A correlation between how a supervisor communicates with the subordinate (one-to-one) and the subordinate's resulting performance.

2. A correlation between how the organization communicates with all employees (the organization to all employees) and the organization's resulting performance.

Accordingly, when a leader tries to effect positive change in how an organization communicates, the first area to address is the manner by which communication occurs between supervisors and subordinates and how this communication impacts individual performance. The second area is how communication occurs collectively within the organization and how that level of communication relates to overall organizational performance. To give leaders even stronger incentive to address organizational communication in their strategy, this book restates each correlation as a law—an absolute necessity in the development and productivity of organization. The *Laws of Communication* state the following:

The Law of Communication #1:

Failure of supervisors to communicate effectively with subordinates results in poor employee performance.

The Law of Communication #2:

Failure of the organization to communicate effectively results in poor organizational performance.

Using the metaphor of a stoplight to highlight different stages of communication development, the remainder of this chapter illuminates how the *Laws of Communication* describe relationships between employee performance and a leader's approach, as well as how well senior leadership and midlevel managers communicate with frontline workers. The stoplight visual provides common qualities of subordinate performance based on how a supervisor communicates to or with subordinates, with the colors red, yellow, and green signifying how best to understand and approach communication at each level:

Red = Danger

Failure to stop could be hazardous for all.

Yellow = Caution

Concern is warranted; danger is looming. Be prepared to stop suddenly.

Green = Continue

All is fine; continue, but remain aware of potential hazards.

The chapter breaks the *Laws of Communication* down according to these color codes, focusing on how leaders might begin to address communication problems in different scenarios. Ideally, these insights can be used to diagnose and evaluate communication problems, as well as to devise strategies that will enhance overall organizational performance by improving the way people in the organization talk to each other.

The Law of Communication #1: Failure of supervisors to communicate effectively with subordinates results in poor employee performance.

The inability of a supervisor to communicate effectively with one, or all, subordinates can result in employee confusion. The outcome can be a stressful work environment that adversely impacts productivity and employee retention. Resulting employee behavior often reveals itself in resistance to change and resentment toward organizational leaders. As such, it is a supervisor's responsibility to communicate with each subordinate clearly and effectively.

Red = Danger: Failure to stop could be hazardous for all.

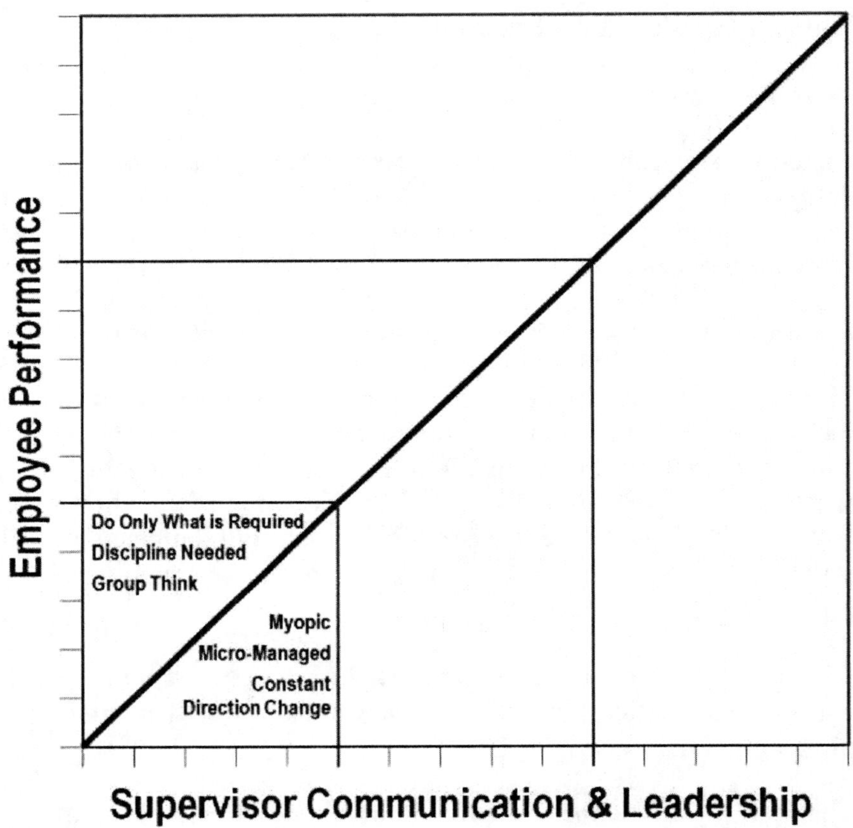

Figure 1.1. Law of Communication #1—the red zone

Managing in the *red zone* tends to require regular employee discipline. In such a situation, employees only do what they are told, and groupthink restricts innovation. Supervisors or managers operating from the *red zone* are often myopic in their perspectives. They fail to notice ways to promote better working conditions, and they tend to micromanage subordinates. Supervisors might also lack consistency, changing policies and procedures before any one method or process can be carried out and become routine.

In such a workplace, employees and supervisors are likely to be adversarial, and morale and productivity are characteristically low. Talented employees seek employment elsewhere, and regular turnover becomes the nature of the business. If labor unions are involved, they have likely filed complaints based on how management is treating employees. In manufacturing, poor cycle times and increased scrap is the norm. In service industries, customer needs are discarded, and service is slow and sloppy at best.

Characteristics of the *red zone* are often symptoms of a larger problem, such as a poor organizational culture or supervisors who are not trained to lead and manage people and processes. Communications from supervisors who are managing in the *red zone* elicit unhappiness from employees. Often, employees find no reason to perform any better than they are, and they may locate everything that is wrong in the organization's leaders. Consequently, the "blame game" is often reflected in communications between workers and supervisors.

Teamwork is uncharacteristic of the *red zone* unless it is to suboptimize the organization for the advantage of the employees at the cost of the organization. In this zone, workers are slow in their work and purposeful in trying to get overtime for their own self-interests. Still, employees do not care for one another, and attempts at setting up workplace self-direct teams are unsuccessful.

Mediocrity and despair trump talent and hope when an organization and its employees are stuck in the *red zone*. Worse yet, if an organization manages in this zone for too long, attempts to bring in new people to effect a positive change will be met with resistance rooted in employees' lack of trust. A change of attitude and consistency over time can move an organization from the *red zone* into the *yellow zone*, but often not without a complete reorganization and the implementation of an entirely new vision and mission in conjunction with all stakeholders. Senior leaders may need to be replaced to move from the *red zone* as they may have failed to identify and correct the root of the problems.

Yellow = Caution: Concern is warranted; danger is looming. Be prepared to stop suddenly.

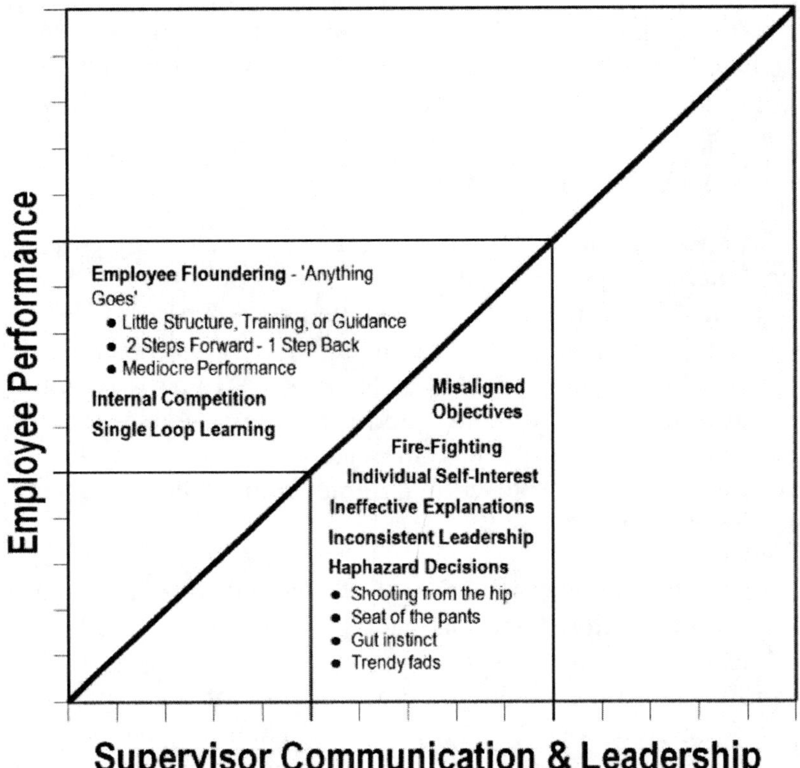

Figure 1.2. Law of Communication #1—the yellow zone

Managing in the *yellow zone* suggests that employees are faring better than those in the *red zone*, but progress may continue to be challenging and tenuous. Signs of success emerge, but they are often overshadowed by other failures of higher severity or even workplace accidents. Competition for limited resources may exist between different groups within the organization and even among employees in the same work unit. Employee turnover in this zone is less prevalent than in the *red zone*, though still a concern as the best talent will not stay long. Morale is not sufficiently high and should be of concern to senior leaders and managers.

When operating in the *yellow zone*, employees continually manage processes within design limits, but they will likely fail to take ownership of these processes. Thus, while some improvements may be noted, senior management's involvement is necessary to spur deeper, lasting changes. If new ideas are introduced by employees, they may be mere copies of popular business fads or failed approaches that were once trendy, such as "moving cheese" or "fish" artifacts. In the *yellow zone*, single-loop learning may be applied during "on-the-job" training, but employees will lack motivation to go beyond the basics to improve their overall performance. Lack of consistency in leadership and management is often the cause. Signs of double-loop learning may emerge; some processes may be improved but not enough that the improvements are contagious to other departments.

The *yellow zone*'s most noticeable qualities are reflected in supervisors, managers, and organizational leaders' cautious approach. Supervisors share some familiarity with their employees and interest in making working conditions better, but they have not found a way to be consistent in their own work habits and how they communicate with their subordinates. Processes and procedures are either too complex or poorly provided. "Fire-fighting" tends to occur without reflection on the cause of each instance, and the same problems are doomed to flare up time and time again. As a result, workers may lose faith in their supervisors, who themselves may be too sensitive, taking employees' work ethics personally and reacting to problems without considering root causes or incorporating input from the workers.

In the *yellow zone*, workplace teams can meet with mixed levels of success. Teams may be formed to solve a problem or improve a process, but little structure, training, or guidance is offered. Teams in this zone tend to struggle and never achieve the "performing" stage of teamwork where a consistently high-level of progress is achieved. Attempts at change by supervisors and senior leaders stem from good intentions, but they are applied in a manner not conducive to gaining higher levels of performance.

An average company, even one maintaining consistent profit margins, may become stuck in the *yellow zone*. Such an organization fails to reach world-class status because it lacks consistency of purpose. The most talented employees will often leave this workplace because they will have no problem finding new employment opportunities. For organizations working within the *yellow zone*, employee turnover is usually above 10% yearly.

Green = Continue: All is fine, continue, but remain aware of potential hazards.

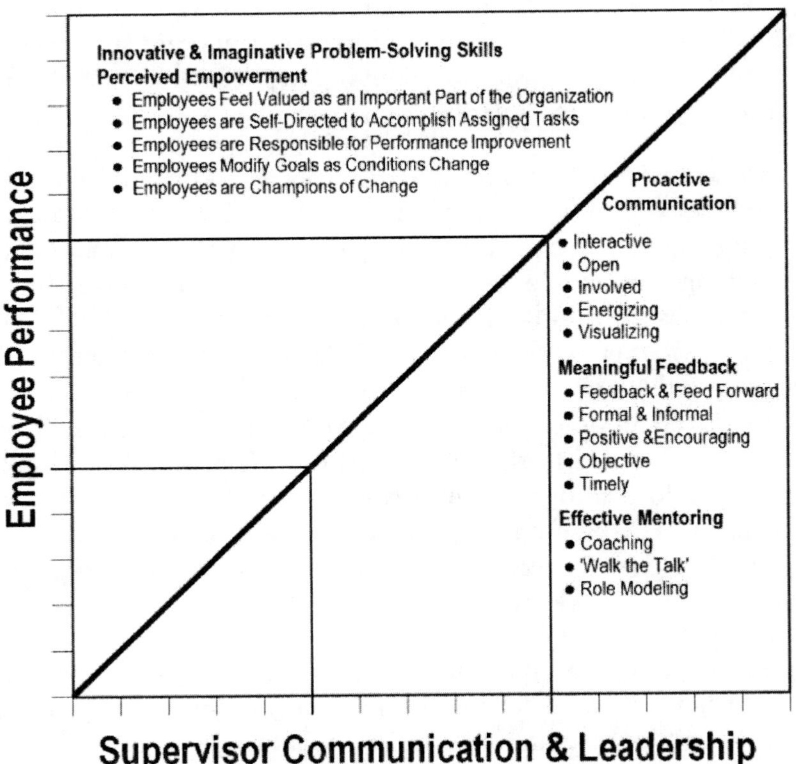

Figure 1.3. Law of Communication #1—the green zone

Managing in the *green zone* indicates that human talent is being maximized and that the organization is leading its industry. Employees and leadership at all levels are well aligned and sustained success is noticeable. When in the *green zone*, cycles of refinement are noted, and managers and workers bring positive attitudes and refined skills to all aspects of their work.

Employees of organizations managing in the *green zone* are open to new ideas and change. Also, these employees are more likely to incite change based on their knowledge and ownership of the process. Employees need not rely solely on senior management to provide motivation; rather, high morale spurs employees to work together and perform efficiently on their own.

In the *green zone*, employees are often self-directed and skilled in problem-solving. They have the confidence to make informed decisions that result in creative and innovative improvements. Employees of these organizations are customer focused. They are not saddled with incremental change, but are motivated to implement large-scale change efforts and socialize the change plan to all stakeholders to ensure greater levels of success. Employees in the *green zone* understand how to maximize limited resources and have a grasp for multiple management methods to gain measurable results. Data-based decisions are noticeable at all levels.

Leaders, managers, and to a large extent, employees are active in business decision making when managing in the *green zone*. Employees interact within their work units and throughout the company as well as with appropriate stakeholders. The organization tends to enjoy a work culture characterized by openness and trust. Senior leaders communicate face-to-face and via other methods such as e-mail, posters, or the Intranet, delivering consistent messages that are also reflected in their actions. Meaningful and objective feedback occurs at all levels of the organization and is considered positive.

Above all, the *green zone* is distinguished by how well the leaders communicate, and their willingness to be involved is especially noteworthy. Coaching and mentoring appear to be routine, as communication tends to help others become better employees. Employees talk with one another to the benefit of all. Employees enjoy working with one another, and they tend to go home at the end of a workday looking forward to returning to the workplace the next day. Those businesses managing in the *green zone* have employees who know that they are valued.

Companies that manage in the *green zone* frequently win industry-related awards or state and national quality-based awards, such as the Malcolm Baldrige National Quality Award and the International Team Excellence Award. These are the world-class companies that others will model. Hardworking employees with good attitudes represent the work culture of *green zone* organizations. Performance excellence at all levels is high, and the organization is continuously undergoing cycles of improvement and refinement to preserve and continue success.

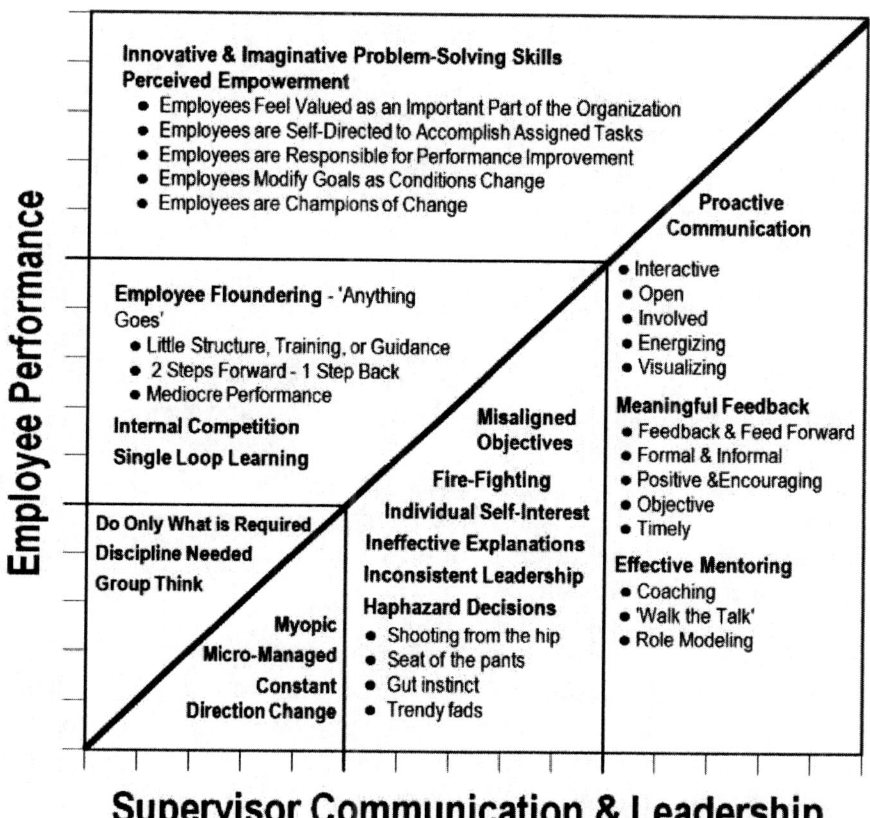

Figure 1.4. Law of Communication #1—all zones

Summary

The manner in which supervisors communicate with their subordinates determines work performance. Employees look to their supervisors at all levels for clear direction, consistency, and encouragement to move in a common direction. The first *Law of Communication* provides a quick glance at common attitudes and behaviors associated with how supervisors communicate. Strong leaders who communicate well are rewarded with loyal and relentless followers.

The first *Law of Communication* offers a three-tiered approach for working toward improved communications. The Law provides an opportunity for organizational leaders to assess how they communicate with their direct reports and where their organization is placed within the model. By doing so, these leaders get a chance to self-reflect on communications for which they are ultimately accountable.

Midlevel managers can then assess what zone (red, yellow, green) they believe their senior level leaders are communicating from. These midlevel managers can also assess how they see their own communication habits with their subordinates and peers. Areas of difference, gaps, or disparity in views can become focal areas for improvement and increased awareness. This level of reflection provides a detailed view of those charged with carrying out policy and procedures in addition to those who directly control and manage organizational resources.

Finally, frontline workers can also evaluate what zone (red, yellow, green) they believe their manager is communicating to them from. If appropriate, the frontline workers can also evaluate how organizational leaders communicate with the midlevel and senior leaders. From this unique perspective stems one of the most important aspects of the Law's application. In most organizations, it is the frontline worker that communicates to or provides the quality of product or service to the customer. As such, this Law strongly suggests that frontline workers' assumptions and beliefs should be identified to ensure they have all the correct information needed for positive customer interactions.

This *Law of Communication* should not be confused with a 360-degree feedback model; there is no direct feedback to one person about his or her abilities, skills, or intentions. However, this Law can help members of an organization identify common communication traits and correlate these characteristics with individual performance. The assessment allows for gaining perspectives from all levels of an organization so that disparities can be identified and gaps in understanding addressed and narrowed. In the end, the organization will bolster individual performance by improving the way in which its members communicate.

The Law of Communication #2: Failure of the organization to effectively communicate results in poor organizational performance.

The first *Law of Communication* displayed the possible organizational consequences of upper- and midlevel management's failure to communicate effectively with their direct reports. The second *Law of Communication* describes the critical role of an organization's communications to its stakeholders—in particular, its employees. This second law provides an enhanced perspective on organizational culture, based on how organizational communications are managed. Many times, organizational culture is identified by the manner in which employees communicate and the types of performance the company produces.

Organizational performance is the noticeable output of how each employee performs his or her job. A work environment that is not based on mutual trust, timely and accurate communication, and socialization of change breeds fear, rumors, and wrong opinions among all constituents. Like the first Law, the second *Law of Communication* also employs the stoplight metaphor, using red, yellow, and green to suggest the communication climate between an organization and its stakeholders.

Red = Danger

Failure to stop could be hazardous for all.

Yellow = Caution

Concern is warranted; danger is looming. Be prepared to stop suddenly.

Green = Continue

All is fine; continue, but remain aware of potential hazards.

Red = Danger: Failure to stop could be hazardous for all.

Figure 1.5. Law of Communication #2—the red zone

When organizations are managing in the *red zone*, leaders, supervisors, and managers are authoritative in their approach. Communication is specific, one-way, and offers little, if any, supporting information about the message being sent. The intent of most *red zone* communication is to tell others what to do, when do it, and how to do it. The message may even appear to be threatening to some subordinates who believe that they will be disciplined, or even fired, if they ask for clarifying information or do not perform exactly as prescribed. Communications in this zone are job and task related only. Supervisors do not appear to be interested in developing working relationships with subordinates, and, even if they were, these relationships would likely be rejected.

Work performed by employees in the *red zone* must exact stipulations from policy, standard managing procedure, or verbal instructions. Workers are not encouraged to do anything different from what they are told to do, and often, an employee could be ridiculed or disciplined, by supervisors, managers, and even peers, for trying to change. Many employees in this zone are only working for the company because they need the job and cannot find a better one.

Organizational morale is low for companies managing in the *red zone*. Turnover may be high if employees are able to find work elsewhere. Otherwise, employees begrudgingly stay with the company until fired or until it goes out of business. Organizations become trapped in the *red zone* when complacency sets in or when unions are unwilling to work closely with management to create a favorable work environment for all stakeholders.

Organizations managing in the *red zone* should not be confused with yellow or green organizations that follow strict procedures and policies out of need. Employment in a nuclear power plant, for example, provides little opportunity (and rightfully so) for workers who want to perform outside of strict policies and procedures. In this case, results could be catastrophic if employees arbitrarily initiate process improvements. The complexities of organizational performance extend beyond the three zones offered in these Laws, yet these models offer insight based on observable employee and organizational traits as well as organizational qualities in the manufacturing and service industries.

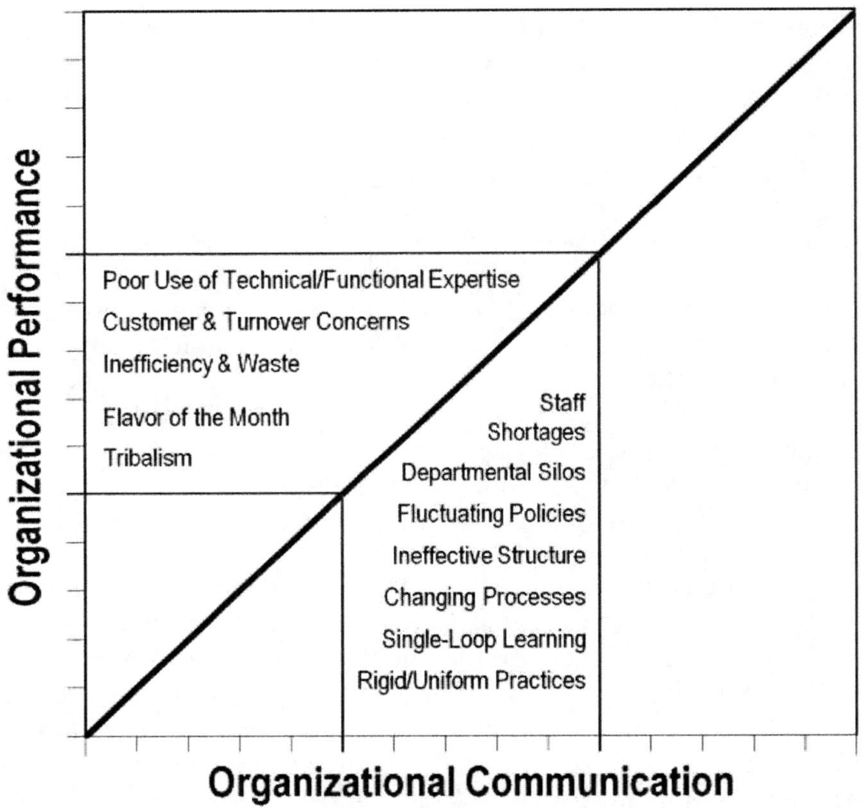

Figure 1.6. Law of Communication #2—the yellow zone

In the *yellow zone*, organizational communications tend to be confusing. Communication might lack the directive nature characteristic of the *red zone*, but messages are neither confident nor consistent. Newer leaders and managers project a lack of confidence because they might not know much about the company or the areas they are responsible for overseeing. Frontline workers are painfully aware that these supervisors and managers lack willingness to learn from them, even while struggling to meet organizational objectives.

For organizations managing in the *yellow zone*, the *Peter Principle* is alive and well for many supervisors who have "attained their highest level of competence" and have been promoted beyond that to a position in which they are not capable. Their level of past success limits their self-awareness and blinds them from seeing opportunities for improvement. As a result, these supervisors may eventually be "let go" or they may become lost in an organizational restructuring. In the worst-case scenario, they are assigned to another part of the organization, doomed to fail there as well.

Whereas more daily communications and exchanges between supervisors and subordinates might occur in the *yellow zone* rather than the *red zone*, the information is fragmented and usually inaccurate. Supervisors may hoard their knowledge as if competing with their peers. This behavior quickly suboptimizes the organization and its capacity to manage limited resources needed at all levels.

In the *yellow zone*, policies tend to change regularly because there is no consistency in supervisors, processes, or frontline workers. This inconsistency contributes to lack of learning, and customers begin to experience reoccurring problematic outcomes. An organization communicating in the *yellow zone* over a significant period of time usually tends to go out of business, or if any of its strategic business units offer value, they are extracted and sold off to another company. Decision making in this zone tends to be more reactive then proactive, as corrective efforts are tried only to make up for market share or loss of customers.

Organizational performance in the *yellow zone* tends to be problematic; as good employees come and go, so do customers. Organizations stuck in this zone will experience a culture where members are willing to do better but are never actually given the opportunity. Talented people leave not because they want or need better jobs; rather, they leave because their supervisors do not listen to them or validate their contributions.

Talented employees of organizations that remain in the *yellow zone* might try to introduce new and valid change. However, when they are not supported or encouraged, they frequently decide to go elsewhere—to companies that appreciate and utilize their talent. High turnover results in inconsistency and a "flavor of the month" approach to positive change. New strategies may be sound, but they are not applied long enough to effect positive results.

With high rates of turnover, talented employees tend to move quickly from technical positions to management without proper training or experience. Accordingly, organizations often make the false assumption that an employee who did a great job leading 5 subordinates can do the same for 50. This common mistake can severely hurt the careers of individuals who cannot make this drastic transition successfully.

Based on levels of rework or waste, such as customer-returned items, it's easy to discover whether manufacturing companies are managing in the *yellow zone*. Customer complaints may go unheeded if an organization lacks satisfactory collection methods or analysis, and correction is more difficult to achieve once a loss of customers is reflected in quarterly balance sheets.

The culture of an organization in the *yellow zone* is ambiguous. To some it looks optimistic; to others, it is frustrating. New and talented employees may be ready to make a difference, yet mixed, inconsistent, and even incoherent messages are common.

Green = Continue: All is fine, continue, but remain aware of potential hazards.

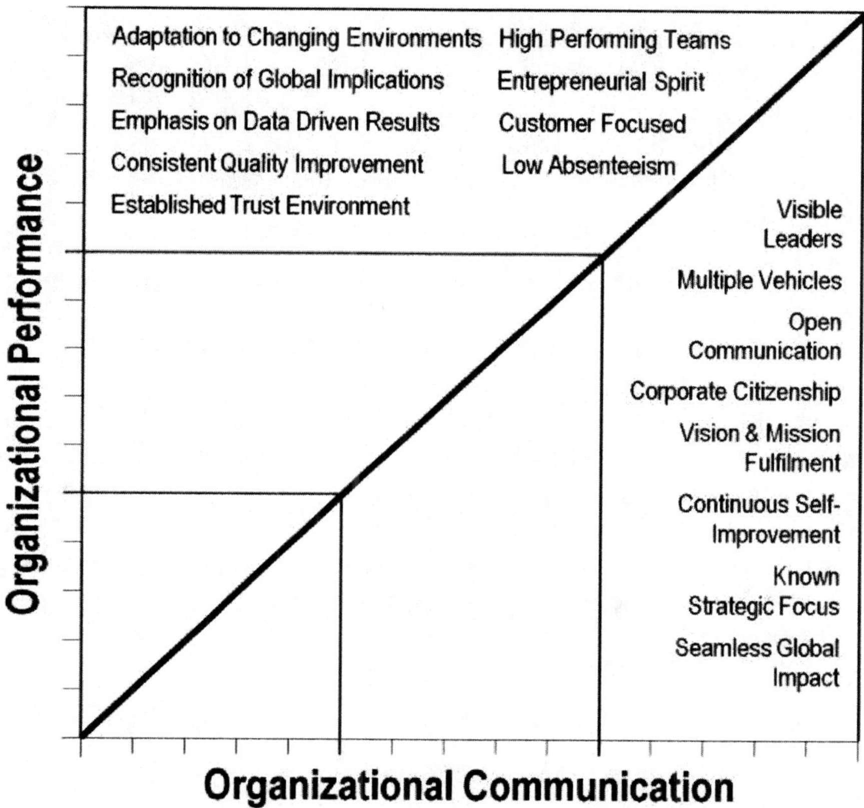

Figure 1.7. Law of Communication #2—the green zone

The most noticeable aspect of organizational communication within the *green zone* is a clear sense of purpose. This clarity can only be achieved when leaders and employees at all levels of an organization know the mission and vision and how they contribute to them. The employee is aware of the organization's purpose because communication is consistent and brought to life through such avenues as town meetings, social events, posters, or customer feedback.

In organizations that manage in the *green zone*, communication is delivered by leaders who are visible and who maintain high levels of commitment and morale. Leaders tend to communicate strategic intent in a manner that attracts followers to buy in and assume accountability and responsibility for their share of the plan. Leaders not only communicate their sound strategies but also deliver follow-up results from previous strategies. As such, leaders and managers at all levels create the path, and then walk down the path alongside employees.

The organizational culture representative of a *green zone* company communicates confidence and enthusiasm for employees at all levels and for all stakeholders. These organizations have a positive impact on all other organizations involved in their supply chain and to all internal and external stakeholders. Managers operating in the *green zone* will not be perfect in every sense, but they are open to discussing opportunities for improvement—whether these suggestions come from frontline employees, new managers, or even suppliers or vendors. Proactive communications with customers are common as the organization seeks feedback to better its product or service.

Organizational performance in the *green zone* might be metaphorically compared with a "well-tuned machine." Each part of such a machine is optimized and functioning at high levels. The machine is oiled, and its user knows what to expect—steady output and easy operations. World-class *Fortune 500* organizations, such as the Ritz Carlton, display qualities as noted in the *green zone*. These organizations have perfected their customer service approaches and treat all stakeholders as employees are expected to treat their guests, like "ladies and gentlemen."

Self-directed and high-performing teams characterize organizations managing in the *green zone*. Trust throughout these organizations is high among all levels of employees. These companies are agile and able to innovate as needed when change is dictated by the competitive landscape. Processes have been refined to become efficient and effective, and data from these processes are used consistently to make decisions throughout the organization.

When managing in the *green zone*, organizational learning is continuous. Double and triple loop learning is evident. Employees listen to the customers and look for ways to offer them new and better products or services. Customer and employee turnover is low. In fact, talented people apply for jobs in these companies and are willing to come in at lower levels if they are given the ability to work their way up through the organization.

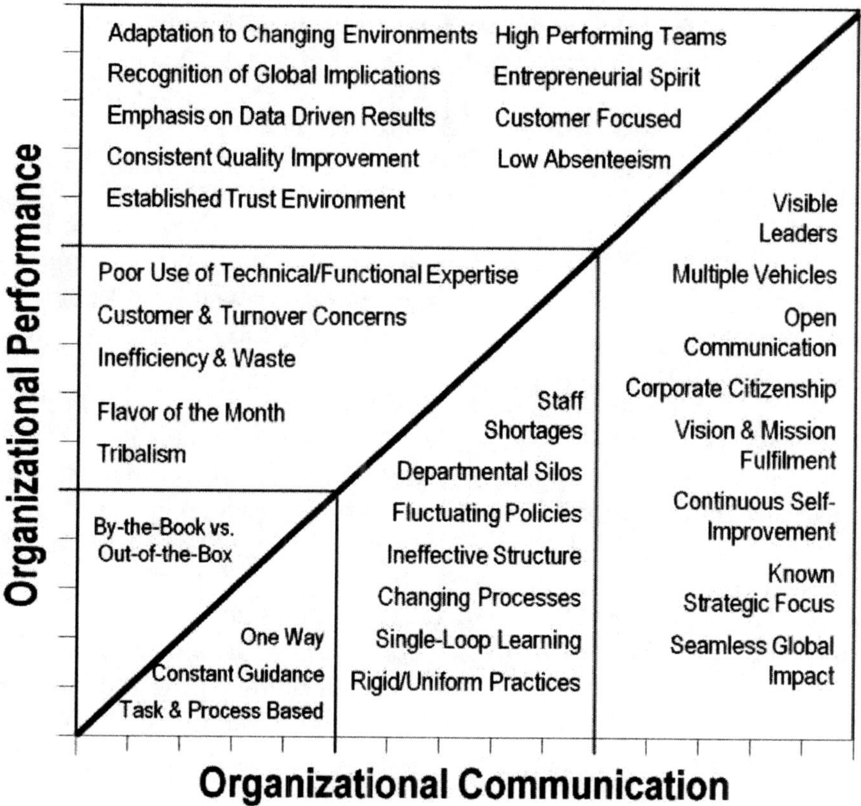

Figure 1.8. Law of Communication #2—all zones

Summary

The manner by which an organization collectively communicates is one of the main drivers for how well that organization can and will perform. Decisions and actions will differ based on whether the organization is struggling to make a return on investment or keeping or gaining market share. Struggling organizations may reorganize often because they lack a structure that will expand and collapse with the market. Reorganizations tend to be associated with secrecy, layoffs, and the elimination of strategic business units. In contrast, increased morale and productivity is both the cause and effect of clear communication, all of which consistently builds trust between the organization and its employees.

Using Law #1 and Law #2 as Diagnostic Tools

It is not uncommon that senior leaders, midlevel supervisors, and frontline workers experience a difference of opinion in how an organization is functioning and communicating. In struggling organizations, senior leaders may falsely sense that they are communicating in the *green zone* whereas subordinates see this communication as stuck in the *yellow* or *red zones*. The rationale for these radically different opinions might be related to the fact that more senior leaders are removed from the day-to-day functions of managing a business. Clearly this hierarchical structure contributes to an organization's propensity for miscommunication.

Both *Laws of Communication* describe employee work performance based on the *Law of Cause and Effect* of how employees believe their supervisors communicate with them. These models can be used as diagnostic tools by conducting an inquiry between any of the following:

- Supervisor and individual subordinate
- Supervisor and all subordinates

- Division supervisors and all subordinates
- Department supervisor and all subordinates
- Senior leaders to all subordinates
- Senior leader to all subordinates

An assessment between an individual supervisor and his or her subordinate will offer two points of data. One point will be how the supervisor believes he or she is communicating with an individual subordinate. The other data point will be how the subordinate sees his or her work based on how the supervisor communicates. Using the *Laws of Communication* model, the differences can be identified, and steps can be taken to align views and improve communication so both individuals can eventually align their perspectives and begin to work in the *green zone*.

A supervisor can conduct the same assessment with more than one subordinate. Then, all data points can be aggregated and differences noted. Using this data, organizational leadership can take steps to align the expectations and views of all subordinates and their supervisor. This process can improve communication, morale, and productivity.

Finally, this assessment approach can be distributed to all employees at all levels. In this manner, the Laws can be used to decide how each employee (senior leader, midlevel manager, and frontline) sees communications and to compare these findings. Each diagnostic application affords a *snapshot* view that is critical to identifying opportunities for improvement or targeting areas within the organization that require increased attention or different kinds of interventions. The assessment and sharing of the information can invoke the *Law of Attraction,* identifying a result that becomes the object of the organization's collective energies.

One of the worst things that can happen to an organization is the presence of poor communication and resulting poor employee performance. However, once leaders and followers are aware of communication issues, the organization can make plans to improve challenging areas and identify strengths that can be applied as best practices for the organization. Various tools are available to identify and standardize communication processes, ensuring that communications, like any other organizational process, can function efficiently and that employees will be led and managed for success. The *Law of Attraction* and *Law of Cause and Effect* have inherent tools of their own that, when applied and practiced, can quickly improve how employees and organizations communicate and dramatically increase the performance they achieve.

Conclusion

Related research indicates that successful communication between employees results in increased satisfaction and morale. Best practices and organizational benchmarking reflects that, when organizational leaders manage and lead communications as a process, organizations experience decreased levels of anxiety and stress along with rising productivity and job satisfaction. These same organizations report greater levels of employee commitment, declines in absenteeism, and decreased employee turnover. Organizations often fail to carry out successful change for two reasons: lack of openness from leaders and failure to recruit subordinates when executing business strategies.

The *Law of Attraction* and the *Law of Cause and Effect* combined with the *Laws of Communication* produce a process consultation perspective that results in a prescription of increased communicational awareness. The increased awareness then provides processes and tools to manage the communication processes and influence individual and organizational efficiency and effectiveness.

Organizations stuck in the *red zone* are doomed to remain problematic, and those stuck in the *yellow zone* will continuously struggle with higher-than-average turnover rates. Organizational cycles tend to follow movement from zone to zone. In the *red zone*, lack of efficiency and effectiveness causes organizations to struggle to stay in business. In the *yellow zone*, organizations are either in the process of climbing from the bottom of a cycle or heading there after being in the *green zone* for some time. However, organizations managing from the *green zone* are world-class, and other organizations can learn from their benchmarking and best practices.

Employees who interact and cooperate with one another and supervisors who give these employees attention are essential to improving productivity and achieving efficiency. The ability to communicate may be the most important leadership quality for individuals who supervise employees. Also, employees who communicate well are good followers. Improving communication within the workplace may cost little, but the return on investment can be huge. All it takes is a little time from people who care.

**Communicate, communicate, communicate,
and then communicate just a bit more!**

CHAPTER 2
SUPPLEMENT CHAPTERS: COMMON THREADS AND THEMES

Richard Schuttler

The supplemental chapters that begin with chapter 3 provide perspectives on how the *Laws of Communication* operationalize in a variety of industries and business. Each chapter is provided by a different subject matter expert with years of experience in their field. Their collective work provides revealing commonalities of problematic organizational communication as well as success stories worthy of emulation and elevation to "best practices."

Whereas there are areas of concern regarding how employees communicate, there are also examples that reflect how current problems might be viewed as future opportunities, allowing for movement from a *red zone* to a *yellow zone* or from a *yellow zone* to a *green zone*. Areas for improvement in the supplemental chapters suggest a lack of *relationship development* between how leaders manage their organizations, as well as how they supervise their subordinates. Accordingly, the supplemental chapters describe easy to learn approaches to immediately improve how employees treat one another. The final chapter of the book also provides several *how to* approaches for improving organizational communications.

Also, among the supplemental chapters, there exists a diversity of new and bold approaches applied and developed by successful leaders in world-class organizations to overcome some of the very challenges described in this book. Table 2.1 provides several approaches advocated in the supplemental chapters. What may be a true and tried philosophy or principle in one discipline is now being adapted and applied to improve organization communication skills and abilities in other settings across industry boundaries.

Table 2.1. Approaches Promoted in Supplemental Chapters

By-Laws of Respect	Meta-Communication
By-Laws of Manifestation	Butterfly Effect
Open Book Management	Slow Versus Fast Learning Companies
Employees as Partners	Language as a Tool
Leadership Rounding	Therapeutic Communication
Amateurism	Organizational Acculturation
Assessments	

The contributors of the supplemental chapters offer practical, yet sensible, information and solutions for anyone regardless of their organizational position—*leader*, *manager*, or *front-line* employee. Whereas the chapters' authors intentionally focus on professional workplace settings, many of these concepts are just as important in one's private life as well. The better one communicates at home and when on the job, the more likely they will achieve greater degrees of success.

Fundamental organizational communications books, especially school textbooks, provide a basic communications *model*. Most communication models originate from the classical metaphor of how people communicate—sender, message, receiver, and feedback loops. In essence, these simple theories are only primers for entry-level workers or young supervisors to gain a fundamental understanding of how people communicate. In discussing organizational communication problems, what is needed more than ever before is a better understanding of how to develop better working relationships. Communicating effectively is far more complex than the simple *sender-receiver* model, as it involves real people with actual needs, wants, and differences. A better understanding of how to approach others and what to be concerned with when communicating would seem to be more important than a model that offers little mention of the increasing complexity of organizational communications in an information-based economy. In essence, what comes into focus throughout this book is that effective communication is an effect of good working relationships.

Themes Found Throughout the 21 Supplemental Chapters

Trust

The most common thread in the 21 supplemental chapters relates to *trust*. Employees must be able to trust their supervisors and co-workers just as senior leaders must be able to trust their employees. Additionally, an organization must collectively communicate to all stakeholders in a confident, consistent, and regular manner to achieve success. Trust is a quality that is earned. Under the *Laws of Communication*, trust is like a two-way street: without trust in one direction, subordinates do not believe in their supervisors, and without trust in the other direction, senior leaders are paranoid about their workers. Trust is an important part of any relationship—professional or otherwise. With trust, followers will listen to leaders and complete any assigned task. Without it, relationships are likely doomed to failure.

High-performing, talented employees will not remain with the same company for long if they do not believe they can trust their co-workers. Trust unites people working together for the common benefit of all. Additionally, trust can relate to how employees feel with regard to how well they will be taken care of by organization policies and procedures. As discussed by Stewart (supplemental chapter 8), "failure to effectively communicate will hinder the change initiative, create uncertainty in the workforce, and cause the departure of highly skilled employees."

Trust in one's coworkers and in one's employer is critical in times of uncertainty. Leaders and supervisors who are visible and who practice open communication can help to improve and build trust. One method to improve employee trust is to consider the *Open Book Management* (OBM) approach highlighted by Tom Box (chapter 4). Box suggests that with an OBM approach, trust is improved via open, honest dialogue about shared business strengths and opportunities for improvement, as well as open discussion regarding the degree to which the business is successfully managed. OBM begins with training employees and making available all the operational and financial information it takes to manage and measure organizational success. This information could exist in terms of financial statements, revenue and expense reports, employee turnover percentages and costs, and other business performance measurements. When this information is shared, employees soon become aware of critical business factors and how their work impacts the organization as a whole entity. This approach does take an initial, likely difficult change effort, but like any other new approach, the time and effort expended is worth the expense in the long term.

Several comments from the following supplemental chapters related to trust are:

- There are a number of specific activities or initiatives that have been shown to increase trust in senior leadership. (Roose)

- Information as a key resource and asset to implement a defined strategy has certain characteristics that should be leveraged by the management. (Heesen)

- When divergence of opinions in the organizational leadership is not reconciled, it can have negative repercussions to the organization because breakdown in communications and consequent disappointment lead to employees' commitment, trust and effective teamwork based on cooperation decline. (Weil)

- Open Book Management demands an environment of trust between employees and management. (Box)
- Communication from leaders and managers will not alleviate uncertainties in the environment, but an informed workforce will experience less stress and have more trust in management. (Stewart)
- The improvement culture breeds trust and loyalty in the department between the leaders and subordinates. (Gobielle)
- The nurse functions as a trusted confident, educational resource, and sounding-board. In times of stress, patients trust that the nurse will help them understand and help them regain control. (Waugh)

Visibility

Another frequent theme within the supplemental chapters is *visibility*. Employees want to see their supervisors and leaders in their daily roles within the organization. Additionally, employees want to be involved in regular dialogue with their supervisors, as well as experience a sense of ownership in improving processes and fixing problems. Good relationships are established from trust as well as visibility. It is difficult to communicate with others that are disengaged or absent. It is also difficult to be a good supervisor if the approach is to lead and manage from behind a closed office door.

Everyone is busy, but are some leaders so busy that they cannot occasionally dialogue, appreciate, and socialize with their subordinates? The best leaders are those individuals who develop proper relationships with their colleagues and employees, and the best organizations have visible leaders. This does not mean daily appointments, or time set aside every Tuesday afternoon, but rather visibility involves an honest effort by leaders to be seen and heard throughout the organization. The term *walk the talk* comes from the notion that leaders display commitment to their words and live by the policies they set forth. Further, positive visibility must be displayed in all actions, including e-mail, memorandums, meetings, and casual conversations—regardless of the audience at hand.

It is easy for some leaders to remain behind closed doors in big offices and not to take time to walk around the facility to talk to employees. Unfortunately, leaders who close themselves off in this fashion do not enjoy the same levels of success in both the tangible and intangible aspects of work. Coaching and mentoring, as described in several of the supplemental chapters, suggests the importance of relationship building. Reflections from world-class organizations indicate that employees are committed to the organization's mission and strategies when their leaders are visible and consistently embodying the organization's philosophy, mission, and vision.

Several comments from the supplemental chapters that relate to visibility are as follows:

- Many of the informal communication strategies used by a hospital organization can demonstrate leadership and visibility and model the values of the organization. (DeLeon)

- In order for community foundations to fulfill their missions, they must exhibit *green zone* behaviors including visibility, being strategically focused, and communicating with elected officials about their vital role in the well being of United States citizens. (East)

- Leadership should be visible and supportive across these three communication methods in facilitating change in the daily functioning of the organization. (Stewart)

- Leaders must be visible across the organization if they are to get successful buy-in of the vision. (Stewart)

- Unable to perceive what was required of them, employees sauntered around the office as automatons reacting to the most menial and routine tasks, such as scheduling an appointment with clients to discuss a staffing strategy, in a knee-jerk-like manner. (Weil)

Education

Another important recurring theme in the supplemental chapters relates to employee education. This should not be a surprise, but many struggling businesses do not offer encouragement, incentives, or financial support for educating their workforce. The more educated an organization's supervisors and subordinates become, the more capacity they hold for improving processes and achieving greater levels of efficiency and effectiveness.

Education can come in the form of academic preparation (university degrees) as well as on-the-job training and corporate universities. Academic work teaches one to learn how to be a better citizen, understand current business paradigms from an interdisciplinary lens, and create improved models for visualizing and solving the complex problems. On-the-job training offers employees opportunities to be better at what they were hired to do by improving their knowledge, skills, and abilities, as well as their ability to learn and adapt. Cross-functional training also helps employees to gain an understanding of the complexities of the overall business, its stakeholders, and its customers.

Education makes it easier for employees to deal with conflict and to solve challenging workplace and private problems. These two skills alone can help employees communicate effectively and better work towards continually improving processes. Self-correcting organizations are frequently characterized by a workforce that operates on trust and competence, but also by a strong disposition toward life-long learning and continual self-improvement. Enhancing the education of employees allows for the refinement of critical thinking skills. The more confident employees are, the more apt they will be to recommend changes, improve operations, and better customer relationships.

Several comments from the supplemental chapters that relate to educated employees are:

- Ongoing communication and training is vital for success. (Box)
- Once an organization establishes a solid foundation of training toward cutting cost and increasing revenue through planning, the next step would be to incorporate training to include your most valuable asset: frontline employees. (St. James)
- Managers receive formal training in interpersonal communication skills. (Roose)
- Competing agendas, family and domestic issues, emotional or psychological problems, health issues, low job satisfaction, lack of confidence, improper training, lack of respect for senior leaders, and personality conflicts all work to further impede and even worsen an already tenuous situation. (Nanna)
- Employees must also receive training on the financial statements. (Box)

Change

Creating an agile and adaptive, as well as forward thinking, organization requires a certain culture that is not commonly found. This culture is accepting and willing to change to remain competitive, even if that change produces uncertainty and ambiguity. In fact, these traits are not only uncommon in organizations, they are not inherent in most people. People tend to gravitate to what they know, believe, and trust—after all, these are the things that made them successful in the first place. Fear of the unknown produces stasis, and few people move too far from their comfort zone if there is risk of future uncertainty.

Most leaders will agree that business planning is easy—all you need is a great team of motivated and competent senior managers to design a brilliant strategic plan. The natural next step would be for these same leaders to follow through with these wonderful plans. Unfortunately, the reality sets in that the plan is far easier to design than to implement. In many situations, senior leaders or managers lack the leadership and communication skills to convince their employees to buy into the plan, or in other instances there is no clear chain of accountability to measure successful outcomes or develop protocols for process improvement. Eventually, the ball is dropped, and the changes do not occur. Worse yet, the plan *is* implemented, but without clear, open communication between leaders and their employees. A supervisor can tell a subordinate what to do, how to do it, and when it needs to be done, but rarely does this micromanagement approach execute well. And if it does, results are typically short term at best.

Some say that "the good is the enemy of great," suggesting that good enough is never enough. Communicating effectively means opening oneself and one's organization to the change process. If a workforce does not trust its leaders and managers, any change effort will be doomed. Change is personal to all those involved—from changes to the parking lot to the development of a new philosophy for enhancing customer satisfaction. The need for change can be the motivation that gets a business started in operating in new ways, but the proliferation of quality communication keeps the change going. Several comments from the supplemental chapters that relate change directly:

- The facility must communicate how they have fulfilled the requirement, or how they are going to change their practice to fulfill the requirement, or even that they have no idea of how to fulfill the requirement! (Fong)

- The key to creating a more successful organizational culture and improve communication within an organization is to be attentive in maintaining those areas of proficiency and also be open enough to change and correction in their *yel-*

low zone that they migrate to the *green zone* rather than decline to the *red zone.* (Anderson)

- Evaluating the communicative structures and pathways within an organization is an essential step toward identifying existing problems and is a first step toward instituting effective change strategies. (Nanna)
- But change is usually scary and threatening because it involves the unknown, the risky, and the uncertain. (Weil)
- Conduct employee opinion surveys or focus groups as part of a change effort. (Roose)
- The more educated a company's workers, the more able they are to do the "little things" necessary to improve the company. (Box)
- Employees are the collective assets that help the organization achieve its vision, and they need to be informed of impending changes. (Stewart)
- Some of the employees were gifted communicators and should have been deployed in much better conceived positions, rather than being considered threats to the apparent order YXV was so keen on defending. (Esposito)

Mentoring / Coaching

Today, coaching and mentoring are popular ideas that are often dismissed as a fad. Yet we see that Marshall Goldsmith, one of the best of the best in terms of management thought, gets outstanding results while providing a great return on the investment for his coaching services (as discussed in his recent book *What Got You Here, Won't Get You There*). Most admit the complexity of running a business, especially in the role of Chief Executive Officer, Chief Financial Officer, or Chief Information Officer, is practically a 24/7 job. The list of what keeps executives up at night is growing as legal, environmental, and humanistic concerns continue to increase. So, why is there any hesitation to ask for personal mentoring or coaching as a means for improving performance and communication?

The answer becomes painfully clear when we examine the reasons why many individuals in leadership positions fail. They are not able to self-reflect or self-assess in a manner that allows them to move beyond their highest level of competence. The *Peter Principle*, as disclosed by Lawrence J. Peter, suggests that employees reach their highest level of competence, then promoted just beyond the range of their experience and skills. Clearly, the Peter Principle is alive and well in most aspects of business and society. Particularly in business, this phenomenon is visible when others begin to question the role and achievements of an existing leader. In business, people are promoted based on their *prior success*, a rationale that resembles driving a car while only looking in the rear-view mirror. When failure occurs, it becomes abundantly clear that these leaders had reached their highest level of competency in their prior position, but were promoted beyond these abilities. We have all seen incompetent people in leadership roles who themselves wonder how they ever were given the job.

Unfortunately, these glaring examples of the *Peter Principle* never sought out a coach or mentor to help them become more self-aware and to learn how to self-assess based on what is happening to and around them. This myopia can also be a failure in part to senior leaders who fail to see the benefit of assigning a mentor to newly promoted executives. Mentoring and coaching only work for individuals who are open to feedback and look at criticism—good or otherwise—as a gift. Mentoring and coaching programs work for people who themselves can mentor well and are willing to be mentored. Furthermore, trust must be inherent in an organization's culture for mentoring and coaching to be effective.

One excellent example of mentoring's ability to produce results occurs during doctoral candidates' completion of their dissertation. A doctoral dissertation is a research project that is much like the workplace—messy, subjective, tedious, and intense. The dissertation research process usually takes over 2 years. A mentor (often called a Dissertation Chair) guides the doctoral candidate through the process. If the mentor is well trained in aspects of the research method and some basic psychology, and wishes to see the mentee achieve success, together they can create a significant, publication-worthy research project. Consequently, if the relationship is strained, breakdowns in trust, respect, and communication tend to occur, much like in the workplace.

The process of organizational and personal improvement is often daunting. Within any change initiative, one must first address flaws in their organization and/or themselves. This knowledge can produce a kind of *cognitive dissonance*, displayed as negative behaviors, such as denial, apathy, and even emotional paralysis. To gain the necessary knowledge and readiness for positive and effective change, leaders often need a positive and open mentoring relationship. This external, objective perspective can help leaders accept the difficult information gained in self-analysis and use this information to achieve levels of success beyond their greatest expectations.

What so many organizations need are individualized and intentional relationships in which organizations and employees are empowered to achieve their full potential though various self-regulating techniques and regular interaction with a mentor. By focusing on a short list of prioritized dimensions, leaders can identify approaches for developing a healthier self-balance, improving their ability to manage their organizations through change processes, and better managing their personal reactions to leadership issues.

Several comments from the supplemental chapters relate to mentoring and coaching:

- As an effective coach and mentor, she consistently upholds a philosophy of giving meaningful and objective feedback. (DeLeon)

- Coach, teach, or guide them. (Huesch)
- The President was made aware of her problems and utilized a coach to stop her from the constant change of direction. (Fong)
- Among some of the initiatives that have helped increase trust in senior leadership are coaching senior leaders in behaviors supporting core values; improve the "walk the talk." (Roose)
- More concise and effective communication is a clear need for improved productivity on the personal and institutional level. (Casey)
- Obviously, through their sincere interest to hear the employees' input, they show respect but, even more so, they inspire respect. (Weil)

Attentiveness

At an executive leadership retreat, Larry Bossidy (author of the book *Execution: The Discipline of Getting Things Done*) asked a simple, yet profound, question: "*When did leaders decide they didn't want to know?*" This question made many people stop in their tracks and question whether they were avoiding the necessary awareness that came with the accountability and responsibility of their roles.

Enron might be the best example of the answer to Bossidy's question. When Enron's CEO failed to recognize what was occurring in the company, his lack of acknowledgement, leadership, and communication with shareholders ultimately led to the demise and bankruptcy of one of the largest corporations in the United States and engendered new regulations and harsher penalties for white collar crime. How long before Enron collapsed were there signs that it was a *house of cards*? How long did leaders fail to pay attention?

Attentiveness goes far beyond providing pay raises and a cafeteria-style health benefits plan. Attentiveness can be a supervisor listening to subordinates who have ideas for improvement. Being attentive often is not so much about doing more work as much as it is being in tune to the work that is ongoing. Being attentive is often displayed by taking feedback from subordinates and using it to make the workplace more efficient and effective.

Attentiveness is being proactive, not reactive, to what is going on inside the walls of a business as well as outside among the stakeholders. Dell Computers temporarily lost its ability to be attentive when the CEO who replaced Michael Dell redirected the company's focus from customer service to reducing costs. This new focus triggered a spiral decline of the superior customer service for which Michael Dell established as his company's key differentiation from the competition. The problems inherent in this kind of change in focus can reveal themselves in many ways—an increase in customer complaints, sizeable equipment returns and warranty work, higher employee turnover, falling stock prices, and a multitude of other key business indicators and symptoms.

The failure to pay attention is often not realized until it is too late, and the organization must change its strategic focus, get lean, and prepare to cope with the turbulent market in which leaders now find themselves. Much like successful people who fall victim to the *Peter Principle*, disaster often results when businesses fail to be able to self-reflect, self-assess, and self-correct in a timely manner—or at all.

Several comments from the supplemental chapters that relate to being attentive are as follows:

- The key to creating a more successful organizational culture and improve communication within an organization is to be attentive. (Anderson)

- Sincere and attentive listening was required and, at a minimum, would have certainly improved relations between the new director and the employees. (Weil)

- Organizations will need to establish a variety of communication channels upwards and downwards the hierarchy. (Heesen)

Morale

The last area common in the supplemental chapters relates to employees' morale. An organization can have the most talent, the best strategic plan, the best providers in their supply chain, the best knowledge management system, and be in the best locations of the world to reach their customers in a timely manner—but all that will mean little if employees do not have high levels of morale. Some leaders consider their workforce to be their most important *asset*; however, great leaders view their employees not as assets but more as *the company* itself. How employees are perceived translates directly to how they are treated. Despite the fact that manipulation has several guises, workers know the difference between being used and being treated skillfully and respectfully, and morale is always what is at stake.

Organizations that tout the *customer comes first* credo often fail to realize that they should be saying *the employees come first*. Rarely will a disgruntled or unhappy employee provide superior customer service, and micromanaged employees tend to only do what they are told, if even that much. Yet, employees who work in a culture that truly believes the employees come first have higher levels of morale and are happier in their organizational lives. At times the customer is not always *right*, and organizational leaders need to purposely build the type of culture that will motivate employees to provide a superior customer service experience.

The United State Navy applies the term *esprit de corp* to their efforts to produce a team that feels as though they *are* the Navy. In fact much of the success of the military is dependent on teamwork.

In movies and on television, we see great examples of *esprit de corp* with scenes that portray the military in life or death situations continuing to battle with a *can do* attitude. This is high morale!

In the workplace, when employees leave at the end of the day looking forward to returning, leaders can be comfortable that they have helped to foster a climate of high morale. Consequently, when employees arrive to work in the morning and are already looking forward to leaving at the end of the day, leaders are confronted with dissatisfied workforce, lacking in morale and satisfaction. The level of morale in an organization is a good signal of the company's culture, the visibility of leaders, the degree of mutual trust, and the leaders' ability to create meaningful work and work-life for their employees.

The morale of the workforce is the responsibility of every leader, manager, and supervisor regardless if it is stated or not in a job description. Some would contend that morale is the responsibility of all employees. However, the chain of accountability of a leader to the organization maintains that they must create an environment wherein employees can flourish, prosper, and grow. If business leaders take care of their employees, the employees will take care of the business.

Most morale problems tend to stem from poor supervisor-to-subordinate communications, as well as from miscommunications from the company to workers. Employees want to be treated with respect and fairness. Improved communication results in improved morale, and the easiest way to improve both communication and morale is to listen to what the problems are (attentiveness), be open to feedback (open and willing to change), help others to do better (provide the tools and resources needed), and gain confidence (trust) from all stakeholders.

Several comments from the supplemental chapters that relate to morale follow:

- Personality conflicts or poor morale among staff may leave people feeling disempowered, dissociated and, as a result, less receptive to hearing what others have to say, thus further inhibiting communication before it even has a chance to start. (Nanna)

- While employee morale is affected by the inevitability of change that is brought about by new technology, globalization, regulatory requirements, and structural changes to the organization; they are affected even more so by the lack of communication. (Stewart)

- Previous leaders in the unit led with a micromanagement, one-way communication style resulting in poor employee morale, high turnover rates, and poor physician satisfaction scores. (DeLeon)

- Joanne had unequivocally stated that those were the mandates from headquarters. That issued in the vein of a military command that percolated from an invisible source—the company's president—to increase revenue. Those faceless words had a devastating effect on the morale of the workers. (Weil)

- Employees cannot be productive nor have high morale when expectations are not communicated with them, and the most consistent communication is the mode of "I'm the director and I make the decisions." This is a true red light situation. (Fong)

- A demoralized workforce is affected by the departure of human capital and prevents the organization from delivering on promised results made to shareholders, analysts, suppliers, and clients. (Stewart)

Conclusion

This chapter began to describe the varied, yet dynamic, insights that follow in the book's 21 supplemental chapters. To achieve effective organizational communications, leaders need to create an environment wherein employees trust one another as well trust their organization as an entity. Visibility and the ability to create a sharing culture of information are important attributes for leaders and supervisors to demonstrate. When leaders successfully achieve trust among employees, the need to micromanage will diminish. This spawns a culture of improvement in which employees at all levels begin to find opportunities for improvement and suggest, as well as champion, change.

If employees are treated professionally and with respect, they will take care of business—namely, their assigned jobs and their responsibility to the organization. In addition, mentoring and coaching programs improve the attentiveness of the organization to help identify growth opportunities. Mentoring and coaching builds strong relationships developed from trust. Improved relationships strengthen communication and respect to nurture a positive work environment for everyone involved. But, fancy and/or expensive mentoring and coaching programs are not needed, just senior leaders who care and who are willing to devote time and effort towards developing a talented and energetic workforce.

Improving communications should not have to be a huge hurdle to overcome. It can begin with a simple organizational assessment in which senior leaders, midlevel managers, and frontline workers are each provided an opportunity to assess to what degree their organization as a whole communicates. Then, differences or gaps in the findings can be determined. With that information, a simple path to improved communications and professional relationships at all levels can easily begin. The simple path begins with regular conversations, meetings, and sharing of expectations.

In chapter 8, Stewart advocates that "Communication is a learned skill." If this philosophy holds true, then one can train and educate and then practice to develop this skill. The 21 supplemental chapters offer perspectives on how best to develop these kinds of skills in both the employee and organization. The *Laws of Communication* provide the overarching umbrella of steps that are then involved in honing the skill of communicating.

SECTION 2
The Significance of Communication

CHAPTER 3
APPLYING SPIRITUAL PRINCIPLES IN BUSINESS COMMUNICATION: THE KEY TO MANIFESTING ORGANIZATIONAL GOALS

Karina A. F. Weil

In the prosperous 1990s, Hong Kong was booming. During that celebrated and affluent decade, Hong Kong, one of the Asian Tigers, lured hundreds of thousands of companies from every corner of the globe as they rushed to establish their presence there. Drake International, a globally operating staffing company, was no exception. I was hired by Drake International Hong Kong as an executive search associate shortly after the company established itself on the island.

Within the company, executive search associates were known for being a breed apart from other company professionals: we worked independently, as if managing our own businesses. Although I was the first and only executive search associate for the Hong Kong branch, I felt confident that I was up to the challenge. Bolstered by Drake International's good standing in the business arena and armed with my list of contacts in the South East Asian business community, I charged ahead.

My job was to provide employment solutions to a clientele of mainstream international banks, and I tapped into an extensive network of high caliber professionals, the best talent available, in order to do so. I reported to the director in the main office a few times a week, but the bulk of my time was spent on the road contacting clients and securing business. I was thrilled with the position because of the quality of life it offered. It simultaneously afforded me the freedom to manage my own time and raise my children—a high priority to me—and the opportunity to remain productive, financially independent, and engaged in my work. I appreciated my ability to work independently, to avoid putting in long hours at the office or being part of corporate politics. For a devoted mother and wife, it was the perfect scenario, but it would not last long.

During those years, Hong Kong was known in the business community as an unforgiving competitive environment, but I was doing extremely well flying solo. While working in this cutthroat milieu gave me a rush, my personal experience had been relatively uncomplicated and trouble-free. Hong Kong was good to me, and I was thankful. However, I could not refute the aggressive style of leadership that thrived in that location.

Although Drake International had been profitable and well established in other continents since the early 1950s, it seemed to be struggling in Hong Kong. Whatever tactic the company had previously used to succeed was not working there, and the Hong Kong office was in dire need of a drastically different approach. I had been working in the Hong Kong subsidiary for about two months when headquarters sent in a new managing director to turn things around.

The Ivory Tower

The day of the new director's arrival occurred without fanfare. No company-wide communication was dispersed, and meetings were held privately in her office. This set the tone for what was to come. Imbued with the drive to make things happen in the shortest period of time possible, the director called in division managers one by one and began pointing out the shortcomings of their performance, demanding an increase in productivity. The managers followed suit and in turn went back to their divisions and relayed the message verbatim, as it had been unloaded on them, to their employees.

I, too, was summoned to meet the new director, and I was surprised to find an intelligent, elegant, and soft-spoken woman. We hit off immediately, but our meeting was short, and our discussions centered primarily on my client portfolio and business strategy for the banking industry. I did not expect much guidance. My previous experience in the consulting business put me in good stead and assured my tenure in the company. Without realizing it at the time, I was in a privileged position because I was working almost entirely autonomously and somewhat removed from the battlefield that Drake had become.

When I first met the director, whom I will call Joanne, the impression she gave me was that of a clear-minded businessperson with a strong sense of direction, but she failed to make this impression with the other employees. Instead, in order to increase revenue, she barked militaristic commands from the safety of her desk, which had a devastating effect on the morale of the workers. Employees sauntered around the office in a mechanized manner. Joanne's cutting words reverberated in the corridors of that elegant Hong Kong business center, undermining the employees' basic belief in themselves.

Instead of reigniting the employees' desire to regroup, reorganize, and recuperate their efforts, a definite and undeniable feeling of inadequacy and incompetence suddenly pervaded the workforce. Not surprisingly, hostility and employee conflict was on the rise, and very little was accomplished in terms of business results. Months rolled by without a single upward move on the revenue charts, and company employees were psychologically weakened to fight the mounting competition. Communications with clients tended to be haphazard, or employees scurried in all directions struggling to secure business from existing clients. Many employees were content with doing the bare minimum to ensure their continued employment.

Speaking Without Listening

Undeniably, Joanne was also under tremendous pressure to show results. Her mission was to salvage the company at all costs. I was there one Monday morning when I witnessed Joanne berating a group of employees with a torrent of disparagement and imperatives. She had a typical nose-to-the-grinding stone management style. Additionally, she was unable to communicate effectively with her subordinates and to see eye-to-eye with them. Joanne remained isolated within the four walls of her office, further alienating those who had the ability to transform the company into a successful one.

Arthur Jue (2006), Director of Human Resources and Leadership Development for Hyperion Solutions Inc., shrewdly pointed out that typical Western management tends to be fixated on the willful exertion of our drive, intentions, and personalities to accomplish and conquer. Other belief systems succeed on the basis of reflection and analysis, which can promote powerful results.

Joanne wanted employees to focus exclusively on budgets, numbers, and sales projections, but I found that they had other concerns. My co-workers' dissatisfaction was obvious, and the grapevine was rampant. Employees huddled in tiny factions in the hallways, in the store and copying rooms, or in the pantry agonizing and speculating what Joanne really expected from them. Whatever *esprit de corps* had formerly existed at this workplace had rapidly deteriorated, and an attitude of each-one-for-himself had sprung up in its place.

Feelings of powerlessness plagued me during those times, but I was able to lend an ear to my colleagues. They were eager to complain and fret about their future, and I had time to observe and learn from what was being said. I began to realize that listening is a vital component of communication, one that is frequently overlooked in personal interactions. By listening, I was gradually becoming able to contextualize the complaints and the feelings of fatigue and exhaustion that had overcome Drake's employees as symptomatic of something larger and more serious.

Everyone was aware that significant change would be needed to confront growing competition and dwindling employee motivation. But, my colleagues, who were so alienated from their new supervisor, had the perception that they were alone. Though self-leadership can exist as a virtue, at the end of the day, employees look to their leaders for guidance and inspiration, and they want confidence that their leader could be the ultimate decision-maker.

At Drake International, employee protests were fueled by their frustration at not being heard or provided with guidance. At the very least, my colleagues resented Joanne's constant bashings. In time, disappointment and cynicism won, and attrition quickly began to erode the company's once vigorous workforce.

A leader was in place, no doubt, but that leader was not engaged. Joanne did not take the time to provide the workers with a general direction. She did not create a strategic plan to harness the immense diversity of talents represented in that office. She did not ask questions so that everyone would feel included in the plan and responsible for the company's fate. In sum, she was not listening! Drake's essential problem was not its competition or the diversity of its workforce—it was a lack of crucial leadership communication savvy.

Listening is the highest form of respect when two or more people communicate. When leaders practice respectful and consistent communication with their teams, not only do they engage employees, but they also create a prototype, a blueprint, which others emulate and duplicate, reinforcing principles and ideals that are also self-perpetuating.

Leaders who are sincere listeners demonstrate respect for their employees. Even more so, they inspire respect. One simple by-product of good listening is that employees often become more motivated to listen. In contrast, aggressively inundating employees with sales targets merely creates anxiety.

Research about communication tends to emphasize the need for leaders to speak, and speak, and speak about what they want employees to do, but very little is said about the need for leaders to listen. In the case of Drake International, the new director should have made a protracted effort to get to know each of the employees on a personal level, to validate their experiences and invite their ideas, before calling them to action.

Sincere and attentive listening would have certainly improved relations between the new director and the employees. Subsequently, leaders need to reinforce and perfect these principles and attitudes. Leaders need to know that communicating with respect is a continuous process, not an event. Communicating with respect is a choice that does not happen perchance. It must be driven by a set of core values and supporting behaviors, grounded on the philosophy that business is people. Communication does not need to subject itself to bureaucracy or a superior's approval.

Suddenly, I found myself in the middle of two polarities. On one side, there was Joanne, with whom I had an excellent relationship. On the other, I had my colleagues who seemed to be capitalizing on my access to Joanne. I decided to volunteer for the role of being the link between the two factions.

The first step was to schedule more frequent meetings with Joanne. Instead of our regular weekly sessions, I began meeting with Joanne twice, sometimes three times, every week. On those occasions, I spoke unabashedly about my colleagues' needs and their opinion of her tactics. I had become their spokesperson. Later in the year, those informal conversations formed the basis for a long and detailed report Joanne prepared to the company's president.

It was in the midst of this turmoil that Joanne asked me if I would consider the position of temporary leader to the executive search division. I was totally taken aback and did not know how to react. There was no job specification for that position, but I intuitively knew that Joanne would expect results. She was either testing me or giving me carte blanche. I chose to believe in the latter.

The Spiritual Laws of Communication

Only a handful of competent employees remained at Drake International. The company was understaffed and had to prepare for significant change, but change is often scary because it involves the unknown. My colleagues in the executive search division were worried and dispirited. They needed to feel secure, competent, and appreciated. They needed to have trust in their leaders, that they could take a risk and emerge victorious, but Joanne had been unable to earn that trust. As a consequence, the employees did not feel empowered, and their productivity had declined. Would they trust me? Would I be able to motivate them?

To make matters more difficult, the only three remaining consultants on my team were of different nationalities. As a result, I expected a great deal of divergence of opinions, perceptions, values, and approaches. How was I to align their views into one cohesive and coherent vision? How could I minimize conflict? The task before me seemed daunting, and I knew my communication style would have a crucial effect on my success.

From an initial state of bewilderment, the answer to my questions sprang into sight. I visualized myself in the employees' situation and asked myself what I would expect in a leader. I reasoned that I would want to feel respected and acknowledged as a person and as a professional. My colleagues were intelligent, capable professionals in their own right. There was little I could tell them that they did not already know or could figure out by themselves.

My role was to harness their knowledge and put it to use by truly communicating with them as a team. We had scheduled our first meeting for the following morning. I decided that instead of telling them what to do, I would listen to them first and offer support to their efforts. I could not think of a better way to show appreciation for their talents. The practical application of this strategy brought our interactions to a higher level of mutual respect and trust. And everybody in the team felt it.

Almost immediately, my colleagues began exchanging ideas and suggestions about how they envisaged the new division should be, how to stand up against the competition, and how to create systems that supported their goals. They were feeling valued, and my selected course of action had proved positive. Most importantly, my colleagues were fueled with the desire to manifest organizational goals, not only because they knew that top management would appreciate their efforts, but also because they knew that their efforts could result in something bigger than themselves.

It has been said that people can conquer all when working together. This union, this bond, becomes a source of strength, a driving force when all else fails. The realities of the market may change, organizations may grow or dwindle, but people remain the same. And, so do their needs.

In the organizational microcosm of that small executive search division, a phenomenon of great proportion was taking place. Employees were voicing their opinions, offering ideas, expressing their creativity, bonding with one another—all without fear. Though I was not aware of it at the time, the forces that came into action sustained the *Laws of Communication*. For Drake International, in particular, two bylaws were also in play:

- The Law of Respect
- The Law of Intention

Every time two or more employees engaged in a verbal interaction with one another, these two forces had to be present in order for true communication to occur.

These by-laws are so far-reaching in their application that they might be considered universal laws, such as those described by Daniel Millman (1993). Millman devoted his life's work to helping people find their life purpose, and he developed a system based on the power of universal laws to transform people's health, personal life, and work by achieving higher levels of lucidity, simplicity, and transparency.

According to Millman (1993), universal laws are not merely rules, suggestions, or codes of ethical behavior. Rather, they transcend the dictates of human society to express a higher order. For example, we can declare gravity illegal, or even immoral, but the law of gravity is still going to apply. These universal laws, such as the law of gravity, have reigned supreme throughout history because of their consistency and consequence, and we discover their power as we apply them. I also refer to them as spiritual laws.

The validity of spiritual law does not require or depend upon any kind of belief. Gravity, for example, works whether we believe in it or not. Thus, whether we believe that these laws are handed down from a Great Spirit or that they simply reflect the mechanisms of the universe, they have the power to change our lives. An infinite number of these spiritual laws exist. They govern the structures, forces, and patterns of our existence, from subatomic particles to swirling galaxies. They govern the ways in which flowers bloom and stretch toward the sun or how waves break and curl onto the beach.

One of these laws is that of respect. Without respect, true communion with others is impossible. The great Paramahansa Yogananda said that respect is the single most important ingredient missing in human relationships—such a simple thought, yet how profound, how insightful.

The Law of Respect

Employees at Drake International were discontented with a leader who spoke but did not know how to communicate. Joanne's verbal conduct had been somewhat abusive and, at the very least, counterproductive. Her conduct was symptomatic of a malady gnawing at the roots of corporate health—failure to establish basic norms of conduct cognizant of human dignity. Robert Sutton (2007), author of a provocative book about corporate behavior, suggested that corporate obsession with winning and obtaining financial results, coupled with a disregard for second place, are the root cause and the impetus for leaders' abusive treatment of employees.

Regardless of whether my colleagues chose to stay on the job or quit, their self-image and self-confidence was shattered. They remained silent because they were fearful of appearing contentious, and their greatest and most creative ideas went unvoiced. But, the tables were turning. I was confronted with the task of finally giving credence to their voices, and I only hoped the harm was irreversible.

Luckily, my colleagues' enthusiasm and faith in themselves had remained intact. Once they realized I was on their side and had not stepped in as a surrogate Joanne, they immediately began to show how much they were capable of accomplishing. I was always an early bird at the office, but I would often come in to find them already on the telephone, either with clients or competitors. Finding out what the competition was up to was a major strategic step, and they enjoyed taking it.

One of my colleagues, whom I shall call Nancy, proved extremely valuable during that phase. She had numerous contacts with members of our competition, and through her bold initiatives, we developed the rudiments of a new executive search division brochure and fee system. Nancy was an average performer in her first months with the company, but now she was generating business leads on her own. A couple of years later, at the end of my tenure with Drake, most of Nancy's clients were repeat businesses. At our last end-of-the-year lunch meeting, Nancy was proudly exhibiting 24-karat gold jewelry that a client had given her in recognition of her outstanding work.

One of the benefits of actively listening to my colleagues was to earn their respect. Respectful communication with my colleagues helped remove erroneous perceptions and misunderstandings that had impeded progress until that point. As I took the time to absorb new information from them, I was rewarded with precious first-hand knowledge about themselves, about the organization, and about the market. Possessing that informal knowledge gave me the tools to help them manifest the division's goals.

Leaders often have a clear vision of where they want their organizations to be, but a vision is only as good as it is communicated, lest it remains a dream. Bridging the gap between vision and reality means communicating in ways that employees understand what is expected of them. Most of all, employees must feel they are a vital part of manifesting that vision. They need to know that the vision is a component of their reality.

Lack of respect, toward the self and others, had been the root cause of the communication breakdown at Drake International. As a result, employees were experiencing broken relationships, thwarted goals and dreams, and even feelings of victimization. But, the Law of Respect had the power to undo these ills. Respect became evident when my colleagues at the executive search division felt that their voices had been heard, and they knew, without a doubt, that they were what Stephen Covey (2005) calls participants in the organizational goals.

Despite our victories in the executive search division, divergence of opinions and clashes in communication did occur. Yet, we all collectively strived to maintain a respectful climate in our discussions. Because we were committed to maintain team cohesion, showing respect for each other as competent professionals, in word and deed, was a priority. We all had witnessed the destructive, humiliating, and divisive power of communication breakdown, so we agreed that all issues would be discussed in *loco*, openly and honestly. Additionally, I knew that my colleagues regarded me as their leader and expected me to be reliable in my words and actions.

As a case in point, during an important marketing campaign, there were five of us, each from a different cultural and professional background, immersed in a heated discussion about which tactic to take. Tempers were out of control, but as soon as we had calmed down, Nancy, with an unruffled and sincere demeanor, turned to another colleague who had been particularly adamant about one point and said, "Your approach turns people off." The other colleague immediately apologized. In our team, there was no room for power plays and demeaning behavior.

Although conflict is a normal part of life, everybody seems to dread it. Management scholars Andrew Ward, Melenie Lankau, Allen Amason, Jeffrey Sonnenfeld, and Bradley Agle (2007) found that leaders of different cultural backgrounds engaged in a debate are likely to have opposing views. This is an unquestionable reality, which is part of human nature. However, there are advantages in intellectual diversity. In their research, the authors' findings reveal that when divergent opinions among organizational leadership are not reconciled, negative repercussions to the entire organization may follow.

The Law of Intention

Thoughts are our intentions physically manifested through words. Words have creative power that leaders can use to achieve their own success and to develop the success of their companies. The Law of Intention is not new. Gary Zukav (1990) explained it beautifully in his book *The Seat of the Soul*, by observing that "every intention sets energy into motion whether you are conscious of it or not" (p.123). The great thinkers of our time warn us that we are constantly co-creating our reality and our circumstances, thus it is only logical to think that we are constantly repeating the consequences of our intentions.

The mental imageries that emerge from the intentions we project have an energy and intelligence of their own, and this energy is perpetually shaping our surroundings. Zukav wrote, for example, that when a person thinks and speaks of marriage, that word invokes a specific consciousness that permeates the experience. From this perspective, leaders can choose to go beyond studying the organization's mission statement and the latest sales report. Instead, leaders can begin by slowing down and making a conscious effort to imbue their words with meaning and intention.

A case in point involves the CEO of Credit Suisse who meets informally with the director of each team every other week to speak about the bank's long-range goals. After a few minutes of personal conversation, he gathers the perceptions and field experiences from each team. Then, he speaks with them about the organization's vision for the future. He clarifies and reiterates his goals, how they fit into organizational goals, and the manner in which each employee can contribute. At this point, the CEO asks if they understand and share his vision. Strategically, he prefers to hold these meetings on Friday afternoons when the impending weekend creates a positive mood. After the meeting, he solicits employees' reactions and comments from the directors.

This corporate leader is able to enlist the enthusiastic commitment of all levels of employees within his organization, and his strategy is a success—the bank is one of the most sought after places for employment. It can be tempting to dismiss this CEO's success as sheer luck, but it is more accurate to say that his intention was to capitalize on workforce dynamism. While exercising control—taking calculating risks and being ultimately accountable—the CEO was entirely cognizant of two fundamental forces impacting any business: (1) the need to gather new knowledge and continuously raise the bar and (2) the need to groom a highly confident, competent, cohesive, and loyal organizational team.

The Power of Words

Corporate leaders desire to be successful, but only those who have mastered the art of communication triumph. Living the Laws of Respect and Intention is one essential step in that journey. Yet, in order to achieve complete mastery, leaders must understand the responsibility they have toward the words they speak. We live in a loquacious culture where focus is often on the quantity, rather than quality, of words used, but words that are charged with purpose and earnestness leave an imprint on people's consciousness. Words have the power to stir emotions and trump skepticism.

The Laws of Respect and Intention may appear unrealistic in everyday application, yet this is precisely why they are often underutilized. Leaders have a responsibility to their organizations and to human beings as a whole. They can become communication agents who instill these principles in their followers by example. And, in believing in these principles, leaders call upon a colossal power generated by the sum energies of any group of people who gather for a single purpose. They just need to believe that they have the power to do so.

CHAPTER 4
SCHUTTLER'S LAWS OF COMMUNICATION: APPLICATION FOR OPEN BOOK MANAGEMENT

Thomas M. Box

In Schuttler's three-level model of organizational communications, the upper level—the *green zone*—represents organizations that have the most effective communications. In many cases, the productivity and profits of these organizations are also better than most of their competitors. Organizations operating in the green zone have a culture of continuous improvement and engage in open two-way communications, and firms wishing to operate in the green zone should seriously consider Open Book Management (OBM).

OBM gained attention in the 1980s, when Missouri's Springfield Remanufacturing Corporation (SRC) implemented this business model. Under the directions of CEO Jack Stack, the company realized great success from following the OBM philosophy. Stack referred to the process as "the Great Game of Business" and a "no-excuses management" technique (Robertson & Matthews, 1997). Stack (1992) offered in his book, *The Great Game of Business*, that the more educated a company's workers are, the more able they are to do the little things necessary to improve the company.

OBM supplies workers with tools that enable them to make the right decisions. Stack affirms that competitors set a company's benchmarks, which can be utilized by the company to motivate all workers to meet the company's goals and objectives. Since its inception, hundreds of companies have implemented OBM with much success, but it is currently estimated that only 1% of U.S. companies are using the philosophy (Dalton, 1999a), a possible indication that the benefits of OBM are not completely understood.

The general basis for OBM seems elementary—teach employees how to read and interpret financial statements, give them an incentive to increase the company profit, and stand back as the money starts rolling in. Implementation of OBM is not quite that simple, however, as it demands an environment of trust between employees and management. Employees must believe they will receive what was promised to them. Management must believe that the information released will not be used against them in any way and that it will be used to help better the company (Stack, 1992).

OBM does involve the sharing of company financial information. It also involves profit sharing, good communication, and employee understanding of the big picture. The idea is to connect company results to each employee's job and make everyone responsible for the company's profit. Thus, each employee must understand how his or her job affects the company's bottom line, and incentives must motivate employees to care if they improve the company (Robertson & Matthews, 1997).

Implementation

Similar to any business technique, top management, especially the CEO, must fully embrace OBM for it to be successful. Management must also embrace and practice the notion that employees are partners, not subordinates (*Shift to OBM*, 1998). Businesses wishing to develop an OBM culture must develop a plan before any action is taken. Ian Jacobsen, Jacobsen Consulting Group President, identified five key questions companies need to answer before implementation (Perry, 1998):

- What are the financial goals for the plan?
- What is the amount of training needed, and who will do the training?
- How will results be communicated to employees?
- How will employee involvement be tracked?

- How will employees be rewarded?

OBM can be slowly implemented to gain acceptance and increase the chance of the plan's success. Of course, these decisions are all dependent on a company's climate and context. As such, leaders should use these ideas as a guide for identifying the best starting point for their business (Perry, 1998).

Education is an essential element of OBM. Employees need to understand the business and the industry, and they need to understand their company's competitive advantage and strategic plan as foundations upon which further knowledge can be built (Cooke, 1996). Employees must also receive training on the company's financial statements, gaining a more nuanced understanding of what the financial statements mean and what affects and influences these numbers (Case, 1998).

With this baseline financial knowledge, employees begin to see how their work performance can influence the company and positively impact the numbers that will eventually translate to their bonuses or other incentives (Perry, 1998). To this end, management must be willing and open to answer employee questions about company finances. This level of knowledge and involvement will likely increase employees' sense of empowerment, as informed and engaged workers are more competent in making informed, sound decisions. All employees should eventually be able to contribute to the discussion of strategic goals and plans as well as the identification of critical numbers (Case).

Companies have developed various training methods to achieve these ends. Wascana Energy Incorporated uses a computer game to help employees learn their business (Robertson & Matthews, 1997). Similarly, Paradigm Learning, Incorporated of Tampa developed Zodiac, a board game designed to teach employees financial statements (Dalton, 1999a). Many training and monitoring systems involve key indicators that are traced regularly and posted for all to see. These indicators, often thought of as a scoreboard, might be translated into a game in which employees are able to monitor their own progress without the pressure normally associated with performance initiatives (Perry, 1998).

Incentives for employees must be put in place to facilitate OBM. Workers will become actively involved only if they are aware of the benefits they will receive. The reward systems for OBM may include bonuses, profit sharing, or stock ownership (Perry, 1998). It is essential that this reward system be carefully planned, evaluated, and monitored. Employees will do what is needed to earn the incentives if given the proper incentive. As such, incentives that were designed to stimulate certain determined outcomes, but have unexpected negative affects or results, need to be offset with additional performance motivation and employee encouragement (Perry). Regardless of how incentives are used, ongoing communication and training is vital for OBM's success, and it is extremely helpful if the process can be fun for all involved (Cooke, 1996).

OBM can be customized to fit different organizations. An example of customization comes from Dean Allison, owner of three Wendy's restaurant franchises. He decided not to choose a traditional approach to management because employees are typically part-time young people. Allison's OBM system currently consists of education on the basic sales less expense results of the profit equation and why return on invested capital is important. In addition, a straightforward bonus system is in place, focusing on sales and profits for each month. A scoreboard is used to track sales and controllable expenses like food costs (Robertson & Matthews, 1997).

Benefits

If properly implemented, OBM can result in many benefits for a company. Whereas companies vary in culture and OBM design, companies successfully implementing OBM characteristics often realize some common benefits. A study completed in 1998 by The National Center for Employee Ownership found that companies who had implemented OBM enjoyed a revenue growth that was up to 16.6% faster than competitors who had not implemented (*The Need to Know*, 1999).

Many managers who are not part of an OBM company attempt to retain their position and status by not sharing information and subscribing to the tired philosophy that "knowledge is power" (Buhler, 1999), but information hoarding can result in employees who simply show up, put in their time, and go home feeling no connection to the company. Workers do not know how the company is doing, how they can or do affect the company positively or negatively, or what their specific focus should be while on the job. This environment can cause employees to feel they are not trusted. In return, the employees do not trust or feel any commitment or loyalty to the company (Buhler).

The result of OBM is a closer focus on the reasons for success and failure. Employees begin to understand how they can positively affect the company and why they are important. They comprehend the whole picture, allowing them to feel more a part of the organization and, thus, more committed to improving the business (Buhler, 1999). Additionally, teamwork will be enhanced as employees join together to better themselves as a group and a company. In this way, OBM can result in more deeply held identification with the company, as well as increases in loyalty towards the business (Buhler). This sense of belonging is vital to successful companies, as it impacts everything an employee might do in regard to his or her work.

OBM enables employees to track their own performance. This ability to monitor their work and their contribution to the company's success is motivating for workers. They work harder when they can see directly how they are improving the company (*Managing by the Book*, 1995). As workers are armed with more knowledge and empowered to make decisions affecting their work and the company, their jobs become more meaningful and satisfying. Workers who feel important will make a greater contribution to the company, feel more content in their jobs, take responsibility for their actions, and feel greater commitment and loyalty to the company (Perry, 1998).

Still, an employee's mere knowledge of how he or she affects the company is not enough to motivate in the long run. Employee incentives are required to ensure employee commitment. OBM strives to make employees behave like owners. In order for employees to act as if they are owners, they must have a stake in the performance of the business—in other words, workers must be rewarded as if they were owners. If they help improve the company, they should know that they will see the direct benefits of their work. Accordingly, incentives are critical to improving a company via OBM. The reward system can be linked to job specific measures, departmental measures, overall company measures, or some combination of these metrics (Robertson & Matthews, 1997).

In the education process, employees should learn how organizational measures are computed, how these numbers affect them, and how they affect the numbers, so that they can influence the numbers and control the incentives they receive (Cooke, 1996). If employees do not understand or cannot affect the numbers, OBM will not be successful, and employees will feel frustrated and hostile toward management. The numbers that determine rewards need to be constantly monitored and displayed so that employees know where they stand and can use measurements as a constant motivator (Case, 1998).

Bonuses typically reward short-term performance that positively impacts the company. To offset this shortsighted emphasis, OBM encourages stock options or other forms of equity ownership to encourage employee decisions and actions that have long-term positive results for the business (Robertson & Matthews, 1997). If the company's profitability is positively affected, so is the worker's personal financial position (Chambers, 1997). Employees' sense of ownership presents many beneficial results for companies. When employees know that they will personally benefit from the success of the company, they care more about their organization. Lower turnover, higher morale, and better performance have all resulted from employee ownership, according to research done on companies which have implemented an ownership culture (Chambers).

OBM does not need to be implemented as a drastic, overnight change. It can be introduced slowly, in phases that work for the company (*Managing by the Book*, 1995). Benefits can be realized through partial implementation, as the complete OBM culture is developed slowly over time (Buhler, 1999). OBM requires increased communication among the various levels of the organization, and management and workers must jointly set effective communication as a target or goal (Robertson & Matthews, 1997). Empowered and knowledgeable employees will have more useful input. They should be included in planning and forecasting, as communication will increase as employees are held accountable for their results. Good and bad numbers will need to be examined and explained via periodic company or departmental results (Buhler).

Potential Problems

Companies attempting to implement OBM must overcome the changing of their company's customs and culture. Management is often hesitant to release formerly undisclosed information in fear of reactions, demands, or disloyal use, and they may not want to devote time to training, explaining, or answering questions. Workers may not be excited about gaining knowledge and empowerment, or they may have no interest in learning about the company and its financial statements. The employees might like having no responsibility or accountability, which enables them to show up, put in their hours, and go home (Dalton, 1999). OBM puts more pressure on employees and managers when they are forced to work together to better their company.

Jack Stack (1992) identified three great OBM fears to overcome in his book *The Great Game of Business*. The first fear identified is the fear that critical numbers will get into competitor's hands. However, this fear can be countered with the belief that the knowledge of a competitor's numbers is a short-term tactical advantage at best. This short-term advantage is nothing that compares with the advantage that comes with educating workers about the company's numbers.

The second fear to be overcome is the fear of employees not understanding the numbers. This fear may be true, but Stack believes that, even so, it is better to be open with workers because workers will often make incorrect assumptions when numbers are hidden. The third and final fear identified in *The Great Game of Business* is the fear of revealing bad numbers. In order to build trust, management must be willing to share the bad news with the good and realize that people can pull together in challenging times (Stack).

According to Julie Carrick Dalton, when OBM does not benefit companies, it is typically a result of the company losing OBM leadership or not fully realizing the extent of the work involved in implementation. She also identified six negative OBM outcomes that managers typically fear. They include workers demanding higher pay, workers misinterpreting numbers, the finance department being bombarded with questions, information being used against the company in union contracts, data ending up in competitor or customer hands, and management being criticized even more severely (Dalton, 1999a).

The necessary use of budgets and incentives can also pose problems in an OBM implementation initiative. Budgets are time consuming and imprecise (Wiersema, 1998), and bonuses or other incentives can often have unforeseen and unplanned results. If bonuses are based on numbers the employee cannot control or does not know how to influence, the bonuses can ultimately prove unmotivating and discouraging.

An example would be targeting material cost as a reduction point, when material cost is figured as a percent of sales. In this scenario, a focus on scrap reduction or other improvements will show no results until the end of the year, long after frustration will set in for many workers (Wiersema). Bonuses can also motivate employees to perform in ways that are not in the best interest of the company.

Some results are production hoarding, fraud, and pursuing personal rewards at the expense of the business (Wiersema). Additionally, bonuses or other payment incentives are only possible if the company is making money, and if promised bonuses are never realized, employees will lose faith and become unproductive (Wiersema).

John Case (1998) identified some of the challenges with OBM companies today. Case begins with the premise that employees are essential to OBM success. If they are not willing to trust, learn, and be motivated by the challenges, OBM will not succeed. Thus, companies must ensure they hire for both ability *and* attitude (Case). OBM also requires a lot of continuous time and attention to be devoted to employee feedback.

The extensive training requires an extremely large resource commitment, including both time and money, and as already mentioned, effective compensation systems must be developed. Case emphasized the danger of an elaborate OBM system forced down from the top, suggesting that step-by-step, gradual implementation will have a greater chance of success. This process will allow members of the organization to get accustomed to the new technique and see that it can produce positive results.

Once the concept is understood and accepted, it will be easier to incorporate the OBM culture into the company's existing culture. As previously mentioned, games are a way to begin to involve employees and focus their attention on key numbers (Case).

The involvement and support of the CFO is also important for OBM success. The main responsibility for training employees often falls on the CFO, even if outside sources are used for training development. Often, it can be hard for the CFO to communicate the meaning of financial statement numbers in terms employees understand (*Shift to OBM*, 1998). It is also difficult for them to find the necessary time to devote to this program, and in some cases there is the question of whether everyone has the ability to learn the financial information and understand the calculations (Dalton, 1999a). Keeping these points in mind, it is crucial that other members of senior leadership work closely with the CFO to achieve buy-in and long-term commitment to the OBM ideals.

Private companies can have another challenge, as company financial data is closely associated with the owner's financial data (Dalton, 1999a). This makes the data even more sensitive and difficult to disclose to employees. In a similar fashion, private companies planning to go public in the future face a unique challenge with OBM, stemming from the Securities and Exchange Commission's restriction on the information that can be shown to employees before it is made available to the general public (Dalton). Companies in this position must consider the options available and pursue the strategy most suited for their company.

OBM can cause too much focus on short-term profit or other key measures. This short-term focus can endanger long-term growth and goals (Dalton, 1999a). As discussed previously, employee ownership programs can be implemented to offset these potential negative effects. If employees are not given ownership, or forced to be a part of the program, they may choose not to purchase stock. The bonuses and other incentives could then cause these employees to pursue personal gain over company goals (Dalton).

When developing OBM systems, companies confront the tough question of what level of salary information they are willing to release. Many companies do not publish individual salaries because they believe it would only lead to jealousy or resentment. Some common practices are to disclose only CEO or top executive salaries, to group salaries in department totals, or to disclose salary averages for positions. Other companies truly disclose everything by publishing every employee's salary. These companies commonly share a view that this openness will motivate employees to try harder to move up (Dalton, 1999b).

Management must also realize that OBM entails an ongoing commitment. Creating a successful OBM culture requires hard work and does not happen overnight. Management must be committed to the change and willing to work on all the challenges they will confront. They must fully understand the concept and all of its implications. This process cannot be a fad that will die out in a few months, or it will be an extreme waste of time and money. The company has to be committed to creating a successful OBM culture within the company for the life of the company. Tom Duening, Assistant Dean of the College of Business Administration at the University of Houston, stated, "Where I've seen [OBM] work most effectively is in organizations that have taken it on as a complete organizational/cultural transformation" (as cited in Prince, 1999).

The Future of OBM

Although much has been published about OBM, the vast majority of writings have been in practitioner, rather than academic, journals. Attracting academics to the rigorous examination of a new construct or model is not easy. One of the problems is the question of convergent and discriminant validity. Do the various writers who have extolled the virtues of OBM seem to agree on the basic principles? If one looks at the writings of Stack (1992) and Case (1998), there is an obvious parallel in terms of basic principles, so convergent validity seems not to be a problem. Still, the question of discriminant validity remains open.

It is difficult, in many ways, to separate the principles of OBM from other business models like Quality of Work Life and Total Quality Management. One approach for earning academic attention might be to examine OBM through the lenses of other well-known business gurus. Gary Hamel (2000), for example, has written extensively about a business model he calls Gray-Haired Revolutionaries—firms that rapidly innovate and change their strategies to address the problems of surviving, thriving, and excelling in the chaotic age in which we live.

Hamel (2000) proposed five design rules for firms wishing to become Gray-Haired Revolutionaries:

- **Design Rule 1** is to have unreasonably high expectations. Clearly, SRC met this criterion. In 1983, they had an 81 to 1 debt equity ratio. The expectation of survival and success was an extraordinarily high expectation.

- **Design Rule 2** is to have an elastic business definition. In the last 27 years, SRC has moved into a staggering group of new business opportunities; for example, they have spun off 22 new businesses in the Springfield, Missouri region alone—a remarkable record.

- **Design Rule 3** is to have a cause, not a business. SRC's cause, basically, is to create wealth for all employees, and they have achieved this goal consistently.

- **Design Rule 4** is to encourage new voices. SRC meets the test here as well—virtually every employee is tasked not only with learning his or her job well, but also in coming up with ideas for new businesses, new processes, and cost saving innovations. The payoff to the individual employee is direct bonus payments, quarterly performance bonuses, and equity (ESOP).

- **Design Rule 5** is to create an open market for ideas. This achievement, too, has been met by SRC. SRC employees—frequently hourly employees who originated business ideas—head most of their new businesses. Thus, OBM, as implemented at SRC, clearly qualifies as a model for a new Gray-Haired Revolutionary.

SRC, under the leadership of Jack Stack, has certainly done more than one might expect to bring OBM to the attention of business leaders. At present, SRC offers regional and national meetings, a catalog of training modules, films, and on-site tutorials to popularize this new business model and teach its principles.

Conclusion

OBM has provided evidence that informed, dedicated employees who have an ownership interest in their work could have a profound influence on the success of their companies. This news is hardly surprising. What is surprising is that less than 1% of American businesses have adopted this business model despite the overwhelming evidence that the old command and control philosophies seem less and less able to cope successfully with the dynamics of the late-20th and early-21st centuries. In summary, is probably safe to say that OBM is a business model well worth examining from an empirical perspective and certainly worth thinking about for firms facing the exigencies and uncertainties of business in the early 21st century.

Operating in Schuttler's noted green zone affords the leadership and organizational willingness to adopt OBM. Even those businesses that are in the yellow zone can use OBM as a means to increase open communications and build trust and thus move into the green zone. Effective communication at all levels allows leaders and subordinates to collaborate for their mutual benefit as well as for their organization and its many stakeholders.

CHAPTER 5
LEAN SIX SIGMA AND COMMUNICATION: OBSERVING THE LAWS OF COMMUNICATION

Francisco J. Melero

The way people communicate within an organization has an impact on how well and how quickly things get done. The message of what is being communicated is important from both the content of what is being delivered as well as the process of delivery. Paying close attention to these elements is not always easy—people may believe that they have no problem getting their points across, but results may prove the contrary.

Schuttler's *Laws of Communication* are always in effect during message exchanges within organizations, especially when change initiatives are introduced with the aims of performance improvement. The cause-and-effect graphical relationship is simple: the better the communication, the better the performance. The *red*, *yellow*, and *green zones* of the stoplight metaphor are, respectively, areas of undesired, cautious, and desirable actions and behaviors.

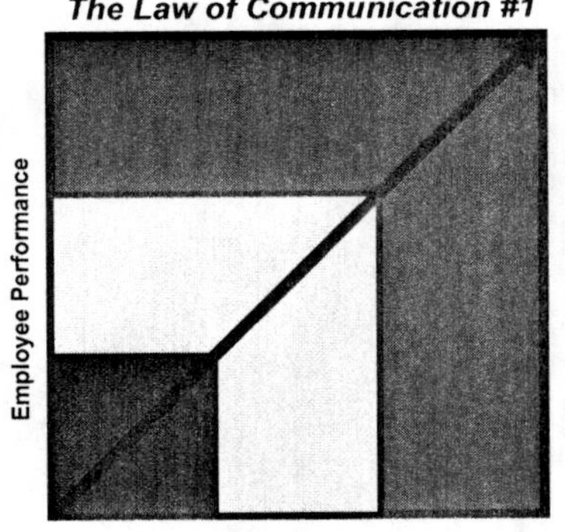

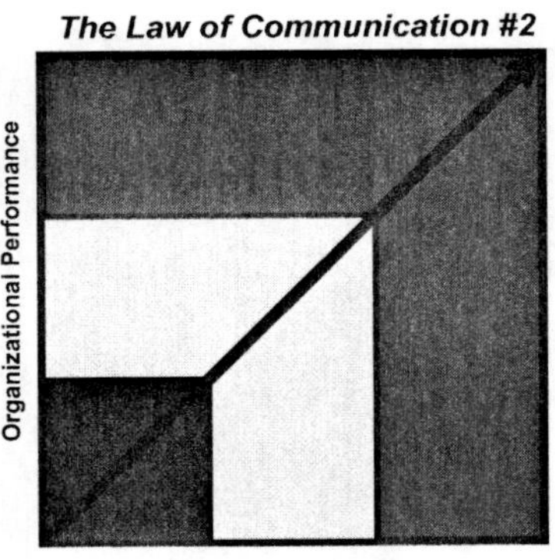

Figure 5.1. The Laws of Communication

The rollout process of Lean Six Sigma (LSS) initiatives, used for organizations of varied industries and sizes, provides a context for illustrating the importance of the *Laws of Communication*. Simple tables can be used to demonstrate prevailing colored zones by exposing the causal relationship that often exists between a leader's communication and behavior and an individual's delivered performance.

Lean Six Sigma

For more than a decade now, many organizations worldwide have been implementing a performance improvement methodology called Lean Six Sigma (LSS). As an organizational philosophy, or methodology, LSS initiatives rely on a disciplined approach to defining problems that are based on factual evidence (i.e. using data), and seeking solutions to these problems using the creativity of a team.

In a nutshell, Lean Six Sigma combines the tenets of Lean (eliminating waste to increase process speed) and those of Six Sigma (reducing process variation to increase quality). The marriage of both Lean and Six Sigma approaches, which were independently developed, has found favor as a comprehensive way to achieve organizational health.

The Approach and Deployment

LSS initiatives use a disciplined framework called DMAIC to structure the way in which LSS projects are designed and executed. DMAIC is an acronym formed by the first letter of each of the five phases of the LSS methodology—**D**efine, **M**easure, **A**nalyze, **I**mprove, and **C**ontrol. Each of these phases consists of a number of activities that must be completed prior to advancing to the next phase. To ensure the activities are completed, a gate review is held between phases with a go or no-go decision to move ahead based on the project team's performance to date.

LSS initiatives are often implemented by executive management coupled with the message of change towards continuous improvement. These improvements are carried out within LSS projects that focus on problematic areas of the organization. To enhance the probability of success of the projects, a number of roles are identified and filled, more in theory than in practice, with top performers. These roles are as follows:

- **Champion**: The executive in charge of the LSS initiative.
- **Sponsors**: Managers that have LSS projects in their areas.
- **Belts**: Individuals responsible for the day-to-day execution of the LSS projects. The most common are the Black Belts who are devoted to projects on a full-time basis and are considered top performers in the organization. Sometimes, individuals may be trained as Green Belts who dedicate 25%–50% of their time to projects in their own areas. In large organizations, a number of Master Black Belt positions may be created to serve as internal advisors to other belts.
- **Team Members**: LSS projects are team-based. As such, the belts will select team members to accomplish the work using the DMAIC process.
- **Stakeholders**: Individuals from all areas that have an interest, or stake, in the success of the LSS projects.

LSS initiatives, when successful, provide organizations with leaner processes, which deliver value to the customer and impact positively the bottom line.

Importance of Effective Communication

To be successful, LSS initiatives require heavy doses of one-on-one as well as all-hands communications—both of which are advocated by the *Laws of Communication*. Even though organizations may have had previous experience with continuous improvement programs, a LSS initiative, with its corresponding LSS projects, bring a new dimension in required discipline in data acquisition, its analysis, and creative approaches to solution generation. Good communication is required from Sponsor, Black Belt, all other Belts, the Champion, and the entire organization. Table 5.1 highlights the essential DMAIC activities involved in LSS projects led by Black Belts.

Table 5.1. DMAIC Activities

DMAIC Phase	Purpose	Activities
Define	Understand a Problem	Assigning a Black Belt
		Creating a Project Charter
		Forming a Project Team
		Uncovering Customer Requirements
		Performing the Define Gate Review
Measure	Set a Baseline	Developing Detailed Process Maps
		Identifying Potential Areas for Improvement
		Gathering Data
		Determining a Process Performance Baseline
		Performing the Measure Gate Review

Analyze	Uncover the Problem's Root Cause(s)	Identifying the Critical Factors Baselining the Critical Factors Stabilizing the Critical Factors Testing Hypotheses about Cause/Effect Relationships Performing the Analyze Gate Review
Improve	Create a Solution	Experimenting and Optimizing Cause/Effect Relationships Proposing Solutions Selecting Solutions Piloting Solutions Performing the Improve Gate Review
Control	Assimilate into Day-to-Day Operations	Documenting the New Process Establishing the New Baseline Creating a Control Plan Returning Control of Process to Owner Performing the Control Gate Review

All of these activities are important, and all are in need of high levels of communication in order to be properly executed. The next section highlights the application of both *Laws of Communication* for the first two activities within the Define phase (as listed in Table 5.1), *Assigning a Black Belt* and *Creating a Project Charter*.

The LSS Define Phase

In the context of an LSS project, the Define phase is designed to identify what processes are important to the organization and to gain preliminary assessments as to the state of these processes in terms of quality and speed. Processes that are deemed important but are not operating at the desired level of effectiveness and/or efficiency are candidates for further study within the DMAIC methodology.

The activities of this Define phase include the following:

- Assigning a Black Belt
- Creating a Project Charter
- Forming a Project Team
- Uncovering Customer Requirements
- Performing the Define Gate Review

Each of these five activities requires constant communication from the Sponsor to the Belt (Black Belt, for purposes of the example) as well as from the Champion to the entire organization. The *Laws of Communication* can be applied to all five activities; however, the first two are selected on the basis that good LSS projects start out with the right person and the right project—conditions acquired by these two initial activities.

1) Assigning a Black Belt

Once a business area with a potential problem in need of resolution is identified, a Sponsor invites a top performer to participate in the LSS initiative as a Black Belt. Early in a Black Belt's career, assigned projects are typically close to the Black Belt's operational area; future projects may be assigned in areas unrelated to the Black Belt's expertise.

Law of Communication #1: Inviting and selecting a Black Belt is no easy task for a Sponsor. This first activity in a LSS project can be a make or break proposition, depending on how the communication is handled between a Sponsor and potential Black Belt. As such, the Sponsor may experience some anxiety when approaching a top performer to work on the project, and this condition may alter the invitation message to potential Black Belts. Table 5.2 highlights some examples of messages in their respective colored zones for this first law of communication. It is important to note the cause-and-effect relationship predicted by the IF/THEN link.

Table 5.2. Law of Communication #1 with Activity 1

Zone Level	Examples of Sponsor Behaviors	Potential Black Belt Performance
RED	If the Sponsor downplays the importance and impact of the LSS project when discussing the LSS initiative with potential Black Belt...	Then, the potential Black Belt resists the new role and delays/declines the decision to volunteer for the seemingly unattractive offering of being a Black Belt.
YELLOW	If the Sponsor challenges a good performer to sign up as a Black Belt and allows only 50% of the work time for the new role...	Then, the potential Black Belt is honored by the new role, attends training, starts the LSS project, and often times experiences burnout due to the demands of the job and LSS project.

GREEN	If the Sponsor rewards a top performer with the new role at 100% of work time dedicated to the project coupled with a well-defined and desirable career path…	Then, the potential Black Belt executes the disciplined methodology with enthusiasm and plenty of discretionary effort devoted to continuous learning of LSS tools and techniques.

Law of Communication #2: Before a Sponsor invites individuals to fill the Black Belt role, a properly conducted LSS initiative rollout must communicate the importance of the improvement approach and generate a desire for people to engage in the effort. The Champion has to take the lead of informing the organization at large of the overview and details of LSS in a continuous manner, and he or she is ill-advised to delegate this responsibility. Table 5.3 depicts some examples of messages in their respective colored zones for this second law of communication. Again, it is important to note the cause-and-effect relationship predicted by the IF/THEN link.

Table 5.3. Law of Communication #2 with Activity 1

Zone Level	Examples of Champion Behaviors	Organizational Performance
RED	If the Champion fails to disseminate the criteria and expectations of the different roles within a LSS initiative…	Then, the organization displays little interest in stepping up to volunteer in a Black Belt capacity.

YELLOW	If the Champion communicates the rigor of being a Black Belt but fails to outline a clear career path for those who volunteer or are assigned into the role…	Then, the organization lacks the confidence to take on challenging roles that may detract from existing career tracks, thus creating difficulties for the Sponsor to invite/select individuals for the Black Belt role.
GREEN	If the Champion discloses challenges, expectations, and rewarding career paths for those individuals invited to take on roles within the LSS initiative…	Then, the organization generates enthusiasm and interest in looking into the role of being a Black Belt.

These simple examples illustrate the importance information dissemination plays in a successful rollout of change initiatives. When poorly done (i.e. the *red zone*), engaging individuals to participate in the improvement approach is a difficult task. When done correctly (i.e. the *green zone*), more than critical mass is achieved towards program success.

2) Creating a Project Charter

A Project Charter is the cornerstone document of an LSS project. The Sponsor is responsible for creating the initial draft of the charter and then works closely with the Black Belt to refine its contents as the project gets underway. A Project Charter typically addresses the problem definition, benefits of finding a solution, the scope of the issue, the nature of the team, and a timeline for project completion.

Law of Communication #1: An LSS initiative is often viewed as an attempt towards organizational change. As such, an LSS project is the application of this change and may be resisted from the start. During this charter creation step, the Sponsor-Black Belt interaction may affect the performance of the Black Belt and, thus, the project. Table 5.4 presents examples of the messages sent by a Sponsor and their possible effects on a Black Belt. The cause-and-effect relationship read by the IF/THEN link can be appreciated.

Table 5.4. Law of Communication #1 with Activity 2

Zone Level	Examples of Sponsor Behaviors	Black Belt Performance
RED	If the Sponsor provides an incomplete charter to the Black Belt…	Then, the Black Belt delays the start of the LSS project.
YELLOW	If the Sponsor provides a complete charter with anecdotal data to the Black Belt…	Then, the Black Belt initiates the LSS project with limited confidence and maximum distrust in the data provided.
GREEN	If the Sponsor provides a timely, complete, accurate, and data-rich charter to the Black Belt…	Then, the Black Belt initiates the LSS project on time, with enthusiasm, and high expectations.

The table illustrates how a Sponsor's deliverables send different messages to the Black Belt. The Sponsor's actions, as evident in the quality of the deliverables, speak louder than his or her words.

Law of Communication #2: The step of creating a Project Charter is one where the Sponsor-Black Belt interaction is foundational. To a lesser degree, yet still important in this step, is the manner in which the Champion communicates the need for the LSS initiative to the organization and to the key stakeholders of LSS project. This organizational communication outreach originates at the Champion level and represents Law of Communication #2. The following table depicts some Champion behaviors and their repercussions within the organization in the different colored zones.

Table 5.5. Law of Communication #2 with Activity 2

Zone Level	Examples of Champion Behaviors	Organizational Performance
RED	If the Champion limits the LSS initiative communication to Sponsors and Black Belts only…	Then, the organization disengages from any activity pertaining to helping Sponsors create and review the Project Charter.
YELLOW	If the Champion highlights aspects of the LSS initiative in a one-shot “all-hands” meeting…	Then, the organization initially meets localized charter activities with enthusiasm only to be unmotivated due to the lack of ongoing top-down communications on the LSS initiative as a whole.
GREEN	If the Champion details positive impacts of LSS initiative using frequent and varied modes of communication to all areas of the organization…	Then, the organization engages with high interest in helping Sponsors create valuable charters that reflect actual problems.

Again, via a threaded example, it is easy to see how continuous information dissemination aids in maintaining the vision and sense of urgency demanded by organizational change efforts. A Sponsor-Black Belt communication in the *green zone* of *Law of Communication* #1 can be pulled back to the red zone if complementary *Law of Communication* #2 messages are in short supply.

The Multiplicative Effect of the Laws

The *Laws of Communication* can aid initiatives, like Lean Six Sigma, to flourish during implementation. This last section discusses how their effect may be magnified. On their own, both of Schuttler's *Laws of Communication* have the power to elevate the performance of an organization by enhancing the manner in which messages are sent and received. This is good news for every organization engaged in some sort of change initiative, such as Lean Six Sigma. Even better news is the realization that focusing on both laws at the same time can actually *multiply* the impact of organizational initiatives and projects. This phenomenon is based on the synergistic effects at play. The following figure shows the effect of this synergy.

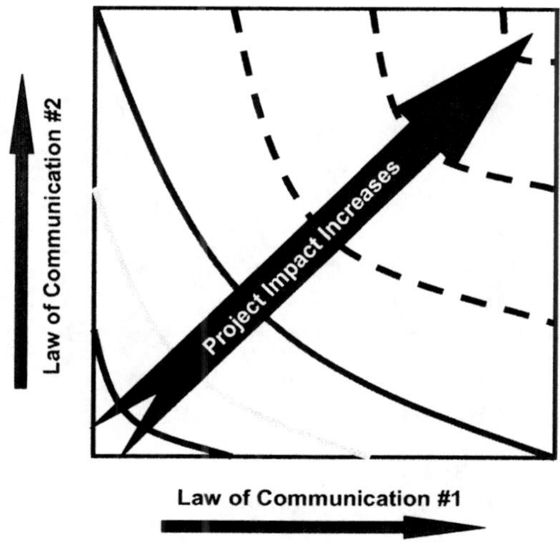

Figure 5.2. Effect of the Laws of Communication on project impact

Synergy can be defined as the interaction of forces that result in a combined effect greater than the sum of the individual forces; this result is said to be multiplicative. In reference to the *Laws of Communication*, the payback of moving from the red and yellow zones to the *green zone* will be realized in organizational performance when focusing on either of the laws. Synergistic results are realized when both laws are implemented interdependently.

An organization that operates in the *green zone* in the context of the *Law of Communication* #1 will be at a higher level of performance if it also operates in the *green zone* from the perspective of the *Law of Communication* #2. Other positive intended and unintended consequences stemming from interacting communication forces (i.e. synergy) will be at play. The following figure depicts this concept.

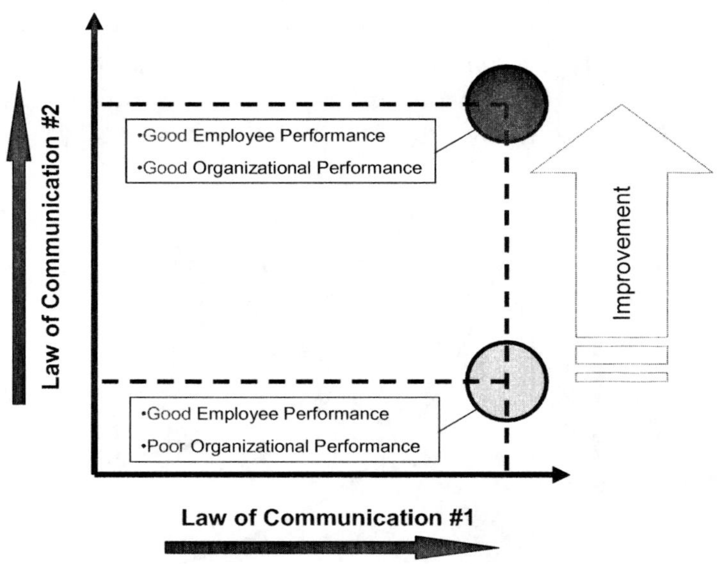

Figure 5.3. Effect of the Laws of Communication on performance

As pictured in the figure above, the lighter-colored green circle represents an organization that has a handle on the *Law of Communication* #1 but is ineffective at the *Law of Communication* #2.

In contrast, the darker green circle represents an organization with solid performance in both communication laws. The latter organization is able to reap the benefits of communication synergy across all levels of the organizational structure. Communication, behavioral, and performance assessments may help organizations find their existing placement on this figure and afford them the opportunity to take action in the appropriate direction. It goes without saying that the top right corner is the ideal placement for harnessing the positive effects of the communication laws.

Summary

Talk is cheap—but an awareness of what is said and how it is said is of value to an organization. These dynamics are the essence of Schuttler's *Laws of Communication.* Some activities from the complex world of Lean Six Sigma illustrate these laws at work. The intent is not to be exhaustive in the portrayal of the laws but to generate some insight as to how one may awaken this awareness within an organization. It is important to recognize that these laws are not independent but are better characterized as interdependent. When working together, they can help each other or hurt each other. It is the responsibility of those individuals in charge of leading and optimizing organizations to focus on communication as an important element of organizational success.

CHAPTER 6
ORGANIZATIONAL ACCULTURATION: FOSTERING INCLUSION IN THE *GREEN ZONE*

P. S. Perkins

In 2007, Harvard political scientist Robert Putnam released a study indicating that ethnically diverse communities engaged less often in civic and social connectedness activities. Understanding the in-group versus out-group worldview of many collective cultures may help explain this phenomenon as it occurs in heterogeneous communities. However, despite the study's dismal social implications, the findings suggested some benefit related to diverse organizational environments, such as exposure to new ideas and creative tension. Such is the case in a diverse workplace setting composed of high-skill workers. It is with this understanding that organizational acculturation is introduced as a viable alternative to the archetype of assimilation in achieving organizational inclusion.

Organizational acculturation is a model designed to create organizational environments that incorporate and value varying points of view and cultural identities. The field of cross-cultural or intercultural communication offers this model of inclusion as a way to embrace differences under the umbrella of mutual benefits and goals. Diversity includes all aspects of culture that differ from the dominant culture's experience—a mix of gender, age, sexual orientation, disability, socio-economic class, ethnicity, co-cultural groupings, and religion.

How do we take such a mix and operate within the *green zone* of organizational effectiveness? Schuttler's *Laws of Communication* shed light on the complex issue of organizational diversity. *Law of Communication* #2 suggests: "Failure of the organization to effectively communicate within results in poor organizational performance," and it is logical to infer that cross-cultural communication dynamics of an organization are an integral part of this law.

Schuttler further suggests, "This second law provides a sense of an organization's culture based on how organizational communications are managed. Many times, organizational culture is identified by the manner in which employees communicate and the types of performance the company produces." The formal and informal networks of communication within the organizational structure acknowledge organizational culture.

The *green zone* of *Law of Communication* #2 recognizes the need for "corporate citizenship," a "seamless global impact," and a "culture of continuous self-improvement." The *green zone* of *Law of Communication* #2 recognizes that inclusion of other, such as in organizational acculturation, is a vital part of organizational effectiveness and success.

Organizational acculturation is a concept introduced by Albert J. Mills (1988) in his writings on gender discrimination and refers to the process by which co-cultures adapt to the cultural patterns of the dominant culture without losing their unique customs, values, or traditions. It requires adjustment on both sides of the cultural paradigm in a process of cross-cultural diffusion, or give and take. Acculturation is the process of adapting to cultural attitudes, values, and beliefs that are not part of the primary culture. It differs from assimilation in that, in addition to learning how to fit in, an individual is encouraged to bring his or her unique perspective and experience to the table, adding to the collective mission. It is the process of diffusion, a blending of perspectives.

In contrast, the paradigm of corporate *assimilation* has long been preserved as a formula of inclusion within U.S. organizations, where co-cultures were expected to absorb and "become like" the dominant culture—typically, white males. Most corporate analysts concur that assimilation has done little to advance the aim of inclusion in corporate America, except for minute gains made by European-American females. The United States Bureau of Labor

Statistics in 2005 revealed that Blacks and Hispanics are less likely to hold corporate management positions. Also, vast numbers of ethnic co-cultures and other co-cultural groupings are not even represented in these statistics.

Why hasn't assimilation created equal opportunity for co-cultural advancement in the corporate environment? It is nearly impossible for one individual playing another's game to effectively compete and win when he or she has no creative input in the game's design. The playing field is created with only one winner in mind—the creator. In order to win, the opponent must think, act, and play like the creator, but most co-cultures have no interest in giving up their cultural heritage in order to engage in such a game. They, too, are ethnocentric in their need for self-identification and preserving heritage. As such, organizations cannot experience the full benefit of a diverse work environment and successfully move forward without creating a newer, more inclusive game.

In order to survive in a global market, the U.S. corporate worldview must expand to embrace the pluralistic points of view they would like to represent. The global market encompasses an ideological and pedagogical framework that expands beyond linear and analytical approaches to problem solving. As such, traditional paradigms should be expanded to include viewpoints that are collective, intuitive, and multi-dimensional, but this shift is often a major challenge for organizations operating from the Western worldview.

Successful organizations understand that true diversity is more than diverse members being invited to the organizational culture to "fit in." True diversity is more than co-cultures providing support services for those who make decisions. Their input, imagination, and innovation must be valued at the top levels.

In the corporate environment, organizational acculturation offers a working solution for inclusion. For example, an organization may enforce an "English only" policy on the work floor, but it provides designated areas where groups can comfortably use their first language. Another organization may create mentoring programs that aggressively groom and promote diverse members, or it may sponsor in-house celebrations in recognition of major co-cultural holidays. An organization might also include a diverse management team dedicated to encouraging and promoting diversity or decision-making bodies purposefully integrated to include critical thinking and innovation from a global perspective.

Similarly, cross-cultural communication clinics as a part of orientation programs help diverse members learn American cultural values and their significance to the organizational culture and how these values affect bottom-line results. Such orientations would also help foster the type of trust and confidence in organizational inclusion that would break down the barriers described in Putnam's Harvard research. These same classes would offer the dominant culture a skills-based formula for how to effectively communicate across cultures. Interpersonal and nonverbal communication clinics offer strategies for speaking and listening to others who differ in communication styles and perspectives. Yes, as Schuttler notes, success is all about communication.

As a tool of cross-cultural communication, organizational acculturation allows an organization to focus on cultural issues that affect institutional achievement, such as the use of space and time. Organizations can examine spatial relationships with an understanding of how cultures operate within *their* reality. Many of us bring a unique reality to the workplace, and we will maintain that reality unless we acculturate into the organization's culture.

An organizational culture that honors everyone's unique contribution can increase communication effectiveness within the organization as strangers come together to work toward a common goal. The paradigm of organizational acculturation is a win-win model of organizational effectiveness that ensures success in the 21st century global market. As organizations expand their boundaries to deliver goods and services to people of all cultural groups and regions, it is imperative that these organizations make room for a new reality, and they cannot do so as long as they maintain homogenous boardrooms. True inclusion brings mutual satisfaction and realized expectations to all involved.

CHAPTER 7
EMPIRICAL SUPPORT FOR THE *LAWS OF COMMUNICATION* AND IMPLICATIONS FOR BUILDING A SUCCESSFUL ORGANIZATION

Jack Roose

Schuttler's *Laws of Communication* focus on two levels of communication that will improve employee and organizational performance. *Law of Communication #1* describes communications that occur at the supervisory or management level with employees. This law states that more effective communication between the supervisor/manager and employee will result in higher levels of employee performance. *Law of Communication #2* describes communication at the organizational level. This law states that more effective organizational communication will yield higher performing employees and, ultimately, better performing organizations. This organizational communication is a major determinant of an organization's culture.

The *Laws of Communication* serve a number of important roles and can be used in several ways to improve an organization's performance. For example, they can help define the parameters within which people are expected to interact with fellow employees, customers, and other stakeholders. They can also form the basis of training programs for managers, supervisors, and front line employees.

Assessment surveys, tools and processes can be developed to monitor how consistently people behave according to the laws. Organizational assessments can be developed and used to evaluate communication practices and their impact on desired organizational results. Likewise, an organization can identify and define benchmarks based on the laws to help develop a focus on continu-

Disclaimer: The opinions and conclusions stated here are the author's and should not be construed as those of Watson Wyatt Worldwide or any of its associates.

ous improvement opportunities. The laws can also be used to help define measurements, tools, and processes used to manage people and their performance within organizations.

In his description of the *Laws of Communication*, Schuttler presents a number of organizational culture attributes often present in high performing organizations. This chapter summarizes data and evidence supporting the fact that these characteristics do in fact relate to the success of an organization. Those previously mentioned characteristics reinforced in this chapter include the following:

- Continuous improvement
- Shared strategic focus
- High morale
- Trusting environment
- Little confusion
- Two-way communications
- Feedback regularly and constantly sought
- Active customer participation
- Clear focus on priorities
- Visible leaders
- Multiple vehicles of communication

In this chapter, I will explore a data-based model of employee effectiveness and organizational performance that reinforces these two *Laws of Communication*. The focus will be on those characteristics of supervisory/management and organizational communication that differentiate highly successful organizations from those that are less successful. In Schuttler's terminology, I will investigate those communications-related aspects of organizations that differentiate between the *red* and *green zones* of the two laws. I will also identify and briefly describe four important tools, programs, or initiatives that involve communications from *Laws of Communication #1 and #2*, and that drive organizational performance. These four initiatives, already commonly addressed in most organizations in one way or another, provide practical examples of programs for improving an organization's performance.

It has long been suspected, with limited evidence, that if employees were treated well and became more involved in company operations, they would be more committed to the organization and perform more effectively, thereby helping the organization perform better. Research on employee opinions and attitudes has evolved over the past 20 years. Initially, consulting firms and organizations focused on various aspects of employee satisfaction (e.g., morale). Up through the 1990s, enlightened organizations tried to build "better" work environments, with an increase in open communication and active employee participation. These organizations implemented initiatives such as quality improvement teams, continuous improvement efforts, team-based processes, and participatory management efforts.

As research and understanding of the relationships between employee opinions and organizational performance improved, the emphasis shifted in the late 1990s and the early 2000s to employee commitment and the extent to which employees were motivated to help the organization succeed. This shift has often led organizations to strive to become known by their employees, communities, and stakeholders as "best places to work," "employers of choice," etc. During this time, research by Watson Wyatt, a global consulting company, clearly demonstrated the relationships among high employee commitment and desirable outcomes, such as an organization's financial success.

Watson Wyatt has been conducting this evolving research since 1987, with an updated understanding of the relationship between employee opinions and organizational performance every two years. Understanding these relationships is critical for organizations, as they can focus their priorities and resources on those efforts with employees that are likely to make a difference in organizational performance.

This evolution has continued during the past several years. The term frequently used today is *engagement*. Highly engaged employees are not only committed to helping organizations succeed, but they also know what to do in their jobs to help produce desired organizational outcomes. Watson Wyatt defines *Engagement* as the combination of Commitment and what is called *Line of Sight*, which includes the following:

- Understanding the organization's goals
- Knowing the steps the organization is taking to achieve those goals
- Understanding how one's job contributes to achieving those goals
- Knowing how well the organization is doing relative to those goals

There are many indicators that an employee is highly engaged, such as the following:

- Highly focused on priorities aligned with broader organizational goals
- Going above and beyond what is expected and required
- Taking on new initiatives and demonstrating innovation
- Passionate about one's work and the organization, and motivated to succeed individually and to help the larger organization succeed
- A team player motivated to help the team succeed

- Continuously improving both individually and offering suggestions for process and organizational improvement

- An ambassador for the organization by speaking positively about it within the work place and in the community, and recommending the employer as a good place to work

These are characteristics of employees whose organizations are operating within the *green zone* of the *Laws of Communication.*

Watson Wyatt's research has shown that financially successful organizations are associated with high levels of employee engagement. However, organizational performance is even further improved if two other organizational characteristics are present. The first of these characteristics is referred to as *enablement*, the extent to which employees have the resources, tools, and equipment required to perform their jobs well.

The second characteristic is referred to as *integrity*, and it is an indicator of the extent to which employees understand and live up to the organization's values, and expect and see other people doing the same. This characteristic has often been called "walk the talk." The "talk" describes desired organizational values, e.g., the ways in which employees at all levels are expected to interact with each other and with customers, suppliers, and other stakeholders. Organizational leaders and their employees display Integrity when they model the values and the normative behaviors that demonstrate the organization's values. Integrity is an outcome of "walking the talk," which is one of the ways leaders communicate within *Law of Communication #1*.

It is the combination of these four characteristics—Commitment, Line of Sight, Enablement, and Integrity—that allows an employee to be truly effective. Having high Commitment, or the combination of Commitment and Line of Sight, is not enough. The latter two factors must also be present in order to have highly effective employees. All four factors combined make up the Watson Wyatt four-factor model.

As noted in the introductory chapter, the critical aspect of organizational communication in the *green zone* of *Law of Communication #2* is creating a clear sense of purpose. The Line of Sight and Integrity factors are the outcomes of the communications that create this sense of purpose, in terms of the following:

- Goals and objectives
- Strategies to achieve them
- Individual contribution to these goals
- Expectations around behavior consistent with desired organizational values

While having effective employees is certainly a desirable goal, and is a high priority for many organizations, most Boards of Directors, CEOs, CFOs, and senior leadership teams must also focus on the organization's bottom line. Fortunately, there is evidence that creating an environment that allows employees to be highly effective also pays dividends in terms of financial success. Watson Wyatt data from the 2006/2007 WorkUSA® survey indicate the following:

- Organizations with high employee Commitment have a total return to shareholders (TRS, a measure of financial success for publicly traded companies) of 18% compared to 12% for the typical company included in the survey; this is an increase in TRS of 50%
- Organizations with high Commitment and high Line of Sight have a TRS of 28%, which is over twice that of the typical company, and 55% higher than companies with only high Commitment
- Organizations scoring high on all four factors have an average TRS of 33%, which is 83% higher than companies with

only high Commitment, and 18% higher than those companies with high commitment and high Line of Sight.

Clearly, creating an environment and culture that allows employees to be highly effective, as defined within the Watson Wyatt four-factor model, can have a substantial impact on the financial success of an organization. Demonstrating these relationships can often make the difference between obtaining the investment dollars needed to create that environment, and not obtaining adequate senior leadership commitment, funding, and resources to do so.

Many organizations today are focusing on how to create a larger group of high performance employees as one way to improve overall organizational performance. In a report focusing on strategic rewards and high performance, Watson Wyatt (2007/2008) demonstrates the relationships between Commitment, Line of Sight, and top performing employees. Highly engaged employees, reporting both a high level of Commitment and Line of Sight, are much more likely to be viewed as high performers in their organizations.

According to this report, over one-quarter of all highly engaged employees are top performers, which is 2.5 times the likelihood of employees who are not highly engaged. Line of Sight tends to be more critical to enabling high performance than Commitment. Employees with high Line of Sight are more than twice as likely to be top performers as are other employees, while employees with high Commitment are only 60% more likely to be top performers. The implication is that to improve the performance of the typical employee, the highest priority should be creating higher Line of Sight.

Two of these four factors describing highly effective employees, Line of Sight and Integrity, are directly related to the *Laws of Communication*. Another of the four factors, Commitment, is an outcome measure driven by many aspects of the *Laws of Communication*, and employee engagement is linked directly to the two laws. To better understand the direct linkages between the two laws and organizational performance, especially the characteristics shown by organizations in the *green zone*, it is important to understand the drivers of these various factors.

If employee engagement has been shown to relate to organizational success, what are the important drivers of engagement? What can an organization do to improve levels of employee engagement? The Watson Wyatt (2006/2007) data point to three primary drivers:

- Customer focus
- Trust and confidence in senior leadership
- Effective reward systems

Data indicate that customer focus is the strongest driver of high employee engagement. Customer focus areas that best differentiate between organizations with high and low employee engagement include the following employee beliefs:

- Customer satisfaction is a top priority
- Employees have the decision making authority to meet customer needs
- Employees are held accountable for the quality of products and services provided

All three beliefs are highly dependent upon communications as described for organizations in the *green zone*.

Trust and confidence in senior leadership is the second major driver of employee engagement. The primary differentiators among companies with high and low employee engagement in this area are as follows:

- Employees have confidence in the long-term success of the organization

- Employees believe that senior management is making the changes needed to help the organization compete effectively

- Employees have trust and confidence in the job being done by senior leadership

Although trust is a prime driver of employee engagement, many organizations today suffer from relatively low levels of trust, for a wide variety of reasons, often independent of senior leadership. A number of specific activities or initiatives have been shown to increase trust in senior leadership. Increasing this trust is not the result of any one activity, action, or initiative, but is the combined effect of many focused communications and activities. As a result, trust levels rarely change quickly, but require a consistent, well-planned, and persistent approach.

Some initiatives that have helped increase trust in senior leadership are as follows:

- Coaching senior leaders in behaviors supporting core values; improving the "walk the talk"

- Designing and implementing a communications plan that involves the *direct involvement* of senior leaders

- Designing and conducting a process for obtaining employee input/feedback *and* facilitating a process by which leaders act upon the results

- Facilitating sessions in which senior leaders discuss the business with employees *and* implications for employees' work

- Designing and conducting an upward feedback leadership development process *and* following up with individual coaching

Trust in senior leadership is a requirement for creating the type of environment present among organizations in the *green zone* of *Law of Communication #2. Laws #1* and *#2* provide ideas and suggestions for how to increase this trust. Employee confidence in the success of the organization, described as an outcome of *Law of Communication #2*, is an essential driver of employee engagement.

The third driver of employee engagement relates to accountability and reward systems. The primary differentiators of high and low employee engagement organizations include the following:

- Employees sensing that high performers are rewarded for their performance

- Employees perceiving that there is external equity for their total compensation package, e.g., their pay and benefits as a total are competitive with those of other employers

- Employees are satisfied with pay and benefits

An effective reward program is designed to meet the needs of both the organization and its employees. Additionally, the impact of effective communications cannot be minimized. Even a well-designed reward program will likely only succeed if it is well communicated. The *Laws of Communication* for organizations operating in the *green zone* provide valuable insights into how the specific details of reward programs can be effectively communicated to employees.

There is often a disconnect between what employers view as drivers of a reward program and what employees perceive those drivers to be. This disconnect, which is most likely to occur in the absence of effective communication, can create a lack of focus, misdirected attention to activities and results that are not organizational priorities, and misplaced employee motivation. In these cases, the organization is likely to be operating in the *red zone*, or at best the *yellow zone*, as described by the laws.

For example, the Watson Wyatt (2007/2008) report on the use of strategic rewards indicates the following:

- 88% of employers believe that annual raises are based on meeting individual goals, while only 46% of employees believe this
- 84% of employers believe that demonstrating knowledge and skills leads to annual increases, while only 46% of employees believe so
- 53% of employers indicate that annual raises are based on demonstrating company values, while only 28% of employees believe so
- In a reversal, while 26% of employers feel annual increases are based on meeting overall company goals, 39% of employees believe so

Today, many employees believe that there is little differentiation in annual increases based on performance. In fact, these increases typically have a small range of approximately 3–5% of base pay for most employees in most organizations. As a result, these employees believe that it is the organization's financial performance, beyond other individual performance factors, that determines the company's ability to pay larger annual increases, and, therefore, company performance is the primary determinant of their annual increase.

Highly engaged, top performing employees are much more likely to see the linkage between their performance and annual pay increases. For example, 81% of highly engaged top performers believe that their annual pay increases are based on demonstration of their knowledge and skills, while only 47% of less engaged employees and 52% of less engaged top performers believe so. This data provides support that improving communication around Line of Sight, and thus Engagement, will improve this linkage among the general employee population.

Likewise, 75% of highly engaged top performing employees believe performance objectives are motivating, compared to 36% of less engaged top performers. Some 89% of highly engaged top performers indicate their supervisor does a good job of providing direct feedback on their performance, while only 43% of less engaged employees indicate so. This data points out the importance of the type of supervisory communication highlighted in *Law of Communication #1*, and it shows the impact of this communication on the motivation of employees to achieve objectives.

Finally, when organizations actively communicate reward programs, employees understand expectations for their performance. They develop Line of Sight to broader organizational goals, know what to do to earn the rewards, and are more satisfied with reward programs. For example, 71% of employees who report active communication are satisfied with base pay, compared to 42% satisfaction among those employees who report less active communication. Some 61% of employees experiencing active communication are satisfied with their incentive pay opportunities, while only 21% of employees who receive less active communication are satisfied.

Similar relationships exist for satisfaction with career development goals and trust and confidence in senior management. These are all important drivers for creating a highly engaged workforce, which leads to better organizational performance. Active communication is based on the practices of managers/supervisors and the larger organization described in the *green zone* of the *Laws of Communication.* Unless they are operating in the *green zone* of communication to support their reward programs, organizations lose a major opportunity to create Line of Sight and to motivate employees to strive for the appropriate goals.

Additional analyses of the Watson Wyatt (2006/2007) WorkUSA® data provide further support for the *Laws of Communication*. The author performed additional analyses to determine those areas in which employees in high performing companies responded most differently from those in low performing companies. These broad areas included the following:

- Communication by senior management about the business and goals
- Trust and confidence in senior leadership
- Continuous improvement and efficiency
- Employee involvement
- Accountability, performance management, and rewards
- Career development

These characteristics of high performing companies reinforce the importance of many of the attributes cited in the introductory chapter and those that are descriptive of organizations operating in the *green zone* of *Laws of Communication #1* and *#2*.

Another Watson Wyatt (2003/2004) report addresses the return on investment for organizational communication. It describes communication practices among 335 companies and differentiates them in terms of financial performance. Three of the primary areas of differentiation were as follows:

- Coaching of senior leadership
- Use of employee feedback
- The ability of managers and supervisors to deliver effective communications in several specific areas

There were often dramatic differences in these practices between companies that demonstrated high vs. low organizational performance. The difference ratios ranged from 2 (high performing) to 1 (low performing) in terms of employees who reported these behaviors, and the ratio was often as high as 4 to 1 or greater. For example, in organizations with high performance, 52% of employees indicated that changes made as a result of employee opinion surveys are communicated effectively to employees, while only 20% of employees in low performing companies indicated so.

Specific differentiating areas in *coaching* were as follows:

- Providing guidance, coaching, and insight to the CEO and senior management team
- Communicating regularly with business unit leaders to discuss business communication issues and opportunities
- Communicating regularly with the CEO to discuss business communication issues and opportunities

Specific differentiating practices related to the *use of employee feedback to make changes and to continuously improve* include the following:

- Conducting employee opinion surveys or focus groups as part of a change effort
- Developing action plans and implementing policy changes as a result of employee opinion survey results
- Designing employee opinion surveys to obtain feedback relating directly to key business objectives
- Using employee opinion surveys to verify employee understanding of key internal communications
- Communicating changes made as a result of internal opinion surveys to employees

Successful companies not only collect employee feedback, but also use this feedback to implement change, by focusing on business objectives (Line of Sight), verifying understanding of internal messages, and providing additional feedback to employees. These are all characteristics attributed to organizations operating in the *green zone*.

The ability of managers and supervisors to effectively deliver various communications is a critical part of *Law of Communication #1*. Those behaviors that best differentiate high from low performing companies include the following:

- Providing feedback to employees about their job performance
- Helping employees with career development
- Giving recognition to employees
- Developing a more participatory style
- Provide formal training in interpersonal communication skills

The data differentiating high and low organizational performance in all of the above areas reinforce specific outcomes in the Laws of Communication, especially as cited for organizations operating in the *green zone*.

Implications for Improving Your Organization

There are a number of practical examples of initiatives and programs in which organizations typically engage that can be designed and improved upon by applying the concepts contained within the *Laws of Communication*. Organizations can use these laws and the data-based evidence supporting them to design and implement effective practices that will improve employee performance and organizational results.

The *Laws of Communication*, as described in this book, and the evidence supporting them, as summarized in this chapter, provide strong direction and help establish priorities for improving an organization. Many, if not most, organizations have already established programs, processes, and tools that can drive better employee and organizational performance. However, many of these same organizations can learn from the implications of the

Laws of Communication to modify and improve upon their current, or planned, practices.

A few of these relatively common organizational practices are briefly described below. When implemented effectively, these practices will provide opportunities for applying the laws and will produce the desired outcomes noted for organizations in the *green zone.*

This chapter has demonstrated the importance of Line of Sight, or, as stated in the introductory chapter, creating a highly focused organization with a clear sense of common purpose. A number of commonly implemented programs serve as a foundation for creating this common purpose. A few selected examples include the following:

- The Balanced Scorecard, or a similar strategic organizational measurement system

- Identification and definition of competencies

- Performance review processes and performance management

- Variable pay or incentive programs

The Balanced Scorecard

Organizations use a number of effective measurement, monitoring, and improvement tools and processes. The Balanced Scorecard is one such process and management system, first described by Robert Kaplan and David Norton (2001). When properly developed and used, this *overall management system* describes, monitors, and aligns performance against explicitly defined organizational strategies and desired outcomes. The balanced scorecard is an excellent system for creating Line of Sight and Engagement throughout an organization.

Initially, the Balanced Scorecard was used primarily as a measurement tool in many organizations. Today, organizations more frequently use it as an overall management system and process for stating expectations relative to strategies, defining desired outcomes, identifying the strategic drivers of success, relating those drivers to desired outcomes, and even measuring reward systems. The fundamental concept is that the organization's strategies are defined as strategic expectations, desired outcomes, and targets in terms of four perspectives:

1. Financial, or the ultimate purpose and outcomes of an organization: typically involves strategies and outcomes for growth, revenues, profitability, etc., as viewed as key outcomes for the investor, owner, key stakeholder, or shareholder

2. Customer expectations: strategies and outcomes that create value for the customer and differentiate the organization from others, as viewed by customers

3. Internal business processes, or process excellence: strategic priorities that create value for customers and shareholders/key stakeholders and lead to customer and stakeholder satisfaction

4. Learning and growth: often viewed as the people, technology, and compliance infrastructures that enable the organization to achieve the above perspectives; these strategies and outcomes support and enable innovation, growth, organizational stability and sustainability, and the organizational change needed to compete and succeed

These four perspectives describe the balanced approach needed by organizations to build and sustain success over time. The financial perspective tends to be associated with lagging indicators, e.g., these are outcomes that occur as a result of the leading indicators in the customer, business process, and learning and growth areas. It is important that the measures included be at the level of strategic measures, rather than tactical annual goal areas that may differ from year-to-year.

As the system has evolved, the Balanced Scorecard has become the center of an overall system that aligns people and resources throughout the organization. The system focuses every employee on his or her role in implementing the organization's strategies and producing at least some subset of the desired organizational results. The system does so in the following ways:

- Beginning with mission and vision
- Developing a strategic measurement system at the level of senior leadership
- Translating strategy to operational terms through corporate Balanced Scorecards and division/unit scorecards aligned with the corporate scorecard
- Creating strategic awareness for every employee through effective communication and possibly through rewards linked to the scorecards
- Making the scorecard(s) a continual, driving process by linking operating budgets, resource allocation, information systems, and other internal support systems to the scorecard(s)

When used as a system as briefly described above, the Balanced Scorecard embodies the types of communication and outcomes defined in the *Laws of Communication* when operating in the *green zone*. The system creates clear expectations and enables alignment from individual jobs performed to the organizational strategies and desired outcomes. It is a primary tool for building and clarifying Line of Sight. It provides a clear focus on priorities and a shared strategic focus. Periodic feedback on performance is a key feature of the system, which leads to continuous improvement.

This management system provides a strong foundation upon which to build other major people management and Line of Sight tools and processes commonly used in organizations today. Brief descriptions of three of these follow.

Development and Use of Competencies

Competencies are the knowledge, skills, behaviors, and attributes needed by employees to succeed in their jobs and to contribute to the organization's success. Properly defined, they can form the foundation for many people management programs and initiatives, for example:

- As an aid to selecting either internal or external candidates for filling positions
- To describe expectations for the work and what is needed to perform it successfully
- In a training needs analysis to determine training and development needs and appropriate programs and curricula
- In performance management systems (see below) to define expectations and provide measurement areas for the performance assessment
- In succession planning to best pair selected candidates with developmental opportunities, and to determine best fit and career progression decisions
- In compensation programs as the performance characteristics that add value to the organization and, therefore, as building blocks of job value

Competencies have a natural synergy with the Balanced Scorecard concept. Some measure of competency assessment and progress is sometimes used as a strategic measure in the Learning and Growth area. Competencies can provide the strategic link between what employees need to do to satisfy, delight, and exceed the expectations of customers, as well as what competencies are needed to perform the key business processes identified.

If organizations develop the appropriate strategic and operational competencies in the right employees, these employees will perform the critical operational processes with excellence. They will produce outstanding results that are valued by customers, and the organization will produce desired financial results. The challenge in the Balanced Scorecard is identifying these linkages (e.g., from enabling employees to performing processes to satisfying customers to generating financial results). Then, the challenge is to develop competencies within the workforce that enable employees to deliver on these linkages.

Competencies can help create the alignment between employee priorities and efforts and organizational goals and outcomes. There are many models for describing and developing organizational competencies. One common model includes three levels of competencies: 1) core, 2) leadership, and 3) role or job specific. Each competency is typically defined at multiple levels, with each level described by a series of behavioral statements describing that level of competency. While there are common competency models and definitions that have been developed in many organizations, each organization should identify and develop (or at least modify) competencies and their definitions to reflect the strategic intent, competitive advantage, values, and nature of the work of that organization.

Core competencies are those that all employees are expected to display with at least some minimum proficiency. These core competencies often help define the culture of an organization. For example, accountability might be a core competency and might be defined at the most basic or introductory level as follows:

- Ensures one's work is done in ways that meet or exceed expectations

- Clarifies expectations when they are not clear or well understood
- Follows up to ensure work products meet the expectations of the user
- Brings errors or possible improvement to the attention of others quickly to improve work and minimize potential problems
- Takes responsibility for one's actions and the results achieved

A higher level of accountability might be described as follows:

- Encourages others to learn from errors and to suggest ways for improving work and results
- Holds others accountable by providing periodic, specific performance feedback, both positive and constructive, and formally assesses others' performance
- Coaches others for achievement of objectives and success

A few other frequently described core competencies include Customer Service/Focus, Flexibility/Adaptability, Continuous Improvement, Growth and Learning, Respect for Others, etc.

Leadership competencies are those that the organization expects all leaders, formal or informal, to display with some minimum proficiency. A few examples include Managing/Leading Change, Managing for Results, Developing and Motivating People, Managing Financial Resources, Establishing and Communicating Direction, etc. Role specific competencies are ones that reflect more specific job skills. Everyone in the organization is expected to display core competencies at one level or another and all leaders are expected to display leadership competencies. However, each job or role will be expected to display a subset of all the role specific competencies defined, depending upon the functions performed, responsibilities, and the skills set needed. Examples of role specific competencies include Written Communication, Oral Communication, Use of Technology, Mathematical Knowledge/Quantitative Analysis, Problem Solving, Persuasion and Negotiation, Product Knowledge, Relationship Management, etc.

Competencies are another tool to help create Line of Sight. They have broad applicability to many processes and tools used to manage people, their expectations, their performance, their careers, and their rewards. They help create the link between a strategic measurement system, such as the Balanced Scorecard, and applications, such as performance management. Properly developed and used, they embody many of the principles contained in the *Laws of Communication.* They are a powerful tool to assist in building and sustaining cultural characteristics of the high performing organizations cited in the *Laws of Communication*, e.g., continuous improvement, shared strategic focus, clear focus on priorities, and two-way communication.

Performance Management

Performance management as a process is one of the primary tools most organizations use to create Line of Sight. In some organizations it is a very effective process, while in many others there are tremendous opportunities for improvement. In those organizations in which it is not as effective, the emphasis is merely on a one-time discussion, often cursory and brief, that justifies a merit or annual pay increase. This use of performance management is what is characterized as operating within the *red* and perhaps *yellow zone* of the *Laws of Communication*.

This chapter has emphasized the importance of Integrity and Line of Sight in terms of creating more effective employees and better organizational performance. A well-defined performance management process provides opportunities to create high levels of both factors. Integrity is emphasized by including the measurement of behaviors descriptive of organizational values on the performance appraisal form.

Line of Sight is enhanced by measuring performance on individual goals and objectives that are aligned with and cascaded down from department, business unit, or organizational goals. Line of Sight is also increased by measuring and providing feedback on behavioral competencies that set expectations for those behaviors seen as important drivers of individual contribution and organizational performance.

The *Laws of Communication*, as described by supervisor/manager behaviors and organizational practices operating in the *green zone*, relate well to the best practices associated with performance management. An effective performance management process is characterized by the following:

- Creation of clear expectations and a clear sense of purpose
- Alignment between individual and organizational goals
- Focus on common goals and objectives
- Accountability and rewards linked to performance
- Two-way communication and dialogue
- Periodic feedback and focus on self-improvement
- Coaching and mentoring
- "Walking the talk," as measured as part of performance, and also as displayed in the interactions between supervisors and employees throughout the process

In summary, an effective performance management process is one of the most important tools an organization can use to create highly engaged, top performing employees and, ultimately, to improve organizational performance. Line of Sight and Integrity are two factors that can be reinforced through performance management. Schuttler's *Laws of Communication* provide useful guidance for designing and implementing an effective process.

Variable Pay or Incentive Programs

The use of well-designed variable pay or incentive programs is a primary means by which an organization can communicate priorities and goals and objectives to employees. Incentive programs help to clearly identify Line of Sight and create alignment to goals and objectives of the organizational unit or the larger organization. Use of incentive programs in a balanced portfolio of rewards helps fulfill the third driver of engagement described earlier in this chapter: accountability and effective reward systems. In today's environment of relatively low and stable merit increase budgets, incentive plans are often the primary mechanism to deliver true and meaningful differentiation in total cash compensation and pay for performance.

Short-term or annual incentives are becoming progressively more important in delivering total compensation. Organizations are increasing the eligibility of short-term incentives to larger employee groups, while also increasing the size of the target incentive amounts. At the same time, organizations are increasing both the company financial and individual performance expectations needed to earn incentives (Watson Wyatt, 2007/2008). As a result, a larger proportion of all employees are becoming eligible for incentives, and incentive awards are becoming a larger proportion of an employee's total pay.

This trend, and the significance of the dollars employers are investing in incentives, highlights the need for effective communication. Three times as many employees who report active communication are satisfied with incentive opportunities than employees who report less communication (Watson Wyatt, 2007/2008). Incentive plans are only effective if they drive desired behaviors and improve desired results. To do so, participants must clearly understand the mechanics of the incentive plan, how their work will impact the measures in the plan, and the awards they will receive. This understanding helps create a Line of Sight that is also a driver of company financial performance.

If employees do not adequately understand the incentive plan, they may view it as merely a bonus plan. If perceived as an incentive plan, employees are driven by the motivation to display the desired behaviors and achieve the desired results, but with a bonus plan, employees are less focused on desired outcomes. They may view the bonus as an entitlement, rather than payment for a specific purpose and performance.

Too often organizations spend considerable time and effort designing incentive plans, sometimes overly complex plans requiring a detailed understanding. Then, at implementation, these organizations operate within the *red* or *yellow zones* of the *Laws of Communication*. In these cases, the organization is not receiving the optimal return on its investment in incentive dollars. In order to achieve the best return on their incentive investments, organizations must operate in the *green zone.*

To operate within the *green zone*, organizations must both clearly communicate and deliver the incentive plan. Communicating the plan establishes clear expectations and creates Line of Sight. Paying awards for specific performance levels tends to produce higher levels of performance, increases employee commitment, and improves trust and confidence in senior leadership. These factors are all essential in creating a highly engaged workforce, and these highly engaged employees are more likely to be top performers (Watson Wyatt, 2007/2008).

Summary

Schuttler's *Laws of Communication* are supported by evidence relating effective employees and organizational practices to organizational success. High levels of employee Commitment and Line of Sight help employees become engaged in their work and the organization. These highly engaged employees are more likely to be top performers. The behaviors, practices, and outcomes described as belonging to organizations operating in the *green zone* of the *Laws of Communication* are also associated with developing highly engaged employees who demonstrate Integrity and whose organizations have provided them with Enablement. These organizations perform more successfully overall, and those using tools and management systems, such as the Balanced Scorecard, competencies, performance management, and variable or incentive compensation, can apply the concepts described in the *Laws of Communication* to generate the outcomes and characteristics of successful organizations.

CHAPTER 8
BUSINESS COMMUNICATION: OPERATING WITHIN SCHUTTLER'S STOPLIGHT METAPHOR

Michael Stewart

What is the purpose of business communication if not to improve an organization's overall productivity and performance? In almost every situation, the fundamental goal has been the same: to help employees cope with a challenging market environment. It is hard to imagine a conversation about business strategy that does not include the word *communication*. In fact, its frequent use would suggest that the meaning of the term is well understood, but its inherent complexity and subtlety makes a simple, one-sentence description nearly impossible.

Schuttler's *Law of Communication #1* demonstrates communication as a social interaction. It is the giving and receiving of information for the purpose of understanding and providing social interconnectedness. Leaders lead and communicate through feedback and feed-forward. They welcome active, interactive, and open dialog mechanisms that in turn foster an atmosphere where employees are innovative and imaginative. In this environment, employees can become champions of change who understand how to attain business goals. But, communication is a learned skill. We learn to speak, listen, and understand verbal and nonverbal meanings through observing other people and modeling our behavior based on what is seen.

In a complex and changing environment, such as the financial services industry, maintaining commercial success becomes a tremendous challenge. With emerging technologies, new knowledge-creation, and the launch of new products or services, survival is based on the ability to communicate effectively with customers, co-workers, superiors, and subordinates. Organizational leaders, middle-managers, front-line supervisors, and employees can ill afford not to communicate with each other, lest they end up operating in the *red zone* of the stoplight metaphor.

Communication Between Superiors and Subordinates

The success of communication between superiors and subordinates is gauged by the reactions of the individuals affected by the change and the impact such reactions have on productivity. New technology, globalization, regulatory requirements, and organizational structural changes are inevitable, and they will no doubt influence employee morale in one way or another, but employees are affected even more so by a lack of communication. Employees help the organization achieve its vision, so they need to be informed of impending changes.

Communication from leaders and managers will not eliminate uncertainties in the environment, but an informed workforce will experience less stress and have more trust in management. The well-being of employees will always be an issue as organizations experience continuous change and uncertainty, but the level of communication from their leaders will determine the zone of the stoplight metaphor from which they operate, whether under stable or uncertain conditions.

Leaders and those they lead are impacted by continuous change. Thus, superiors must find successful ways to continuously engage subordinates. To achieve planned results, leaders must engage workers with systematic communication throughout the change process. Failure to effectively communicate will hinder any change initiative, create uncertainty in the workforce, and cause the departure of highly skilled employees. Communication from top-management, middle-management, and front-line supervisors is a useful tool for dealing with uncertainty and change, and it brings about equilibrium between employees and leaders when done effectively.

Employees who operate within the *green zone* will deliver the services and products required by customers. In contrast, an unmotivated workforce and high levels of attrition prevent the delivery of promised results to shareholders, analysts, suppliers, and clients—a sure sign that the organization is operating in the *red zone* of the stoplight metaphor. Employees are demoralized when command lines are unclear, arbitrary changes of procedures are later reversed, and decisions are made to increase one's power rather than the financial performance of the organization.

Lines of communication between supervisors and employees are not always clear, especially when a supervisor is lacking certain communication skills. Leaders in the regular course of business activities, and in periods of uncertainty and change, should create messages specific to the needs of employees. Senior executives, middle-managers, and front-line supervisors must design effective modes of communication specific to bringing about changes to the employees, structure, and design in their organization. Leaders must know what communication method best meets the needs of their unique workforce—a communication method that was successful in another environment might not be applicable to the present situation.

While uncertainty and change are inevitable, the manner in which they are communicated impacts the well-being of employee performance and productivity. With globalization, the emergence of the knowledge worker, new technologies, and a shrinking workforce, an organization's manner of coping with uncertainty and change determines the well-being of employees. Managers and empowered employees need to devote considerable time and resources to helping other employees deal with uncertainty.

New technology can bring fear to employees. There is the fear of losing one's job to automation, or fear of learned skills becoming redundant. The fear of losing a job creates paralysis that in turn impacts productivity in a negative way. While supervisors cannot guarantee employment in the face of new technology and automated processes, they can communicate to employees the benefits of such changes to the workforce. To alleviate paralysis, supervisors can explain that automation eliminates manual activities that are otherwise menial. By communicating the value of new technology, these leaders can steer performance into the *green zone* of the stoplight metaphor.

Newly-Promoted Supervisors

Schuttler's *Law of Communication #1* is that failure of supervisors to effectively communicate with subordinates results in poor employee performance. To avoid this pitfall, organizations should ensure that newly- promoted supervisors have strong communication skills. Many managers confront the problem of determining meaningful approaches that will achieve results and improve performance, but supervisors can determine where their communication skills rest on the stoplight metaphor. When supervisors are myopic and micro-manage, the end result is a group of employees who do only what is required of them. New supervisors are responsible for developing, deploying, and communicating an agenda for their entire group of employees, but their prior positions as individual performers may not have prepared them for these tasks.

To function effectively in the newly promoted role of manager or supervisor, an individual must build operational, personal, and strategic networks. Newly-promoted employees generally go through a training period, whether in a day or one week, where leadership and strategic development are addressed. Unfortunately, these sessions often lack training devoted to communication.

Most people are born with the physical ability to talk, and organizations mistakenly perceive this ability as effective communication. They do not see a need to teach employees to communicate, but for communication to be effective, it must be taught and practiced in its various forms (face-to-face, verbal, written, emails, etc.) and to match the needs of the audience.

Communicating is not simple—at least effective communicating, that is. For communication to be effective and reach its intended audience, it must be learned, practiced, and exercised. Effective communication requires continuous learning. Organizations operating from the red zone can better their performance by seeking outside help or help from another more functional area of the organization, one with a proven track record of effective communication with employees, customers, clients, stakeholders, and other important constituents.

While outside help, such as consultants with communication training, will cost the organization initially, the benefits and return on investment will far outweigh the costs as employee performance improves over time. Unless organizations have the requisite in-house communications expertise, it is recommended that they seek outside help from industry experts. Outside experts can tailor communication mechanisms to fit the needs of the supervisor and the intended audience because communication modes are not a one-size-fits-all. A mode of communication that was quite effective in one environment can be doomed to failure in another.

Presentation skills, interpreting dialogue, learning to listen, and understanding body language and gestures are communication techniques that can be taught and learned over a period of time, but there is no substitute for authentic communication that comes from the heart and head of the person speaking. Effective communication that creates a vision of a better future and improved employee performance must be authentic. Employees tend to trust a supervisor who is genuine, but not someone who has been taught to say the right thing and use the right gestures. Knowledgeable employees are quick to recognize insincerity and respond negatively to it.

Communication can also occur even when nothing is said. The unanswered inquiry from a customer, for example, speaks volumes. The message may be that the organization does not care about the customer's business or their relationship with the customer. To avoid this type of error, communication must be clear and tailored to its audience. Organizations and people are different, and the mode of communication used should match each situation.

Developing mechanisms for customer satisfaction and employee performance is not the sole responsibility of supervisors. Employees have a responsibility to ensure that personal goals, personal development plans, adequate training, and career paths are well designed. This can only be achieved through open dialog, face-to-face communication, double-loop learning, and a feedback feed-forward process.

Improved Employee Performance

Supervisors should openly and consistently communicate change initiatives to the workforce. This practice alleviates uncertainty and maintains normalcy. Supervisors who communicate with employees only once or twice during the year, generally during performance review periods, do not create a high performance environment. In contrast, continuous communication between supervisors and employees provides the opportunity for learning about each other, the strategy of the organization, and how the strategies and goals of the individual correlate with those of the organization. Interpersonal communication between the supervisor and employee is not simple, but it creates an open atmosphere for growth and improved employee performance.

Improved employee performance will not only enhance the financial growth of the organization, but also provide employees with a sense that they are adding value and not merely collecting a paycheck. Through open and continuous communication, supervisors can look to the workforce to identify knowledgeable employees who need to be retained because they are critical to maintaining productivity levels through a change initiative. Front line supervisors know that cooperation and support for change is gained in individual situations rather than in groups or large meetings. When supervisors delay communicating changes, uncertainty among employees, investors, shareholders, stakeholders, and analysts will fester.

When employees sense uncertainty, they become distracted and lose focus. Losing external focus places the organization at risk.

When standards are not clearly linked to goals, the workforce flounders and talented employees and customers are lost to other companies. This type of activity does not necessarily place an organization in the *red zone*, but an organization firmly rooted in the *yellow zone* will be prevented from operating as a *green zone* organization. As such, effective communication and open dialogue between management and workers should be a shared interest if organizational and individual goals are to be met.

To gain support from employees and create an organization of performance excellence, supervisors must spend time communicating the nature of strategic, technological, structural, and human resource changes. At minimum, supervisors should communicate the reasons for the change and the scope of the change, even if the message contains bad news. Supervisors should also develop a graphic representation of the change project—one that people can understand and point to. In addition, supervisors should provide analysis to predict the negative aspects of implementation. When supervisors provide an explanation of the success criteria, how they will be measured, and how people will be rewarded, a win-win situation is possible.

Best Intentions

Leaders of every type of organization—for-profit, non-profit, public and private—must be aware of communication issues and how the lack of effective communication can derail the best-intended vision, strategy, or goal. Communicating the new vision and strategies will not be successful if done through a single communication from top management to employees. Even with constant communication through emails, newsletters, and speeches, the effort can fail if a very visible senior executive behaves in a way that contradicts the new vision and strategy.

The behavioral integrity of the leader will lead to organizational success. Employees want to perceive that management is credible in what is being communicated, and the credibility of the management team starts at the top. To ensure that the right people are in the right jobs, the board of directors of the organization must select a CEO who is of the highest ethical standard to lead the organization. The board of directors has a fiduciary responsibility to protect the shareholders of the organization.

Organizational strength lies in leadership and total involvement of employees in the strategic planning process. An organization's strategy is not fixed—the strategic plan should be continuously revised, a living document, to reflect external and internal environmental changes. An organization that continuously communicates with the workforce will avoid the negative implications of "constant direction change," a trait that is representative of the *red zone* in the stoplight metaphor. Open and continuous communication from senior and middle managers can ensure employees that any change in strategy is a response to environmental changes.

Like all processes, the strategic process will confront resistance if it does not have buy-in from employees. Organizational leaders and designers of the process should be mindful of the challenges in undertaking new tasks and challenges. In particular, employees may be unclear about who is responsible for what and who is supposed to report to whom. There is difficulty in getting people to communicate and coordinate the change process, but traversing the different color zones of the stoplight metaphor will provide the leaders with important insight when communicating strategy, vision, and goals.

Communication Plan

In order to earn buy-in, organizational leaders must be effective in communicating the organization's strategy and goals—a communications plan is highly recommended. The CEO of the organization should introduce strategies at the annual all-employee meeting, and each division and department manager should then meet with employees to discuss the organization's strategies in more detail and incorporate them in their division or department plan. These meetings deliver a consistent message and foster employee understanding of organizational priorities. Organizations that involve employees in this process will generally operate in the *green zone* of the stoplight metaphor.

Once the organization's strategies, including division and departmental plans, have been communicated, managers should work with employees to develop supporting unit action plans. Managers should have a discussion of goals with employees. Employees should agree on four to six specific, measurable, action-oriented, realistic, and timely goals on their personal development plan.

Each goal should be linked to the specific success factors and strategies they impact to ensure alignment at all levels. A workforce that shares in the overall strategy, vision, and goals of the organization and relates them to their own development plans will create greater organizational performance, and organizational workforces that are part of a strategic process have greater latitude in creative processes.

Communicating Change

People have an unquenchable desire for change, especially those with an entrepreneurial spirit. As long as this desire continues, creativity will always be prevalent. The creative employee influences change to system design and technological processes, and the design of strategy and process from the top will ultimately fail. To prevent failure in new system designs, senior leadership should conduct an analysis of the organization's workforce and build coalitions through communication and collaboration to achieve desired changes to the organization. Middle managers might be one of the organization's best resources with which to form these coalitions.

Many middle managers are working within the areas of technology or operations. Through job rotations within the same organization, middle managers have developed extensive networks. Leveraging the skills of the middle managers and making them effective communicators of change is a critical resource that leaders of the organization can tap into.

A change in an organization's system design will allow the organization to anticipate what the rapidly changing environment will be like. An organization that reacts to external and internal environmental factors, as opposed to proactively planning for the unthinkable, is at a disadvantage in a rapidly changing global market place.

Creating trusted allies in middle managers improve the odds of top-level management realizing complex but necessary organizational change. Leaders and managers can bring about change to the organization's current system design by involving middle managers who have an established network among employees, customers, and stakeholders. By aligning knowledge management, customer satisfaction, product and service, human resource, and social responsibility, organizational effectiveness and financial and market results are achieved through the effective execution of the organization's strategy and business governance plan.

Business governance plans dictate that an organization's board of directors, CEO, and other senior managers implement, communicate, and execute change to the organization's culture. Senior leadership can bring about change to the current system design by involving all employees in changing from a culture of questionable practices to one that demonstrates ethics, integrity, honesty, and transparency.

The way management goes about creating a learning environment, creating new knowledge, and having open dialogue to embrace strategy planning and execution will determine the organization's success. Environmental changes are inevitable, but how the organization manages this inevitability makes all the difference. To react to change is always too late, as it means catching up to the competition. Organizations must be proactive and create, manage, and communicate change if they are to somewhat accurately forecast the next unexpected and unthinkable environmental event.

Leaders of organizations seeking growth through various means, such as alliances, mergers, acquisitions, or through partnerships, should understand the importance of strategic, collaborative, and interactive communication to effectively achieve performance excellence. Leaders should be visible and supportive in facilitating change in the daily functioning of the organization. How leaders communicate and execute organizational changes to the workforce will determine the organization's financial health, customer and stakeholder satisfaction, and the well-being of employees and their performance.

With globalization comes the emergence of knowledge workers, new technologies, and a shrinking workforce. As such, effective coping with change and uncertainty will be an important determinant in employee well-being. Managers and empowered employees will need to devote considerable time and resources to establishing open and continuous communication.

Lateral Communications

Not all communication needs to come from the top, but an organization that operates in an environment lacking structure, and in which systems and processes are continuously revised, is operating from the *yellow zone*, and major strategic changes will need to be made from the top. Some changes in the organization will also come from divisional and functional unit heads. In this case, collaborative and interactive communication is needed for the sharing of limited resources in meeting organization performance goals.

Organizational performance is important to the leaders of the organization, investing public, stakeholders, and other important constituencies. Equal in importance are the results the organization achieves over time, as these results have a direct impact on employee well-being in terms of personal and professional development.

Organizational results are directly linked to employee morale and performance, but employees will not know how well the organization is performing unless those results are communicated regularly to the workforce. Hearing about the company's performance from street analysts does not build an environment of openness and trust. Leaders at all levels of the organization must communicate with the workforce if organizational performance excellence is to be repeated in the long-term.

Clear and continuous communication from organizational leaders will help in developing and deploying the strategic plan to individual employees. With this information, they will be able to monitor their performance against goals and identify training and development needs. By taking this approach, the organization is better able to enhance the well-being of its human capital and, at the same time, maintain processes that deliver desired organizational results. An organization with open and clear communication channels will create employees who can better meet the needs of customers, clients, and suppliers and who are better informed of what the competition is doing.

Many organizations fail to determine meaningful approaches that will achieve results and improve performance during routine or unexpected challenges. As the stoplight metaphor suggests, the best approach to this issue is effective organization-wide communication to achieve planned results. Organizations can achieve stability in their workforce by linking customer and employee needs to high organizational performance. In the case of the customer, the organization can work toward continually improving services. For the employee, the organization can offer some form of monetary reward or appropriate recognition.

Operating in the Zones

Organizations that want to operate in the *green zone* should employ intentional processes that support value creation undertakings for its customers. One critical process would be the communication of values and know-how's to encourage cooperation among cross-functional teams. This structure places rapid decision-making and agility at the points of greatest impact for customer and business needs. Employees' efforts are rewarded with incentive compensation, merit-based performance appraisals, and educational reimbursements. Six Sigma, for example, links accountability for process improvement directly to employees most involved in the process.

In order to operate in the *green zone*, the organization's workforce must have an understanding of organizational processes, customer needs, expected outcomes, and feedback mechanisms to ensure contribution to high performance work systems. Creating equilibrium between organizational and individual needs ensures that employee morale is high in creating, controlling, and improving processes. Without customers, no organization can survive. In any *zone* of the stoplight metaphor, retaining customers and maintaining organizational stability are the two most important, and most difficult, tasks of all.

Organizational stability might be achieved with mechanisms that maintain a balance between the strategic goals of the firm, the needs of the employees, and the maintenance of satisfied customers. These factors can be achieved in the long-term with effective communication. An organization that operates in the *red zone* can have some success, but it will be only for the short-term. Over time, talented employees and customers who are critical to the survival of the firm will depart from a *red zone* organization. *Yellow zone* organizations need to create structure and double-loop learning and address customer concerns through an inquiry and design process if they are to remain viable and operate at the next level. The next level would be where the organization operates in the *green zone*.

While all organizations operate in an environment of complexity and constant change, both planned and unplanned, *green zone* organizations have the advantage of sustained organizational performance. A successful organization communicates a better future through social responsibility and a lived vision and mission where leaders and employees are good corporate citizens, customer focused, and adaptable to the changing environment.

A *green zone* organization is positioned for potential disruption. It must retain flexibility if it is to survive old and new competitive forces in the global marketplace. A primary objective of the strategic organization is to create uninterrupted value for its stakeholders—a goal of any business strategy. To do so, leaders must create a visionary picture of the future that is relatively easy to communicate to employees, customers, and stakeholders.

Conclusion

Leaders must be visible across the organization if they are to earn successful buy-in, and clear, compelling, and multiple communication channels must be used to broadcast their vision. They will be successful when the employee at the lowest rung of the corporate ladder begins communicating this new vision. But, communication is not an end in itself. In *green zone* organizations, open and renewed communication is necessary. For an organization to maintain adaptability, it must stay abreast of the strategy and vision while engaging in the needs of partners and customers, by building relationships and interdependencies among customers, professional organizations, governmental agencies, vendors and suppliers, economic institutions, mass media, international consortiums, and other entities.

An organization operating in the *green zone* functions as a collection of parts, or subsystems, integrated to accomplish an overall goal. It is important that managers and leaders of *green zone* organizations think about their organization as a system and communicate this design to the workforce. The soundness and adaptive effectiveness of any organization's system is done through inquiry or evaluating its strategic position in the environment. The leaders' inquiry and evaluation of the organization will help to recognize global implications for the company and its workforce. An informed workforce is better equipped at becoming adaptable in periods of internal and external disruptiveness.

The culture of a *green zone* organization communicates confidence in the input of employees and stakeholders at all levels. Within this framework, one cannot overlook the political ramifications that arise when organizations try to earn buy-in, as each department may lobby for limited resources and control of the path of organizational change. Each department has the ability to steer the strategy or the structure of the organization in favor of their own interests. Politics can improve the decisions an organization makes, but they can also produce problems and promote conflict if not managed skillfully. To manage organizational politics and gain needed benefits, organizations must establish a balance of power in which dissenting views can be heard and alternative solutions considered.

While politics cannot be eliminated, they must be controlled with open dialog and effective communication. Across functional departments, politics can be managed by involving senior managers, as they are responsible for the implementation of strategic plans and the vision of the organization. Through strategic, collaborative, and interactive communication, senior leaders, middle-managers, supervisors, and subordinates can make clear choices that generate minimal conflicts, provide the right incentives, assign ownership and accountability for strategic and development plans, provide transparency and education, and implement common mechanisms across functional departments.

The creation of an environment that fosters employee learning and motivation is directly linked to the creation of new processes geared towards organizational results and performance excellence. An organization's continued existence or demise, and whether it operates in the *red*, *yellow*, or *green zones*, will depend on whether there is open dialogue and a collaborative workforce. Environmental changes are inevitable, but how the organization manages and communicates this inevitability makes all the difference.

To react to change is always too late, as it means catching up to the competition. Organizations must be proactive in communicating, creating, and managing change if they are to somewhat accurately forecast the next unexpected and unthinkable environmental event that impacts customers, stakeholders, employee productivity, and organizational performance. Organizations that operate in the *green zone* of the stoplight metaphor will meet the challenges of the evolving environment because they are engaged in a culture of continuous self-improvement and drive for data-driven results, where organizational vision and mission are lived through a well-informed workforce.

CHAPTER 9
BUSINESS INTELLIGENCE: CORRELATING PERFORMANCE TO COMMUNICATION

Bernd Heesen

This chapter will demonstrate how a communication strategy can help to improve the performance of an organization. Performance is defined as "the manner in which or the efficiency with which something reacts or fulfills its intended purpose" (Webster, 1996, p. 1439). The intended purpose of an organization is defined by its vision and mission.

Communication should be focused and efficient in order to supply relevant, timely information to support the decision-making process. In 1989, Howard Dresner, a research fellow at Gartner Group, established the term *business intelligence* to describe a set of concepts and methods that might improve business decision-making by using fact-based support systems (Wikipedia, 2007). In an ideal scenario, the decision making process consists of the following steps:

1. Information is collected (data acquisition and data storage).

2. Information is analyzed to understand what happened at what time. The information is interpreted, for example, to suggest cause and effect relationships that help leaders in understanding why problems may have happened.

3. The knowledge gained via analysis is used in the decision-making process to help avoid negative developments and reinforce positive developments.

The decisions should lead to a consequent implementation and an evaluation of the consequences. Adding the following steps creates the *Business Intelligence Framework* (see figure 9.1):

4. Employees and leaders are urged to act in accordance with the decisions made.

5. Feedback is gathered regarding the outcomes of the decision.

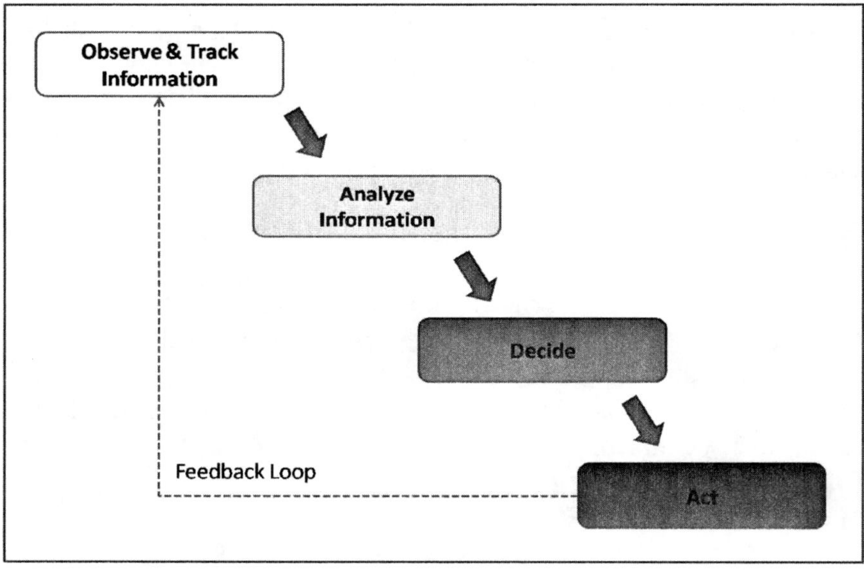

Figure 9.1. Business Intelligence Framework

Motivation

A leader's task is to communicate the vision, mission, intent, and strategy to all members of an organization. The members of an organization should understand their individual roles in contributing to the fulfillment of the corporate strategy. This requires them to be updated on the vision and the supporting strategy. Identifying the activities and initiatives that will be performed to implement the strategy should enhance this process. Finally, it is critical to define performance objectives and develop instruments and processes that will help to facilitate top-down and bottom-up communication (as illustrated in figure 9.2). The second *Law of Communication* mandates the leader to communicate the vision. This creates a clear sense of purpose for the members of the organization.

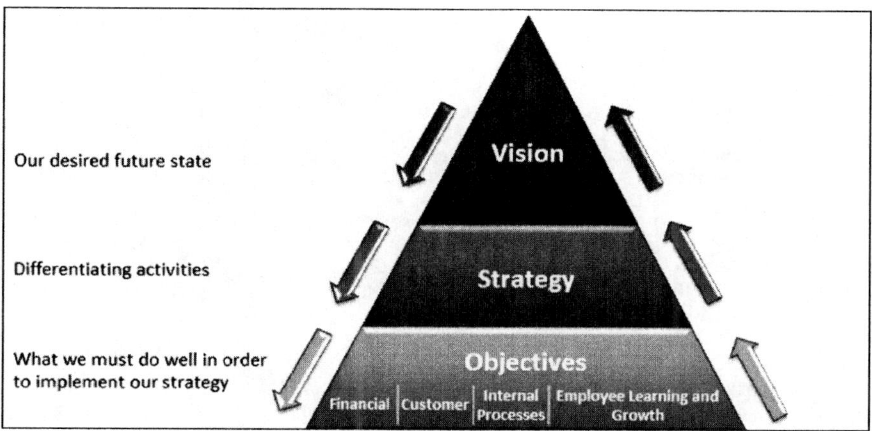

Figure 9.2. Implementing a Strategy with a Balanced Scorecard (reproduced based on Niven, 2002, p. 107)

Based on the first *Law of Communication*, leaders should communicate the organizational performance standards and clearly link them with goals since employees look to their supervisors, at all levels, to provide clear direction. Developing a set of measures or indicators for each of the objectives allows measurement of the progress towards achieving the vision. Sharing their definition and understanding with all individuals who are either meeting or not meeting the set expectations affects is crucial (see figure 9.3).

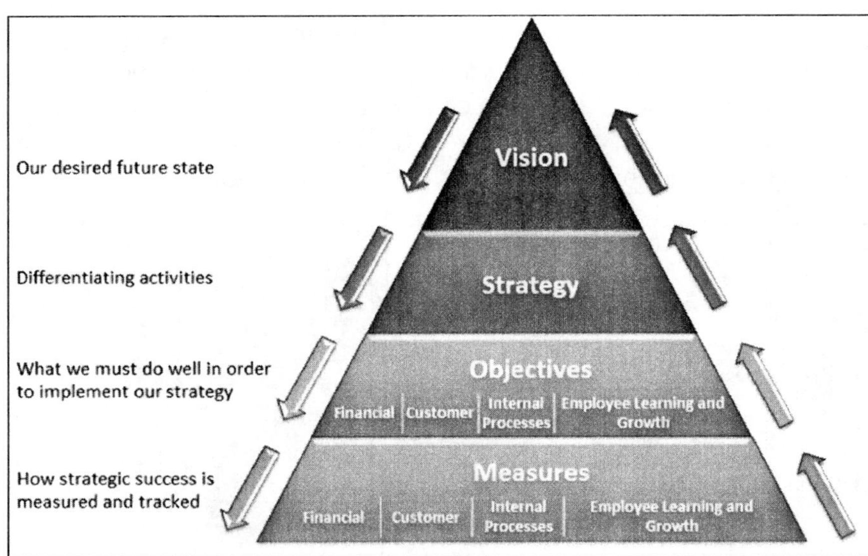

Figure 9.3. Implementing a Strategy with a Balanced Scorecard (reproduced based on Niven, 2002, p. 107)

The Value of Information

Having a shared understanding of the measures is a great starting point to work towards implementing a strategy. In order to enable the *decision-making process loop*, the organization needs to start tracking employee performance toward each of the measures. At defined intervals (e.g. daily, weekly, monthly, quarterly, annually) this information can be communicated. Alternatively, communication might be triggered when a measure deviates significantly from the expected value (exception reporting). This process can be automated via information systems that constantly monitor information streams. This means a significant process improvement over a manual case-by-case investigation or the alternative of waiting for the next periodic report, which might cause a significant delay in realizing the performance gap.

Information as an essential resource and asset to implement a defined strategy has certain characteristics that should be leveraged by management. Companies often invest significant money in information systems to collect data. Apart from the investment in hardware and software, the time users need to maintain, transform, manage, and extract these data create permanent additional costs. Since the production and use of information is so costly, it is important to understand the value of information as an asset itself.

Information systems store data in the form of individual characters, e.g. "2,0,y,e,a,r,s", which only become meaningful when based on a defined syntax of a language, e.g. "20 years." The usefulness and value of this data is limited unless its relevance is understood based on the context it is used in, e.g. the age of an applicant to be 20 years rather than the time since a product has been introduced in the market, thereby transforming the data into information. An interpretation of information based on a correlation with other information can transform data into knowledge—potentially knowing that a management position requires at least 10 years of business experience and a candidate with an age of 20 cannot fulfill this expectation. The value increases as data is transformed into information and into knowledge (see figure 9.4).

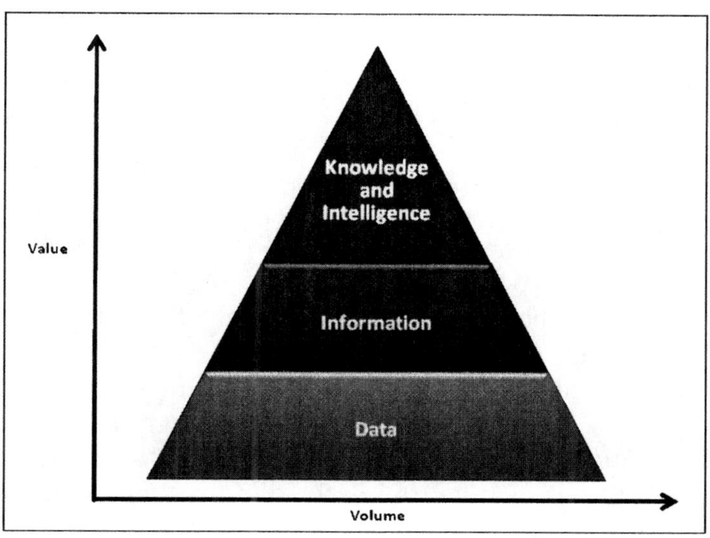

Figure 9.4. Volume versus Value of Information

The total value of sharing available data (value level 1), information (value level 2), or knowledge (value level 3) can be increased by identifying the interested target audience for this asset (step 1) and then leveraging several communication channels to reach the target group. The total value of the asset *information* increases as more individuals benefit from it.

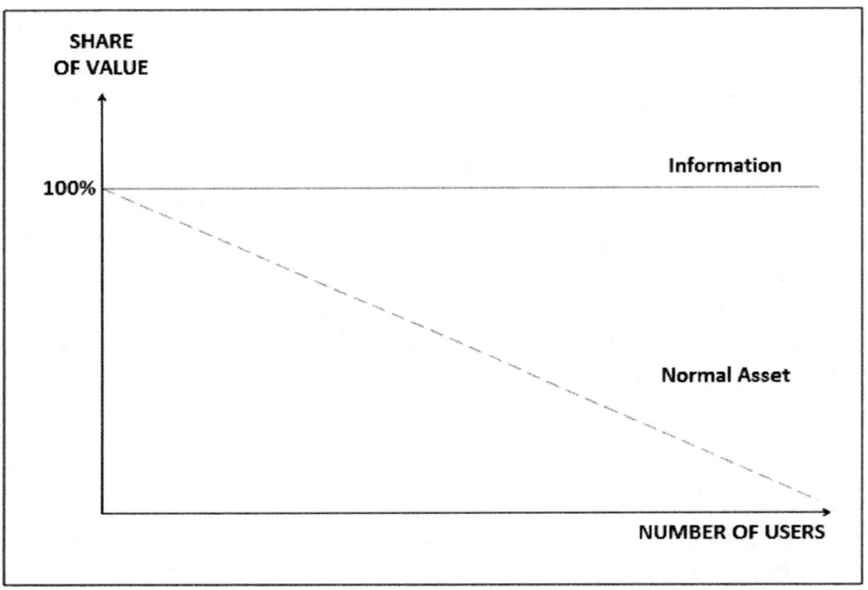

Figure 9.5. Shareability of Information (reproduced based on Moody & Walsh, 1999, p. 500)

In contrast to many types of assets, information does not lose value when used. It can be exploited without depreciating the value (see figure 9.5). This relationship implies that once information is available it should be communicated to as many individuals as possible whom may benefit from it. Information that is not communicated is worthless, and there would likely be a negative contribution to the bottom line for information that is not communicated, as the production and storage costs for the information would not be recovered (see figure 9.6).

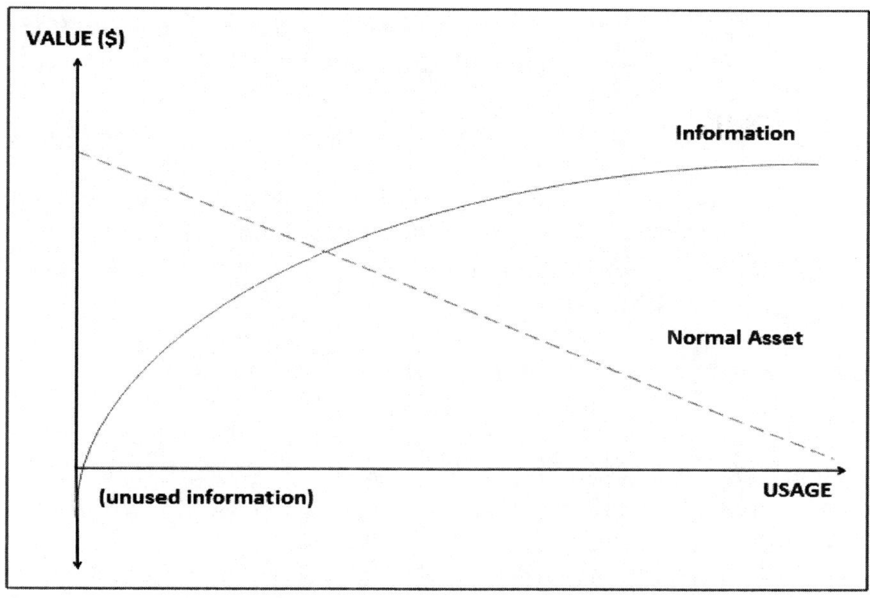

Figure 9.6. Value Increase with Use (reproduced based on Moody & Walsh, 1999, p.501)

Another relevant factor to define the value of information is its accuracy. Decisions based on incorrect information may actually cause a negative value. Incorrect forecast information about market growth may be the foundation for wrong investments and consequent losses for the organization. Accurate information, conversely, can hold a significant added value.

The value of information also increases via integration. For a retail company, it is important to have information about the revenue growth per product. It is also essential to have information about the cost of goods sold. A real increase in value for this information can be realized by combining both information streams with each other to analyze the contribution of each product to the bottom line. Combining different sources of information in a meaningful way thus adds much value.

To define an exact value of information is problematic. Three established valuation models could be used:

1. Historical cost: The amount that has been paid to acquire information (e.g. a mailing list or market research information).

2. Market value: How much the information could be sold for.

3. Utility value: Expected future economic benefits that can be obtained by possessing the information. The utility value is the one most frequently applied to estimate the asset value of information.

Correlation of Performance with Communication

Time is a critical success factor influencing the utility value of information. As displayed in figure 9.7, the delay caused by collecting data, analyzing the information, deciding and finally acting in accordance with the decisions made goes along with a decrease in utility value. An organization that is acting more quickly than their competition can improve their performance and gain strategic advantage.

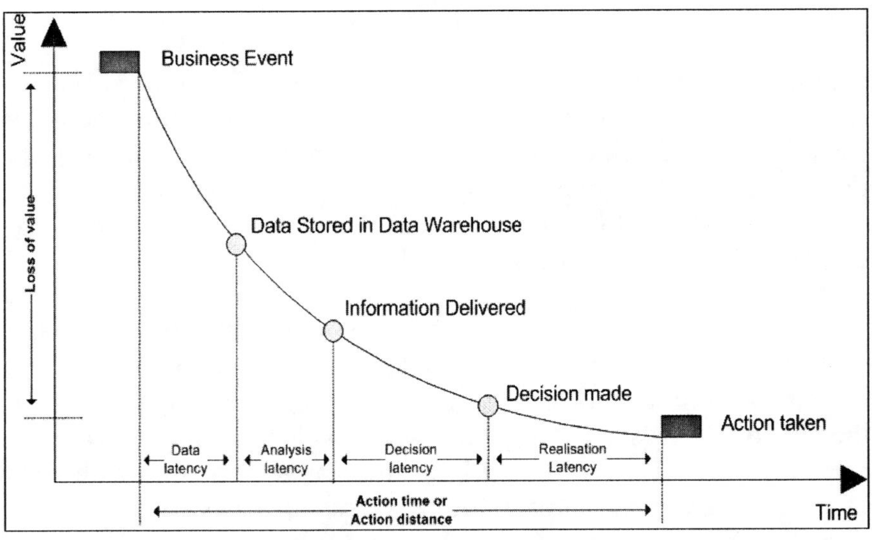

Figure 9.7. Time as Critical Success Factor (reproduced based on Hackathorn, 2004, p. 3)

In order to maximize the utility value of the asset information, organizations need to establish a communication strategy based on the following premises:

1. The most critical information needs are identified.

2. The information recipients are identified.

3. Suited communication channels are utilized to supply the information to the recipients.

4. Information systems are established to support a timely availability of information (minimal data and analysis latency).

Premises one through three require an analysis of the information demand within the organization. With information sharing becoming so easy via communication channels like e-mail and internet/intranets, one of the challenges is to find the right balance between information overload and *underload* (see figure 9.8). Sharing more information does not necessarily generate a higher value as each individual has a limited capacity and time for information processing.

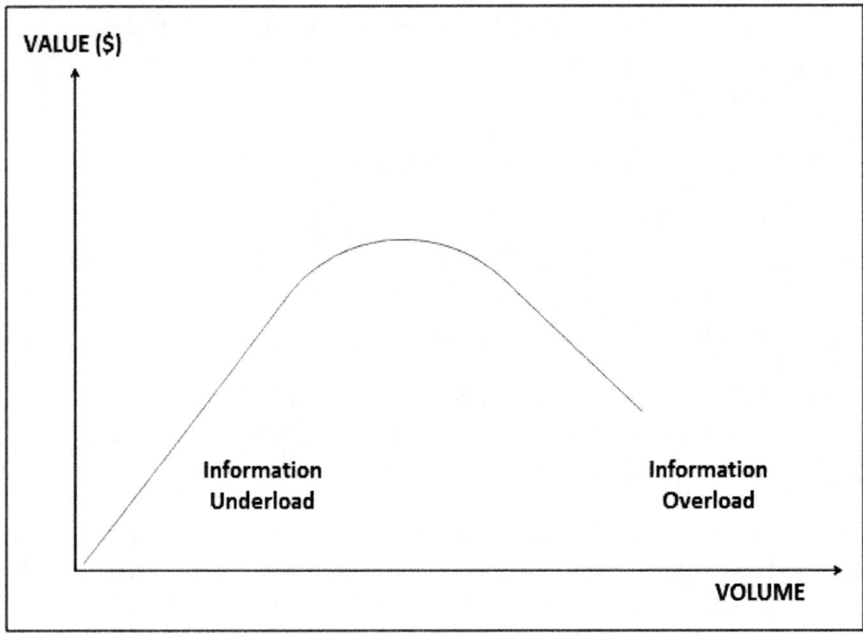

Figure 9.8. Volume versus Value of Information (reproduced based on Moody & Walsh, 1999, p.504)

Information systems can support the distribution of information and offer flexible ways to find the balance between information underload and overload. Reporting can be organized via standard reporting, ad-hoc analysis tools, or exception reporting. Information broadcasting is one of the new solutions offering a proactive information distribution. Information distribution does not depend on the recipients to retrieve the information but instead offers information published in a communication channel by an information producer (publisher). The information consumer subscribes to those information channels suited to supply the relevant information. The consumer then receives information broadcasts from his or her selected information channels and thereby balances supply with information individually. The use of dashboards is another trend. Dashboards present key information in a graphical format, highlighting critical information in colors, and offer the option to drill down to get more detailed information on request. An example of a dashboard is displayed in figure 9.9.

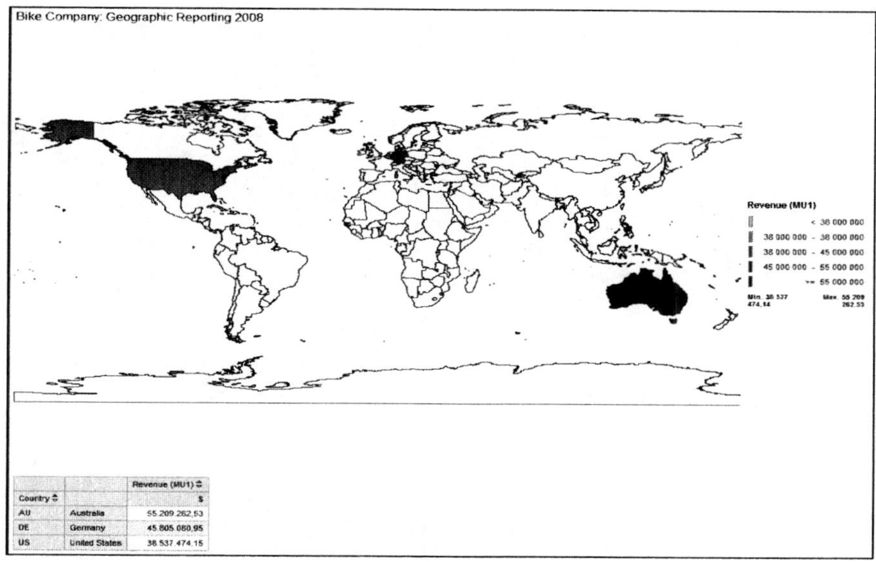

		Revenue (MU1)
Country		$
AU	Australia	55.209.262,53
DE	Germany	45.805.080,95
US	United States	38.537.474,15

Figure 9.9. Web Reporting using SAP® Business Intelligence (SAP, 2008)

The leading information systems for business intelligence offer advanced analytics, information broadcasting, and dashboards as described here. Further information about business intelligence solutions is offered at the Web site http://www.heesenonline.de/BI (Heesen, 2008).

Summary

The old saying, "I know that half of my advertisement is wasted, I just don't know which half," describes the need for accurate and timely information. In an economy with increasing international competition, the need for information is increasing as well. In order to survive, organizations should apply the *Laws of Communication* model. It is well suited to support high performance organizations in which employees share the strategic focus and feedback is regularly sought and appreciated. This way, organizations can better identify areas for improvement. Organizations will need to establish a variety of communication channels upwards and downwards the hierarchy. They need to leverage an up-to-date IT infrastructure in accordance with the business intelligence framework.

CHAPTER 10
THE DOMINO EFFECT TOWARDS CORPORATE EXCELLENCE

Gerald Huesch

Attaining corporate excellence is like the domino effect—when one piece hits another, they all follow suit. The way senior leaders and front-line supervisors follow the *Laws of Communication* shapes the climate of the organization, impacting the organization's behavior and leading to superior, mediocre, or low performance. As one influences the other, it is important to have a strong foundation to build upon.

In this supplement, I will focus on how the *Laws of Communication* support organizational leaders who achieve market and commercial excellence as reflected by profitable growth. First, I will explore the chain reaction of great results, or what I refer to as the *Domino Effect Towards Corporate Excellence*. The second step will address corporate climate, its definition, and its dimensions, including performance, agility, and strength of innovation. Next, I will share how the *Laws of Communication* influence corporate climate. Then, I will offer a short scenario that reflects the domino chain reaction—how one newly appointed CEO transitioned from the *red* to the *green zone* in his behavior and actions.

The Domino Effect on Corporate Excellence

Corporate leaders must learn to deal with complex social contexts and structures (Fulmer, 2000). They must also demonstrate strong competencies to assess, anticipate, and adapt their communication towards the best possible outcomes. Effective leadership depends on an understanding of communication that goes beyond *common sense* and *gut feelings*. By enabling and encouraging communications within the *green zone*, leaders create a workplace atmosphere where employees are proud to belong and give their best efforts, exceeding expectations:

- Creating unique and outstanding products and services
- Surpassing own accomplishments
- Surpassing competitors' accomplishments

By avoiding the *red zone*, leaders greatly reduce destructive behaviors that undermine organizational goals, tasks, resources, and followers' effectiveness, motivation, well-being, and job satisfaction.

The Domino Effect Towards Corporate Excellence

The Domino Effect Towards Corporate Excellence (Figure 10.1) resembles a series of dominos where one impacts the others. Simply, the way senior leaders, mid-level supervisors, and front-line managers align themselves and their actions to the principles set forth in the *Laws of Communication* impacts the corporate climate of an organization. The resulting climate then influences corporate behavior—the engagement and motivation of all employees central to the development of corporate excellence.

Figure 10.1. Corporate Excellence = f{ LE x ME x PE x DE x MarE x CE } (Provided with permission by Gerald Huesch, 2008)

Following the *Laws of Communication,* the corporate climate combines leadership and management excellence to shape the workplace atmosphere. This atmosphere will produce employees whose performance is high, mediocre, or low. The corporate climate influences (directly and/or indirectly) corporate behavior as well as the common key performance indicators of corporate excellence.

Corporate behavior is a combination of people and excellence. It is the ability, motivation, engagement, loyalty, and dedication of all employees visible in the performance they deliver. Corporate excellence, a combination of market excellence and commercial excellence, is defined as a function of Leadership-, Management-, People-, Deliver-, Market-, and Commercial-Excellence. Or, CorpE = f{ LE x ME x PE x DE x MarE x CE}.

Corporate Climate

Corporate climate is commonly considered the perception of how an organization deals with its stakeholders and its environments. A body of literature and other evidence has grown up around the idea that corporate climate significantly impacts the financial performance of a company. That is, the culture of an organization has an indirect but discernible effect on output.

Litwin and Stringer (1968) investigated and suggested linkages between corporate climate and operational performance. Based on my own experiences and research, I reviewed and revised the original dimensions and merged them into what I call the *Excellence Barometer*. The *Laws of Communication* are another important link to this concept. As such, in addition to describing climate and culture within an organization, the *Laws of Communication* can be used to establish a causal link through communication, culture, and performance. We see that effective supervisor and organization communication leads to a conducive corporate climate that results in performance excellence—the *green zone*. Conversely, ineffective communication leads to a dismal culture climate, one that results in substandard performance—the *red zone*.

Dimensions of Corporate Climate

Chapter 1 referred to the *Law of Cause and Effect* in that causes are actions and effects are behaviors. Without ongoing effective communication in all dimensions, corporate excellence cannot be achieved. Table 10.1 provides eight core dimensions of the corporate climate that influence an organization's performance excellence, or cause and effect relationships.

Table 10.1. Corporate Climate: The Excellence Barometer, Eight Core Dimensions (provided with permission by Gerald Huesch, 2008)

Dimension	Working Definition	Causal Mechanisms
Structure "Red Tape"	The degree to which processes, procedures, and working methods constrain individual and organizational behavior.	Too much structure means inflexibility when it comes to seizing opportunities. Lack of structure may make workforce not coherent and inconsistent.
Involvement and Responsibility	The degree of personal autonomy, decision-making capacity, and permissible individual initiative within the organization's structures.	Responsibility arouses people with power motivation. Responsibility reduces the asymmetries of information required to make optimal decisions.

Excellence Performance Standards	The degree to which quality and output are monitored, maintained, and promoted through-out the organization.	Arousal of achievement-motivated people Higher aggregate output levels by discouraging shirking Higher-end quality through monitoring and internalization of standards
Recognition & Rewards	The degree to which workers feel that wages, social recognition, and intrinsic rewards throughout the organiza-tion are justified in terms of expectations on services rendered for every member of the organization.	Retention (purpose, money) Recruitment goals and quality (money) Worker motivation (social recognition, self-esteem)
Social Cohesion "Spirit"	An organizational state in which the members respect the order, share the purpose of the organizational entity, respect others' roles, and are committed to maintain or ameliorate interpersonal and organizational relations.	Synergies through common purpose Low paranoia about doing something wrong (i.e. triple checking an internal document)

Support	Support is the amount of material, social, and psychological resources provided to members and organizational subunits to achieve a given task, goal, or fulfill a purpose.	Under-funded and understaffed departments cannot achieve their intended purpose. Employees receive neither the permission or encouragements for their task do not perform.
Clarity & Transparency	Lack of ambiguity as to what roles, tasks, objectives, and purposes are within the organization.	Ambiguity may produce inaccurate outcomes Too much clarity may leave little creative room Unclear expectations and communication can create conflict that is detrimental to performance

Values and Ethics	Definition of norms and ethics as the creation of negative externalities of a company as an entity or its members individually that are not offset. The dimensions of values and ethics are postulated to comprise three basic ethical relationships. They are: *Interpersonal relationships:* this is the relationship employees have towards one another on a personal level. *Organizational and collective responsibility:* this is the relationship between the organization as a whole with other organizations or individuals. *Principle agent:* this is the relationship that individuals have to others on a functional level.	Retention through legitimacy Reduced misallocation or diversion of company resources Reduced risk and liability through non-compliance

Red-to-Green Zone Scenario

Peter, a newly appointed CEO of a major information technology company described himself as a typical a "*Vēnī, vīdī, vīcī*" manager, "I came, I saw, I conquered." He is what the *Laws of Communication* label as a *firefighter*—one who is known for solving problems quickly but never finding out what caused them, thus finding it necessary to solve the same problem over and over again.

Peter expected the company employees to follow his every order. He did not want to hear what subordinates thought, and he only practiced "one way" communication. His favorite saying was "If it's too hot, then get out of my kitchen!" When he did ask questions, they sounded like orders. He was authoritative and set such a high pace that nobody could follow. And, his goals were unrealistic. They were too difficult to achieve. During meetings and direct reports, no one ever spoke up with ideas or recommendations for improvement. The employees did only what was expected of them (*red zone* behavior).

When first appointed, Peter was proud of his results. He used his power to change many things, and there was an immediate positive outcome. But, this outcome was short-lived. He did not have the ability to self-reflect or self-assess, and he operated under the philosophy that it was *his way or the highway.* As a result, turnover quickly increased, and results were not positive for long.

After a period of time, Peter realized that he was not doing well, and he began to feel that his career was in jeopardy. Luckily, he acknowledged that he needed the help of others. Peter asked for a mentor to help him see the impact of his well-intended but misguided leadership and management approaches. In addition, Peter's boss put him on a performance improvement plan.

The plan consisted of three steps with regular one-on-one consultations and three intense leadership trainings sessions (one each year), plus a systematic 360° training plan. This time investment allowed Peter to see sustainable positive changes in his behavior and his organization. The three steps are listed below with specific information for Steps A and B found in Table 10.2:

- Step A: Assess the "as is" situation connected to the *red zone* behavior.
- Step B: Establish desired end state *green zone* behavior.

- Step C: Identify the gaps, and design a plan of action to close these gaps and move from *red zone* behavior, to *yellow zone* behavior, and then to *green zone* behavior.

Table 10.2. Corporate Climate: The Excellence Barometer, Peter's Red Zone—Green Zone Behavior

	Step A	**Step B**
Dimension	**As-Is Situation (Red Zone behavior)**	**End State Goals (Green Zone behavior)**
Structure "Red Tape"	Peter created a high level of unnecessary administration. Rigid procedures. Everything needed to be double-checked. New ideas were difficult to go through his "checking." New unnecessary rules, policies and reports.	Eliminate unnecessary procedures, reporting, policies, rules and administration. Check ideas and optimize its integration process. Install "innovation days" to create new unconventional ideas and concepts.

Involvement & Responsibility	Peter is the "Master of Micromanagement." All decisions over his table. No brainstorming and involving others. His questions are perceived as decisions. No risk-taking allowed. Every step is controlled. Real Involving-Delegation is not present. Peter takes decisions for his direct reports without discussing it with them. He gives unsolicited advice.	Install open dialog, brainstorming and decision making procedures. Install a clear delegation regulation. Don't change this regulation without agreement with direct reports. Control your voice-pattern so a question does not sound as a decision. Take time to involve people in your thoughts and decision making. Install feedback and learning loops: take one minute before closing a meeting or phone call. Don't give feedback without asking for permission.

Involvement & Responsibility (continued)		Learn motivational speech techniques, so people want to follow and take responsibilities. Learn coaching and question techniques to assess and minimize potential risks in advance.
Excellence Performance Standards	Peter's goals are far too challenging. No feedback and learning loops. Only negative feedback. A lot of double work is necessary. In some areas he does not insist on high quality.	Align strategy and business procedures and optimize goal-setting towards realistic and challenging goals. Install speed-feedback meetings and learning cycles. Install a 30-day goal-setting process. Install 30-day retrospectives. Optimize processes involving key player. Learn situational leadership techniques.

Recognition & Rewards	People have the feeling that Peter is neither really present nor really interested what his direct reports have to say. He is perceived as having always a hidden agenda. Peter provides mostly negative feedback. Good people cannot grow under him. Always held small. Good work is not reflected in money, incentives, or in positive feedback. People are being pushed to their limits without a break and without any acknowledgement. After a great job is done, nothing but the next challenge is offered.	Be really present when people present their work. Recognize good work individually and officially. Learn to give supportive feedback. Bring good people to board meetings. Improve career opportunities and job rotation into other countries. Develop an incentive program. Offer emotional stability. Learn to shape your voice to be soft and approachable so you can be perceived as being open and willing to listen; and learn to use it with right timing. Install a roundtable of experts for important issues.

Recognition & Rewards (continued)		Celebrate successes in the groups. Learn to see the limits of your people. Ask regularly for ideas and input how to do things better and where they need support from you.
Social Cohesion/ "Spirit"	Peter divided and ruled. Talked badly about other employees and their performances. Gave unnecessary tough feedback in front of others. Gave mixed messages to different teams. Asked people to save money but spend it unnecessarily and invited guests to outrageously expensive evenings. And Peter did not share important information to his teams on time.	Start to defend your people. Install positive failure culture. Avoid cynical comments. Learn conflict resolving techniques. Walk-the-talk. Learn to trust. Tell upfront what and how you plan to do something, ask for ideas, decide and follow your plan. Inform more often. Celebrate successes individually.

Social Cohesion/ "Spirit" (continued)		Improve the integration procedures of newly-appointed manager and employees. Learn about intercultural differences. Learn to write e-mails according to the situation. Be the model you want to see in your organization: Save money first.
Support	Peter was perceived as cold and distant. People did not feel supported regarding material, social, and psychological resources.	Learn to use a soft voice pattern. Check and optimize funding and resource management. Learn about the Pygmalion and Galatea effects. Be present in second level meetings and ask real questions and provide supportive talk.

Support (continued)	Learn to talk and communicate professionally with people according to different personality types. Learn to deliver difficult information, without "shooting" the others (one on one, one on team). Learn mediation techniques. Learn about the psychology of communication. Learn how to change resistance to support from his people and groups. Learn motivational speeches. Learn nonverbal leading techniques. Learn patience and relaxation techniques.

Clarity & Transparency	Peter was basically the only one who knew what, when and how to do things. He changed his goals, procedures and policies so fast that nobody could follow. He expected “mind reading” from his subordinates. His orders were not transmitted throughout the company, and if they were, it took very long and was not what he wanted at the beginning. People did not know what he really expected from them and who was doing what, when, how and why. The strategies, goals, and procedures were unclear and too complicated. There was no real planning, not even for the next 30 days.	Improve system to deliver information and communication throughout the organization: fast, easy and clear. Install a 30-day speed planning and retrospective meeting. Show clear aligned strategy, operational and day to day procedures. Make sure of role clarity. Clear lines of authority and responsibilities: who is doing what, when, and how. Give the reason and “why” behind your decisions. Be clear on priorities. Don’t change priorities without consulting and talking to your direct reports. Be present in meetings of your employees with their teams to answer questions.

Clarity & Transparency (cont'd)	All actions were triggered by e-mail. The reasons of his decisions were not clear and understandable. Every two days he changed the priorities of projects and almost "everything" had highest priority.	Ask the whole company: "Where do you need more clarity?" Answer quickly, easily and efficiently. Keep asking in meetings (learn to ask real questions).
Values and Ethics	Peter did not follow the values and ethical standards of his company nor his people. He did not follow his own commitments. Basically, there were no standards of values and ethics present in the organization.	Make ethical compliance-management an important issue for you and your organization. Develop three major rules for everybody of "how we really want to deal with us and others, and how we want to make decisions." Make it visible, measurable and punish if it is not being followed. Give acknowledgement if someone is doing it fantastically. Make "holding commitments" one of the major rules.

Values and Ethics (continued)	Let each division add three major rules that they want to follow and then each department another three. Not more than nine rules. All should be involved in this process. Increase effective and respectful interaction between people at the board, their teams and departments. Announce what will happen and what you will do and follow your word. Inform when things happen that make you change your word. Do this even in short meetings: "Before we begin, how do we want to proceed…?"

After nine months of systematic work toward *green zone* behaviors, a positive change in Peter's organization became noticeable. Peter's direct reports developed trust in him and followed his guidance. Over time, Peter's department became known for their hard work. They had become a self-directed team, adapting to whatever requirements were placed upon them. Department and organizational Key Performance Indicators were changing for the better based on measurable outcomes.

After 18 months, Peter's team was known for being fast learners, and they were credited with improving the overall reputation of the organization. Peter enjoyed a better working reputation with all stakeholders, and his confidence was such that he agreed to increased responsibility. His mentor offered impressive feedback, noting that Peter was able to take time to assess his own performance objectively and with the input and insights of his team, peers, and supervisor.

Conclusion

If the *Domino Effect Towards Corporate Excellence* is purposely planned and then incorporated into the corporate climate, organizational leaders have the opportunity to prevent Peter's mistakes. This purposeful plan allows for a preventive approach that is far less costly in the long run in regards to people and the budget. The *Laws of Communication* offer a tool to identify the zone (red, yellow, or green) from which supervisors and the organization operate at any given moment. They also provide a roadmap, with directions for moving from one zone to another.

The *Laws of Communication* allow for identifying composite scores, via the *Supervisor Communication Inventory* survey that measures supervisors' communication effectiveness and organizational communication traits amongst senior leaders, mid-level supervisors, and frontline managers and their employees. Using the stoplight metaphor to plan a preventive approach, in conjunction with principles from the *Domino Effect Towards Corporate Excellence,* reduces costly corrective actions.

SECTION 3
Applying the Laws of Communication

CHAPTER 11
THE LAWS OF COMMUNICATION IN THE LODGING INDUSTRY

Chris Roberts

The *Laws of Communication* have broad application across industries, but examining each law within a specific industry can reveal the uniqueness of their application. The differences in industry structure, competitive strategies and tactics, regulation, and time to market all work to define characteristics that drive the differences.

Of the many industries that operate in our economy, the tourism industry is the third largest (behind automobiles and food stores), contributing over 6% of the GNP. This industry primarily includes restaurants, hotels and motels, cruise ships, airlines, car rental agencies, and travel and tour operators. The National Restaurant Association (NRA) (2007), for example, reports that there are currently more than 945,000 foodservice locations in the United States, employing more than 13 million workers and producing sales in excess of $558 billion, or an average of about 14 workers per location.

Likewise, the lodging industry generated more than $133 billion in sales during 2006 (AHLA, 2007a). There are currently more than 47,000 hotels, motels, and inns with 15 or more rooms in the United States that employ more than 1.8 million workers, or an average of about 39 workers per location. Of these two tourism industries, lodging employs more workers per facility and, therefore, typically has a more robust organizational structure, making it of greater interest when studying management theories.

Hotel Organization

To examine the application of the *Laws of Communication* within the lodging industry, it is useful to understand how these hotels are typically organized. While the decision of how a business structures its production and delivery operations is often a competitive choice, with the lodging industry virtually all competitors design themselves in essentially the same manner. Hotels usually adopt a highly structured organizational design that is centered on hotel functions.

These functions, such as the front desk, the restaurant, housekeeping, and marketing and sales, create boundaries that are rarely crossed. Employees in each area typically limit their actions to their own functional area, but coordination is essential for the delivery of seamless guest services. Information flows across units in standard patterns that rely upon written reports and key managers who convey necessary data to another group.

Group activities, business meetings, and social functions require additional coordination activities, for these events often include services from multiple departments. Events could include meals and/or refreshment breaks, hotel rooms for participants from outside the local area, and function space plus any of the various meeting services required for the function. Communication between departments is essential to provide the ordered services when planned and at the level of quality desired. Timing, then, is an integral ingredient of successful product delivery in providing meeting and event services.

The manufacturing heart of any hotel is the housekeeping department. It is this group's function to clean and prepare the hotel rooms for sale each day. While production is often an essential function of any business, within the lodging industry production is often viewed as a necessary yet simple (and thus secondary) function. It receives operational information from the front desk as to which rooms to prepare each day and does not typically play a strong role in either sales, planning, or future thinking (Roberts & Shea, 1999, 2003; Shea & Roberts, 2002).

Sales and marketing efforts dominate leadership thinking in this mature yet highly competitive industry. While service delivery is important to the product design, for most lodging firms it is the second priority. Initial efforts are concentrated upon getting the customer in the door, and service efforts are used to keep the customer for repeat business purposes. The staff members who work in sales and marketing are usually higher-skilled, experienced employees who are proficient in selling.

Hotel Employees

The majority of the hotel's workforce is designed for entry-level positions. This applies to all operational departments across the organization. Usually the largest department is housekeeping. Housekeepers often work independently from one another, cleaning a block of rooms on a given floor or wing of a building.

Communication with these fairly autonomous workers is slow due to the distance between where their work is performed (in the guest rooms) and where they are based (usually in a large, centralized facility in the rear of the main floor of the hotel). Assistant housekeepers roam the facility, performing inspection of work completed and responding to worker needs, but as highly mobile supervisors, their presence in any one area is fleeting at best.

Employees at the front desk are also primarily entry-level workers. They often work in small groups or teams that are shift-based, with three shifts during each 24-hour period in order to provide round-the-clock service to guests. Teams can change daily depending upon scheduling needs. Communication is a primary aspect of work in this area. Desk clerks have the most contact with guests. They receive guest requests for services and contact the appropriate workgroup within the hotel to fulfill it.

If a guest encounters another department employee and submits a request, the guest is often directed to the front desk for service. Thus, these entry-level workers perform a vital role in the communication network of daily hotel operations. Supervisors in this area are co-located with the desk clerks, so support and communication are much more immediate than in the housekeeping department.

Food and beverage employees provide labor for the hotel restaurant, bar, and catering departments. Usually the second largest group of employees in the hotel, they generally work in teams classified by the "front of the house" (the public areas such as the dining room or bar) or "back of house" (the production areas such as kitchens, storage, etc.). The wait staff, busboys, cashiers, and hosts fill entry-level positions that require little training. Their tasks are mostly limited to the areas in which they work, and their service for guests is limited to the direct services they provide. Supervision is co-located, so support and communication are typically fairly immediate.

Given the organizational dependence upon entry-level, lower-skill positions, the turnover rate in the lodging industry is much greater than what other industries usually experience. Hotels often have turnover rates of 60-80%. The reasons for this high turnover include the hiring of students, the use of part-time workers for peak seasons, and the ease by which workers can find employment at competitors. This level of turnover requires the firm to design training programs and operational duties that are quickly mastered, simple in nature, and easily performed.

Hospitality Organizational Communication

Communication is typically exercised in a top-down fashion, with managers and supervisors directing subordinates in daily activities. Few cross-functional teams use a matrix or other mixed form of reporting structure. Because the vast majority of lodging operations operate 24 hours per day utilizing three shifts of workers, communication and coordination across shifts is vital. Shift changes create opportunities for information to "slip through the gap" as workers come and go, even though the guest continues to stay at the property.

While there are usually procedures and opportunities for shifts to communicate information, the desire for those of the ending shift to depart sometimes causes a breakdown in the completeness of the communication. Additionally, those starting the new shift are sometimes overwhelmed with a barrage of information and may not adequately absorb it all. Thus, communication across shifts is a prime place for errors to occur in the communication process.

Further complicating the communication dimension is the nature of supervisor/employee relationships. Supervisors and managers tend to work mostly during regular business hours so that they might be available to interact with external contacts as needed or to be available for guest concerns that happen during the busiest portion of the day. There are some supervisors during the evening and night shifts, but certainly fewer than during the busy daytime.

Given these business needs, an employee's direct supervisor may, at times, work during shifts that are different than that of the employee. As such, an employee may work with a variety of supervisors across the week as shift assignments vary. This situation makes it much more difficult for employees and direct supervisors to build a meaningful relationship.

The *Laws of Communication* examine communication between supervisors and subordinates, and those external to the firm. The *Law of Communication #1* focuses upon the internal employer/employee relationship:

Failure of supervisors to communicate with subordinates effectively results in poor employee performance.

With the conditions described within the lodging industry, one can easily understand why hotel employee performance is not optimal—and may never be. The majority of hotel employees are entry-level workers earning at or slightly above minimum wage, and the resulting turnover rate reflects this situation. Thus, their commitment to the work and the organization is certainly different than in other industries where employees desire to build careers and secure long-term employment. Further, hotel employees are often scheduled to work at times that are different than the direct supervisor, weakening the potential for a meaningful relationship. Finally, communication is regularly passed between individual workers, different shifts, and functional areas, creating opportunities for information to be altered or lost completely. Thus, *Law of Communication #1* accurately reflects the limitations of outstanding employee performance in the lodging industry.

Unique Industry Configuration and Ownership Structure

As previously noted, there are more than 47,000 lodging facilities in the United States. Of these, approximately 64% are affiliated under one flag or another; that is, they are either a franchised brand or member of a chain, or a member of an alliance of hotels. Typically, these organizations are large. The largest chain hotel company is Wyndham Hotels, with 6,661 hotels and an average hotel size of 80 rooms (AHLA, 2007b). Other large firms include Choice Hotels (4,919 hotels; average size 83 rooms), Intercontinental Hotels (3,698 hotels; average size 150 rooms), Marriott Hotels (2,648 hotels; average size 180 rooms), Hilton Hotels (2,460 hotels; average size 160 rooms), and Best Western (3,955 hotels; average size 77 rooms).

These companies are widely dispersed across the United States and many nations of the world. Franchising is a common growth strategy, and while it has been very successful, it has resulted in an interlaced and unique ownership structure for each hotel facility. Three aspects of each hotel must be known to gain a full understanding of the ownership structure: (1) who owns the building, (2) who operates the business, and (3) whose name is on the building.

Contrary to brand images, the parent company of the majority of these well-known firms own very few of the actual hotel buildings. They look to small investors to provide the capital for each hotel. Thus, the risk for the individual hotel venture is essentially "transferred" from the large chain organization to the smaller investor.

The small investor/owner will often select a well-known brand as a franchise because of its ability to provide a broad exposure to the market. This is often necessary to build sales, and the well-established brands can affordably provide it. Few individual hotels can fund the regional and/or national marketing efforts required to build market awareness among future customers. Further, as most of these small investors are not experienced in hotel operations, many of the larger companies offer contract management services to individual owners.

Of course, some investors/owners choose to hire their own managers, but hiring experienced firms is a common choice. For example, Marriott International owns the Hyatt Regency in Cambridge, MA. They have contracted with Hyatt to operate the business for them, and they have elected to have the Hyatt brand on the building. Thus, the three aspects of building ownership, building branding, and facility operations are needed in order to truly identify the management structure of an individual hotel property.

This mix of ownership on a building-by-building basis has resulted in large lodging organizations that consist of management teams that do not report to the same hierarchy and do not often share the same goals and objectives. It also has resulted in many independent-minded franchisees that adhere to corporate strategies and policies in order to benefit from the brand value yet wish to maintain their autonomy as a small- or mid-sized business. This ownership structure has resulted in organizational practices that are consistent in terms of marketing and product delivery yet vary wildly in terms of human resource practices. It has led to little consistency in the internal cultures created within each franchisee, as well as the accompanying turnover rates.

The *Law of Communication #2* focuses upon an organization's ability to communicate with stakeholders, especially internally with employees:

Failure of the organization to communicate effectively within results in poor organizational performance.

Given the wide mix of management approaches, cultures, ownership design, brand images, and competitive strategies in the lodging industry, it is challenging for large chain organizations to effectively communicate across all member hotels. In addition, the 24-hour operation of the business generates shifts of workers that often are not paired with direct supervisors.

Daily operations require constant communication to coordinate services and to transfer guest information across shifts. Turnover rates strongly influence the general experience level of the staffs, and the entry-level jobs do not effectively help to build long-term employees who share a common belief in the organization's goals and values. Maximizing organizational performance through effective communication is indeed a major challenge for these industry-leading lodging organizations.

CHAPTER 12
THE LAWS OF COMMUNICATION AS APPLIED TO THE SUCCESS AND FAILURE OF A TELECOMMUNICATIONS FIRM

Paul Ryder

Introduction

In this chapter, the *Laws of Communication* will be used to help explain some successes and failures of a telecommunications firm attempting to re-define itself as an Internet company through the actions of one of the firm's business units. *Law of Communication #2—Failure of the organization to effectively communicate within results in poor organizational performance*—will be used to examine the organizational-wide impact of poor communication on corporate objectives, employee morale, and organizational success. *Law of Communication #1—Failure of supervisors to effectively communicate with subordinates results in poor employee performance*—will next be used to examine the relationships between the supervisory staff and employees at the individual level. Because communication is a multi-faceted concept that, when discussed, can lead down an enormous number of endless directions, this segment will focus on one aspect of communication: the communication of strategy.

To quote Rayburn (2007), "An organization's most important audience is, and has always been its employees" (p. 21). For any organizational strategy to succeed, executive leaders must first ensure that the organization's employees, those responsible for implementing strategy, understand and can connect executive management's strategic direction to tactical actions under the employees' span of control. Miranda and Thiel (2007), when referencing a 2006 McKinsey survey, found that 41% of executives interviewed cite the alignment of corporate strategy to employee performance goals as the principal driver behind enabling organizational speed and agility. Accordingly, "almost nine in ten executives say organizational speed and agility have become increasingly urgent issues for them over the past five years" (Miranda & Thiel, p. 14).

Background

Some background is needed to help set the stage for the anecdotes used in this chapter. To protect the *innocent*, the parent telecommunications company will be referred to as Mobile One, and the Internet business unit will be referred to as Wireless Broadband. Mobile One, like all wireless carriers in the last 10 years, is a blend of a competitive local exchange carrier (CLEC), a long distance provider, a wireless business unit, and countless acquisitions.

Merger mania hit the telecommunications industry hard, creating frequent realignment of personnel, particularly those in leadership positions. Political shrewdness, a keen awareness of environmental influences, and personal connections often determined the middle managers and leaders who survived this constant onslaught of organizational upheaval. Retention and advancement decisions were often made based on connections rather than leadership skills or functional competence.

Entering into the Wireless Broadband Market

Forecasting the erosion of voice margins, Mobile One decided to enter into the wireless broadband market and is currently building out a new network to offer wireless Internet connectivity to the masses at a competitive price. As Mobile One stands up a fourth generation (4G) wireless broadband network, the executive leadership team must develop a cohesive, systematic approach to developing and communicating its wireless broadband strategy, one that will secure a long-term competitive advantage for Wireless Broadband and Mobile One.

The shift from a voice-centric to a data-centric product portfolio will be a transformational change affecting every aspect of Mobile One's business model. Mobile One's intention is to launch what Clayton Christensen (1997) considers a disrupting technology. As such, the product portfolio will be new, the customer base will be different, the underlying technology will be innovative, the mix of suppliers will be more diverse, the distribution model will be unique, and the methods Mobile One uses to reach customers will change.

Successfully launching a disruptive technology amidst the limitations of a corporation's existing bureaucracy processes and organizational politics is extremely difficult, if not impossible. Recognizing this challenge, Mobile One chose to assemble a pseudo-autonomous business unit that would not be bound by Mobile One's processes, structure, and organizational challenges. Mobile One labeled this business unit Wireless Broadband and put a few of Mobile One's strategy executives in charge of building an organization and launching an untested wireless broadband technology that would turn the industry on its ear.

The euphoria of being liberated from Mobile One's organizational boundaries was quickly replaced with the very real sense that a total lack of structure and no defined communication mechanisms was very nearly as bad as being too organized. The first communication blunder would prove to be the most enduring, and Wireless Broadband would suffer under this burden throughout its existence. Within the first two months of Wireless Broadband's existence, the launch date was announced.

An extremely aggressive target for launching the service was released to the marketplace prior to any systematic analysis of an end-to-end schedule. Those who had launched new technologies understood the challenges ahead and began to make decisions that would have the greatest impact on the critical path, only to have those decisions repeatedly second guessed by every executive that turned an eye toward those decisions. One example will serve to underscore this point.

Anyone who has ever built a telecommunications network appreciates that adding backhaul, the telecommunication links that connect communication distribution points to central offices, is always on the critical path. The backhaul plan was debated, decided upon, and revisited no less than eight times in four months of deliberations. Each time the final decision was disseminated, whole teams were spun up to deliver on that plan, only to have a new *final* decision communicated, causing an endless stream of redundant work and wasted effort. Engineers, middle managers, and directors in both Mobile One and Wireless Broadband soon began to wonder aloud whether Wireless Broadband could stick with any game plan.

This is just one example of how decisions were made and subsequently overruled by those on the next rung of the corporate ladder throughout the first six months of Wireless Broadband's startup phase. The frequency with which critical decisions were overturned forced almost all decisions to be made by one person at the very top of Wireless Broadband's hierarchy, the CEO. The CEO was repeatedly called on to make even mundane decisions personally and often had to intercede between factions of the organization that were on opposing sides of a decision. As the business unit gained momentum, the CEO interjected a Chief Operating Officer between himself and the rest of the organization.

Speculation: No Strategic Plan

Any communication of a strategic plan was completely foreign to Wireless Broadband. Every leader was allowed to speculate on the definition of success and how they might contribute to the organization's ill-defined objectives. Not surprisingly, there were as many ideas about Wireless Broadband's strategy for achieving its goals as there were employees in Wireless Broadband. It was as if a race was scheduled and a finish line established. All of the contestants were told that they needed to complete the race in unison; then, they were blind folded and asked to run, skip, or gallop toward the finish line.

This lack of a communicated strategy manifested itself in fierce political battles between vice presidents who all had developed competing priorities based on their understanding of the business unit's objectives. The Product Vice President developed a massive product list, the Marketing Vice President developed a short list of launch priorities that were in perfect conflict with the Product VP's view, the Vice President of Sales ignored both and focused solely on consumer sales, the Network Vice President did not know where to build cell sites nor who to ask where to build cell sites, and the Vice President of Technology Development continued to develop the radio access network to deliver features that would not be needed in the network for years.

It is difficult to measure the impact of these early communication challenges on Wireless Broadband's objectives because, as mentioned, few objectives were ever communicated. But there is quantifiable impact on the one objective that was established: the launch date itself. Each time a launch date drew near, one of two things ensued: one or more organizations began to signal that their deliverables were behind schedule due to another organization's failure, or an organization's leadership asked that the scope of launch be re-defined. Accordingly, the launch date was changed 4 times, and the definition of launch was changed six times. By anyone's standard this one objective, the most sacred of objectives for Wireless Broadband, was significantly impaired by a total lack of any strategy communication. Poor strategy communication impacted Wireless Broadband's ability to meet its objectives, and the launch delays negatively impacted the business unit's performance.

Communication Challenges

The communication challenges, exacerbated by constant rumors of a Wireless Broadband spin-off, began to negatively impact morale at the working level. The constant disagreements between vice presidents crept into the directors' daily activities, and skirmishes frequently surfaced among directors forced to negotiate working agreements on the fly. Visible signs of contempt between functional groups abounded—so much so that e-mails from one function, the IT organization in particular, immediately prompted rebuttals and were pounced upon by constituents in other functions. Because these working agreements were never enforceable, the decisions made at the director level were frequently revisited by the Chief Operations Officer (COO).

The COO was intimately involved in Director level decisions because the ever-present politicking between functions forced all decisions to the COO's desk. Now, a lack of communication was again forcing all decisions to the highest rungs of the corporate decision making process. Directors' decisions were constantly being overturned, injuring their sense of ownership for implementation and ultimately hampering their morale. It wasn't long before the entire business unit's optimistic spirits were depleted and replaced by a sense of impending *underachievement*. The second *Law of Communication—Failure of the organization to effectively communicate within results in poor organizational performance—* seems to have held in this instance.

Any conversation regarding the communication of strategy between supervisors and their staff at Wireless Broadband would need to be a short one given that, as mentioned previously, no strategy was ever communicated. Instead, this segment will focus on the lack of structured communication between supervisors and staff and the deleterious impacts to employee performance. As the organizational communication omissions began to impact the personal communications between management and staff, the morale of the business unit began to turn sour.

The amount of time directors and managers spent battling one another put a toll on the amount of time the management staff spent communicating with their direct reports. Communication lapses between the management staff and employees led to a great deal of wasted effort and redundant work. Efforts proven to be simple tasks, such as launching a trial, took three times as long as they had previously. Prior to Wireless Broadband's inception, Mobile One often did employee and consumer trials. In fact, a few of the Wireless Broadband employees had executed broadband trials that cost less money, were executed in a more timely manner, and required fewer employees to execute. Wireless Broadband had more resources to throw at trials and the very presence of these additional planning resources slowed the trial execution process to a crawl. Trial planning resources were constantly revisiting decisions with their supervisors, which caused them to overanalyze the minutiae of the tasks, and ultimately slowed progress.

Improving Communication

How could communications between supervisors and staff been enhanced? Effective organizational communication should account for relational factors and informational factors in both the creation and dissemination of the communications. The circumstance, environment, and players will influence the degree to which relational and informational roles take precedence; no single model of communication will work in all situations. The management team could not have missed the signs of discontent brewing between functions and knew themselves how the unease over a lack of a communicated strategy could create uncertainty.

All employees began putting in long hours. Because every decision had to be revisited repeatedly, any significant task generated endless meetings. After a full day of meetings, employees had to read an enormous amount of emails to determine what decisions might force their activities in a new direction the next day. As employee morale slipped and employee stamina dwindled, performance declined significantly. Employees, lacking any formal communication regarding their next steps, met their deliverables to the best of their abilities, only to see their work recreated by outsourced contractors.

The management team could have created wikis, established recurring all-hands type meetings with their staff, published weekly updates to a Wireless Broadband intranet, and much more to distribute any and all available information. The management team could have met the lack of strategy head on and begun communicating the available tidbits of information. Management could have confirmed that there was a lack of information about the business unit's strategy and explained this apparent shortcoming. A simple explanation for the lack of a strategy could have been that Wireless Broadband was launching a new technology and targeting a new customer base. Employees would have understood that charting untested waters means learning as you go, but without any communication employees were left to "flail" about on their own.

Management had many tools at their disposal. Widespread use of email, instant messaging, and cell phones; the increased reliance on corporate intranets; and ubiquitous mobile phone use has enabled almost instantaneous engagement and communication among organizational counterparts, and between leaders and their constituents. Today's leaders are able to stay in contact with the workforce like no other time in history. This labyrinth of communications and *always-connected* philosophy does present challenges for the multi-tasker, which is what most organizational participants are becoming. Employees and leaders are constantly assaulted by new communications and the almost constant risk of interruptions adds a new challenge to communicating effectively.

Communicating

Communication is only as effective as the audience's comprehension of the communicated information. Leaders, and anyone who hopes to be understood, need to craft their communication in terms that can readily be understood. Because management needed to motivate and influence employees with their communications, they had the additional onus to ensure that their message was interpreted appropriately. Comprehending the message is only the first, albeit most crucial step, to internalizing the message. In order for the message to be internalized, the message must be retained. Nichols and Stevens (1999) have shown that half of what a person says is immediately forgotten by the average listener. Two months later, the listener is only able to recall 25% of what was said. It is for these reasons that management should have created a communication plan for distributing information between supervisors and their employees early, often, and uniformly.

During periods when strategies need to change to react to evolving environmental events, such as new competitive pressures, more efficient communication strategies are needed. Agile communication structures and processes need to be developed to ensure that as strategy changes tactical responses to these changes in strategy are immediate, efficient, and meet the prescribed objectives. Miranda and Thiel (2007), referencing a 2006 McKinsey Quarterly study of 1562 executive responses in both the private and public sectors worldwide, found that 39% of executives cited the ability to push decision-making authority as far down the organization as possible as the organizational component that could contribute most to an organization's ability to respond quickly to changing circumstances. Some 41% of executives cited the alignment of performance goals to corporate strategy as the organizational component that could contribute most to an organization's ability to respond quickly to changing circumstances.

Individually, directors and managers had all of the information they needed to prepare their communications. Executive management or Human Resources should have noted the declines in performance and brought the management staff together to discuss the communication challenges collectively, but Wireless Broadband's rush to meet the launch date afforded no time for introspection and none of these communication tools or decision-making structures were put in place.

Conclusion

According to Miranda and Thiel (2007), almost 9 of 10 executives who were questioned suggested that the speed with which the organization executes strategic objectives and the organization's ability to change direction quickly had become increasingly urgent issues over the prior five years. Norton and Kaplan (2005) found that 9 out of 10 corporations fail to implement their strategies. The fact that communication is an essential component of implementing strategy is indisputable. Executive management must ensure that they regularly communicate corporate strategy consistently to those employees responsible for implementing.

Some would argue that all employees are responsible for implementing strategy. Hrebiniak (2005) suggested that the number of people needed to effectively implement strategy demands that strategic objectives be linked to the day-to-day tasks and activities of people at all levels of the organizational hierarchy and across all business units and locations. By drawing linkages between employee actions and specific strategic objectives, management can reinforce desired behavior.

All of the authorities on communication of strategy appear to agree that communicators, and leaders in particular, are responsible for convincing constituents to internalize strategy. Gone are the days when employees *toed the line* simply because management drew a line. In today's dynamic and global environment where employee loyalty needs to be earned rather than taken for granted, leaders need to communicate strategy in terms that employees understand, appreciate, and are willing to implement. By flouting Schuttler's first and second *Laws of Communication*, Wireless Broadband condemned its employees to expend more effort to meet ill-defined objectives that may or may not lead to sustained competitive value for the organization.

CHAPTER 13
THE LINKAGE BETWEEN THE LAW OF COMMUNICATION AND UNIVERSITY RESEARCH ADMINISTRATION

James J. Casey

Introduction

Communication is a critical component of working relationships between faculty, staff, and administration in the area of university research administration. Colleges and universities within and outside the U.S. are being called upon to seek increasing levels of grants for non-financial (academic, intellectual) and financial (revenue) reasons. The view of research grants as simply being revenue, while in some ways regrettable, is a necessary component of most university budgets today. For this paper, the primary view is that research grants serve to build the intellectual infrastructure of colleges and universities and, by extension, improve communities and society in general.

This paper discusses the importance of communication within university research administration and discusses its connection to the *Laws of Communication* as outlined in the main body of this book:

Law of Communication #1: Failure of supervisors to communicate effectively with subordinates results in poor employee performance.

Law of Communication #2: Failure of the organization to communicate effectively results in poor organizational performance.

In other words, leaders must lead and communicate.

Disclaimer: The opinions of the author are solely his own, and do not represent the position of any organization or entity that is discussed within the article.

The Current Context of University Research Administration

The field of university research administration illustrates unique characteristics of communication.

First, there is a vertical structure for research grants within most colleges and universities. Grants generally, though not always, flow upward, e.g., from the faculty member to the department chair, then to the dean, and onto the head of research/grants at the institution and the provost/vice chancellor for research/grants. In other words, at most institutions, and in theory, a number of people must "sign-off" on the grant before it can be submitted to an outside source. Most universities struggle with individual faculty and staff who, for whatever reason, do not desire to submit a grant through the university process. This is a problem that is often one of communication.

In my 14 years as a research administrator, the problem of faculty and staff submitting grants without institutional approval occurs in a minority of circumstances (less than 5%). Nevertheless, this problem is one that is often illustrative of the *Laws of Communication* discussed herein.

A second characteristic is that of faculty entrepreneurship, e.g., "doing their own thing" in the pursuit of knowledge. Faculty are generally hired to teach and advance knowledge within their field(s) of expertise. This is especially applicable in the area of university-industry partnerships. Sometimes faculty will not tell administration until after the fact whether they have initiated contact or work with companies, which can lead to significant problems in the areas of intellectual property and liability.

A third characteristic—as exemplified by the University-Industry Demonstration Partnership (UIDP)—is recognition of the importance of good communication. This partnership was an outgrowth of the three-year University-Industry Partnership Project (UIPP), the predecessor to the UIDP. As briefly discussed, the principle of communication is infused within two publications that resulted from the UIPP (Principles, Living Studies).

Institutional Actors

For university research administration to succeed at the research and administrative levels, there needs to be solid and constant communication between three important groups of employees: faculty, staff that support the research activities of the faculty, and central administration staff, which includes everyone from the Vice President for Research (or equivalent position) down to the research office and ancillary departments charged with monitoring the research enterprise (human subjects, animal care, biosafety, export controls, etc.). Each of these institutional actors will be described in turn.

Faculty

Faculty are the bedrock of university research. They design, propose, and conduct the research. Focusing on disciplinary, interdisciplinary, or multidisciplinary projects, they are the professionals who move the state of knowledge forward. As such, they are the central focus of the research administration enterprise.

As a group, faculty are a diverse lot. Some are quite humble about their achievements, while others are quite vocal. Some want to work in partnership with administrative actors and "the system," while others seem to relish in challenging the system on a periodic basis.

This is the challenge. Given their central importance in the research enterprise, faculty must be treated the same as a group, but they must be handled in a nuanced fashion by the other actors in the university research system. In short, they benefit from a system that respects and facilitates their work and contributions while making sure they function as part of the university "team"—tall order, for sure.

Staff

University staff is a critical, often underappreciated, component of success in managing university research. Located within departments, colleges, and central administration, they provide the grease and/or glue (as the case may be) for research and research management. The range of their responsibilities is broad: basic office tasks, preparing grant budgets, conference planning, finding funding opportunities, communicating with internal and external constituencies, and project report writing and editing. In many cases, they are the right hand to the faculty, so central is their work.

Over my career, it has been apparent at times that communication with departmental, college, and central administrative staff is not as strong as it should be. This deficit leads to misunderstandings, technical problems, and under performance in that unit. Communication from and with staff is a critical component of success in university research.

Central Administration

Central administrators have a significant role to play in research management. Often maligned for being "the brick wall" by faculty, they serve dual roles simultaneously. From one perspective, they encourage the faculty to pursue their academic goals through research proposals. Yet, they sometimes have to serve in a "bad cop" capacity because they have to ensure the proper stewardship of grant funds that come from outside sources. For example, central administration must make sure that financial and non-financial aspects of grants are consistent with sponsor and governmental requirements, and sometimes they need to take stands that put them at odds with faculty.

Communication is critical in these situations, as miscommunication can lead to reduced morale and productivity. Faculty may take their research elsewhere, to an environment where they will not be watched so closely. Or, they may do the research on a consulting basis, outside the realm of their employment with the university or college.

Some faculty consider central administrators to be overbearing, requiring too many rules, and only interested in administration and not the research. While that is probably true, it is not true to such an extent as claimed. Thoughtful research managers simultaneously recognize that it is important to have the necessary rules in place while at the same time encouraging faculty to explore new areas and lines of research. Faculty need to remember that most requirements associated with research grants do not come from the universities themselves, but from the sponsors and governmental agencies (particularly the U.S. Government).

Ultimately, my experience in research administration has taught me that consistent and accurate communication is important between all three groups of institutional actors. If every category made the same amount of effort to be consistent and accurate, miscommunication and bad feelings can be largely avoided.

Applicability of the Rules to University Research

Considering the two *Laws of Communication* and applying them to higher education research administration, it is clear that failure to communicate clearly at the department, college, and central administrative levels leads to exactly the type of failures described by Schuttler.

The failure of higher level administrators (faculty, central administration policy makers, deans, etc.) to communicate effectively with subordinates results in poor employee (primarily staff) performance and less than optimal research productivity (measured in the amount of research dollars for the fiscal or calendar year) at the organizational level.

It is also important to point out that poor morale at the departmental, college, or central administrative office levels can lead to reduced individual and institutional performance. In this sense, higher education research administration is often quite similar to private sector business.

The discussion now turns from the university research administration in general to a specific case study, the University-Industry Demonstration Partnership (UIDP), and how communication is addressed in that context.

Special Focus: The University-Industry Demonstration Partnership (UIDP)

The *Harvard Business Review* in its July/August 2007 issue had two phrases that sum up the goals of university-industry collaboration: "Managing for the Long Term" and "Going the Distance." These phrases accurately reflect what university-industry collaborations and the University-Industry Demonstration Partnership (UIDP) are all about. University-industry collaborations are critical long-term infrastructure developments and should be managed accordingly. In that respect, university research management diverges from private sector companies that are concerned about quarter to quarter profit and loss results.

University-Industry collaboration is a critical topic in academic, industry, and government circles. With federal research funding being in a state of zero growth or actual decline, colleges and universities are being forced to diversify their research portfolios (looking for new funding sources from private business, corporate foundations, and other non-profit foundations).

The new and expensive costs of U.S. homeland security and the wars in Afghanistan and Iraq are having a significant fiscal impact upon the future shape of the U.S. budget. Research funding in the United States does not occur in a vacuum. It is tied to other policy choices that the President and Congress make. The choices the federal government makes with respect to allocating funding and resources is not unique: these choices occur in all other western democratic societies.

How industry is investing its research funds is another important dimension; from 2000-07, industry research has focused on new projects rather than on directed basic research. As Jim Scinta (2007), chair of the Industrial Research Institute's Research-on-Research Committee points out, firms that dedicate a disproportionate amount of their research and development (R&D) to new projects rather than basic research will probably satisfy some of their intermediate business goals but will fail to cultivate broad-based knowledge that will ultimately lead to long-term growth through innovation. Although Scinta does not specifically address business collaboration with colleges and universities, a decline in basic research will most probably impact higher education research facilities that are capable of engaging in basic research.

Over the past few decades, American universities have enjoyed a strong productive relationship with private companies that have led to wins by both sides. In a general sense, there seems to be a broad consensus that domestic and international university-industry partnerships are important to the United States. Higher education and industry have generally found these relationships to meet their requirements, given the significant differences that can exist among missions. There is much to celebrate in this recent history of collaboration.

Why Universities and Industry Collaborate

Why do universities and industry collaborate? As previously written, the reasons are many, and this list is by no means exhaustive:

- Technical opportunities exist in industry for faculty and students that may not exist at colleges and universities.

- Materials exist in industry for research and educational purposes that are often lacking at some colleges and universities.

- Universities receive research funding from companies, a need that has become increasingly apparent over the past ten years. Universities come to rely on the generation of extramural funding as they structure their budgets.

- A ready pool of graduate and undergraduate students exists at colleges and universities that industry may access for their work requirements. Students in return receive critical workforce training that supplements coursework. Workforce training is increasingly recognized within the U.S. as a critical component of education in a knowledge-based, international economy.

- University-industry collaborations can advance the service mission of colleges and universities. Service missions are an increasing component of universities as they become more involved in their local communities. Such service has also been demanded by local and state governments within which the institutions are located; this could be considered a quid pro quo for tax-exempt status—or at least to forestall political retaliation against universities that are perceived to be "rich islands" within some communities.

- Local and regional economic development can occur from university-industry partnerships. There is evidence to suggest that university-industry collaborations contribute to the overall economic development of the United States. This is necessary in a post-industrial, knowledge-based economy.

- Collaborations between universities and industry often are novel to high technology areas, as opposed to low technology areas (such as basic manufacturing). Nanotechnology and materials science/engineering are examples of such high technology fields. However, the argument is being increasingly made that basic manufacturing is now "high technology" and hence is equally important to the U.S. economy.

- College and university internal reward structures often provide for financial incentives to faculty. These financial structures are critical for research development and retention of "star" faculty. If colleges and universities seek to increase their research portfolios, they must create reward structures for faculty and staff that bring in such extramural funding.

- Industry often desires the research infrastructure that is present at colleges and universities. For many companies, it is simply more cost effective to contract out research to universities that have the research infrastructure instead of building new facilities or renovating existing facilities.

- The United States Government encourages university-industry collaboration. The Bayh-Dole Act of 1980 and the National Science Foundation (NSF) Partnerships for Innovation Program (NSF-PFI) are perfect examples of this encouragement. The NSF-PFI Program is an excellent example of combining intellectual property, workforce development, and R&D components into a consistent funding program. (Casey, 2004)

As this list illustrates, university-industry partnerships are and should be symbiotic relationships. Benefits should accrue to each partner in the relationship. This is one strong characteristic of university-industry collaboration.

Despite the historic strength of university-industry partnerships in the United States, there have been recent indications that this relationship is strained and needs some tending to. This is particularly true in the areas of contract negotiation and intellectual property.[1]

According to recent statistics from the American Association for the Advancement of Science (AAAS), there has been a recent decline in the level of industry support for university research in the United States.

There is also evidence that suggests foreign universities are conducting increasing amounts of U.S. industry sponsored research because they are willing to forgo ownership of intellectual property (IP) resulting from research. American universities are more likely to demand sole ownership of IP generated from university research than their foreign counterparts. As a September 2006 NSF InfoBrief stated: "A three-decades-long trend of increasingly strong ties between industry and universities may have ended."

All of these factors lead to the conclusion that, despite a strong historical relationship between U.S. higher education and industry, the present time is an uncertain era for these collaborations. Thankfully, it has been recognized by universities, companies, and the U.S. Government that this trend must be reversed by more vigorous and successful collaborations.

---

[1] For additional background information on university-industry collaboration, the Bayh-Dole Act of 1980, the positives and negatives of Bayh-Dole, and suggested improvements in the law and regulations to make Bayh-Dole even more effective, see the testimony of Dr. Susan B. Butts, Senior Director, External Science and Technology Programs for the Dow Chemical Company. Her testimony of July 17, 2007, given before the U.S. House of Representatives Committee on Science and Technology, Subcommittee on Technology and Innovation, recommends small changes in Bayh-Dole and tax regulations to clarify the intent of Congress relative to ownership/control of IP resulting from industry-sponsored research, with the intent to improve the climate for university-industry research partnerships in the United States. Testimony of Dr. Susan B. Butts, p. 1 (July 17, 2007). She also reiterated an issue (p. 1) that surfaced during the University-Industry Partnership Project; namely, that foreign universities are more flexible with IP ownership and control, causing more sponsored research to be conducted abroad.

Prior Efforts by the Government-University-Industry Research Roundtable (GUIRR) and the Industrial Research Institute (IRI)

From the 1980s until the convening of the University-Industry Congress in 2003, the Government-University-Industry Research Roundtable (GUIRR, part of the National Academies in Washington, D.C.) and the Industrial Research Institute, Inc. (IRI) were concerned with strengthening and improving university-industry partnerships.

Established in 1984, GUIRR was created in response to the report on the National Commission on Research, which called for an institutional forum to facilitate dialog among the top leaders of government and non-government research organizations. The year 1995 saw GUIRR's formal mission being revised to

> convene senior-most representatives from government, universities, and industry to define and explore critical issues related to the national and global science and technology agenda that are of shared interest; to frame the next critical question stemming from current debate and analysis; and to incubate activities of on-going value to the stakeholders. This forum will be designed to facilitate candid dialogue among participants, to foster self-implementing activities, and, where appropriate, to carry awareness of consequences to the wider public. (GUIRR, 2002, p. 2)

Founded in 1938, the IRI is the foremost business association of leaders in R&D working together to enhance the effectiveness of technological innovation in industry (www.iriinc.org). The IRI is comprised of senior executives from a diverse range of industries whose member companies are investing $70 billion annually in R&D projects worldwide. The IRI is the only cross-industry organization providing the R&D community with insights, solutions, and best practices in innovation management developed through collaborative knowledge creation.

The GUIRR/IRI efforts were primarily concerned with the creation and modification of a variety of standard/boilerplate contractual agreements. Publications were released for university and private sector use, and over the years these model and boilerplate agreements became part of the university-industry partnership culture. There is no doubt that these model and boilerplate agreements served their roles well, and helped advance the growth of these partnerships. However, it is generally recognized that these publications only addressed part of the relationship, and certainly did not have a profound impact on improving and managing these relationships in the more dynamic, internet-driven world of the past two decades.

Based on this history, GUIRR and IRI recognized that more needed to be done within the relationship than promulgate new contract templates. They decided, as a result, to partner with NCURA (National Council of University Research Administrators). The next section discusses the new initiatives.

University-Industry Congress/University-Industry Partnership Project (UIPP)

The University-Industry Congress was established in 2003 by NCURA and the IRI, with GUIRR serving as the neutral convener. In 2004 the University-Industry Congress was renamed the University-Industry Partnership Project (UIPP).[2] This project existed from August, 2003 through its national summit in April, 2006.

---

[2] For additional information regarding the UIPP and UIDP, please see the appropriate sections of the *GUIRR 2006 Annual Report*. This report provides sections on the following: 1) Deemed Exports: Promoting Change on Critical National Issues; 2) *The Here or There?* Report: Bringing New Knowledge to the Debate Over Corporate R&D Globalization; 3) The University-Industry Partnership: An Action Agenda for More Effective Cooperation; 4) UIDP: A New Institution to Strengthen the U.S. Research Enterprise; 5) Major Workshops and Convocations: Advancing National Science and Technology Policy; and 6) The Federal Demonstration Partnership (FDP): A Track Record of Success in Raising Research Productivity.

NCURA was founded in 1959 as a professional organization of individuals with interests in the administration of sponsored programs (research, education, and training) primarily at colleges and universities. With over 6,000 domestic and international members, NCURA serves its members and advances the field of research administration through cutting edge professional development programs (www.ncura.edu/).

The UIPP brought together approximately 35 handpicked people from academia, industry, and the U.S. Government. A significant strength was the wide breath of participants, representing small and large universities, small and large companies, different sectors of the U.S. economy, and members from the major federal research agencies (National Institutes of Health, National Science Foundation, Department of Commerce, and others). I was chosen as a delegate because of my legal expertise and experience working at research and non-research universities. The purpose of the UIPP was to discuss the university-industry relationship, ascertain what was working and what was not, and to establish deliverables that would strengthen these relationships.

In somewhat broad terms, the UIPP focused on the following:

- Turning challenges into successes, i.e., surmounting the primary challenges of contract negotiations and intellectual property into positive results.

- Building trust and teamwork. In the first year of the project, it was readily apparent that there was significant distrust among some of the participants, either on a general level or based upon prior bad experiences.

- Defining and prioritizing the issues. The participants needed to ascertain what the major problem areas were and decide which ones needed to be addressed first.

- Finding a "common cause." This is primarily based upon building trust, finding common areas of concern and redress, and creating a plan.

- Developing flexibility. This is a recognition that university-industry partnerships, to be truly productive and long-term, must be flexible to meet future demands and changes of an internal and external nature.

- Building on existing efforts, such as the Business-Higher Education Forum (BHEF) publication "Working Together, Creating Knowledge" and the Responsible Partnership Initiative by EARMA (European Association of Research Managers & Administrators.

A significant benefit from the UIPP was greater communication and understanding between the project participants and the institutions/sectors they represented. The change was remarkable between the first and third years: whereas the first year represented significant distrust and strained conversations, the third year saw significant progress being made. Communication was more open and solution-focused. Calling this transformational change is not an overstatement.

One of the major contentious issues identified by the UIPP was poor communication between university and industry partners. This problem is exactly why the UIDP is a case study for this portion of the supplement.

A primary conclusion of this project was that negotiation of sponsored research agreements is a barrier to industry-university research collaboration in the United States. This barrier is exemplified by longer contract negotiation times, contentious negotiation processes, increasing costs resulting from the increase in length and contention, and little or no benefits resulting from the conclusion of the contract negotiation. This conclusion is not surprising given the efforts dedicated to the issue prior to the establishment of the UIPP. TurboNegotiator (TN)—the first demonstration project of the UIDP—is meant to start addressing this problematic area.

The UIPP ended with a national summit on April 23, 2006. At that time, two publications were rolled out that reflected project deliverables:

- *Guiding Principles for University-Industry Endeavors*, which articulated a preamble and guiding principles for such collaborations, and

- *Living Studies in University-Industry Negotiations*, which illustrated a variety of successful and problematic partnerships.

The *Living Studies* crossed different sectors of the U.S. economy and represented a variety of private sector, university, and government actors, and mapped perfectly with the *Guiding Principles*. The *Living Studies* illustrated the *Guiding Principles* in action. While it is true that the *Living Studies* publication is primarily historical in nature, it is equally true that these studies are meant to be learned from and applied to the present. That is the essence of a "living document."

University-Industry Demonstration Partnership (UIDP) and TurboNegotiator (TN)

The conclusion of the UIPP at the national summit occurred simultaneously with the kickoff of the UIDP as its successor project. Membership in the UIDP is dues-based, drawing on the idea that institutions that pay to belong have a vested interest to make the UIDP succeed. A membership drive for the UIDP started even before the national summit closed out the work of the UIPP. The membership drive, so to speak, continues to this day. The UIDP had its first meeting in December, 2006 and generally meets every quarter.

The UIDP was modeled after the Federal Demonstration Partnership (FDP), which began as the Florida Demonstration Project in

1986. The FDP is an association of federal agencies, academic research institutions with administrative, faculty and technical representation, and research policy organizations that work to streamline the administration of federally sponsored research (FDP Mission Statement, www.thefdp.org/about_FDP). FDP members of all sectors cooperate in identifying, testing, and implementing new, more effective ways of managing more than $15 billion in federal research grants. The goal of improving the productivity of research without compromising its stewardship has benefits for the entire nation (FDP Mission Statement, (www.thefdp.org/about_FDP).

Now over 20 years old, the FDP is widely accepted as a success by universities and the federal government. It is considered a model for driving institutional change on a national level. FDP continues to move forward, seeking to improve institutional stewardship of federal research money while ensuring the timely and expeditious conduct of research.

Transforming the UIPP results into reality, and using 20+ years of FDP experience, the UIDP mission is to nourish and expand collaborative partnerships between universities and industry in the United States. How will this mission be accomplished? As the UIDP main web page states (www.uidp.org/about_uidp),

> The UIDP accomplishes this mission via a coalition of universities and companies who engage in voluntary collaborative experiments or new approaches to sponsored research, licensing arrangements, and the broader strategic elements of a healthy, long-term university-industry relationship. Institutional experiments are chosen and jointly pursued by willing members when they have the potential to increase the level, degree, or ease of university-industry collaboration. A primary focus for the UIDP's initial work will be on streamlining intellectual property negotiations.

The National Science Foundation (NSF) is a Founder's Circle Member, a category reserved for institutions that make a substantial resource contribution to UIDP. Other members in this category include Pfizer, Ex One, Hewlett Packard, the Kauffman Foundation, and the University of California-Los Angeles.

The potential benefits of the UIDP include the following:

- Improving the research relationship between universities and industry (the focus right now is not on licensing existing university technology funded by the federal government)
- Attracting more industry investment into American universities
- Improving American innovation and competitiveness in a knowledge-based global economy
- Delivering solutions, not just talk

UIDP Characteristics

The UIDP focuses on *collaborative* beta-testing of new approaches to sponsored research, licensing arrangements, and strategic university-industry partnerships. Working groups will be focused on designing institutional experiments.

In addition to these practical, project-related initiatives, UIDP is a forum for the wide dissemination of the latest news, best practices, etc. in the area of university-industry collaboration. Institutions that join the UIDP not only belong to demonstration projects, they are also part of a broader forum designed to enhance collaboration.

One of the unique characteristics of the UIDP is that it requires a paradigm shift. Whereas the current/past paradigm is characterized by *policy-based contract negotiation* (e.g., the partners have IP policies that drive terms and conditions in agreements), the new paradigm requires a *principle-based paradigm*, one that is characterized by the partners determining the parameters that should be considered in selecting appropriate contract terms and conditions.

TurboNegotiator

The first UIDP demonstration project is TurboNegotiator, a tool to allow university and industry negotiators to rapidly navigate towards mutual agreement on intellectual property provisions. This initiative came out of the UIPP; the latter found that research agreements and intellectual property provisions were among the most significant impediments to past, present, and future collaboration between universities and companies. TN is currently in a conceptualization phase (Phase I). Beta testing of TN is at least a year away (late 2008 if not 2009). As demonstrated in the following discussion, communication is critical to university-industry partnership success.

The following steps give the reader a strong idea about how TN will work:

1. Define and describe the "Project Space."

2. Populate Project Space with examples of suitable agreement terms.

3. Develop a questionnaire to probe parameters for the proposed project and use the answers to map the project into the corresponding sector in Project Space.

4. Develop software that will guide the process further. This includes 1) asking questions based upon input provided by project participants, 2) using responses to map projects to a sector within Project Space, and 3) providing sample agreement terms for that sector, which may include explanations and the positives/negatives for such terminology choices. TN, in theory and in practice, is a multifaceted tool.

TN is a rational basis for building an agreement that accurately reflects the project parameters and what the partners want. It uses example terms as the starting place for negotiations. TN is also a process rather than a solution; it improves the understanding of needs and contributions. More importantly, it is an educational process from which all contract negotiators will benefit.

TN is interactive. It will encourage discussion and include input from all key stakeholders. All relevant parties to the agreement should answer the questions. This includes faculty, company researchers, and contract negotiators from all sides involved in the negotiation.

TN is constructive. It suggests terms that are fair and reasonable, and it results in less time for negotiation. Projects commence earlier, which is in everyone's interest. TN will include a time-to-agreement metric, similar to a tickler file but more sophisticated. This latter component can be an excellent managerial tool to spur quality and time improvements. Quality and speed of negotiation should be the goals and passion of all contract negotiators, regardless of institutional affiliation.

What TurboNegotiator Is Not

TN is not a *proscriptive* tool. It does not provide the *right* answer or the *only* answer. *It is not coercive.* If either party is not happy with the outcome, the parties can always walk away from the negotiation or take a different approach or attitude. Maybe the parties have not answered the questions honestly or completely—though this is critical for TN success. This illustrates the importance of communication.

TN does not force or mandate a win-lose outcome. TN seeks to forge agreements that result in productive research, meet the missions of the parties, and possibly lead to long-term relationships. In the end, TN seeks to foster mission compatibility on a project-by-project basis with the desirable outcome of spurring greater thought towards future collaboration.

Summary Features of TurboNegotiator

The major summary features of TN, given project status at the present time, are as follows:

- TN requires parties to agree on project scope before proceeding to clause selection. While this sounds like common sense (and it is), it seems harder in reality. As a contract negotiator, I always nailed down the project scope before negotiating terms and conditions. As an attorney, it always seemed to me to be negligent to negotiate in the absence of necessary technical/project information. This requires effective and timely communication.

- TN measures its own success by a "time to agreement" module. Timeliness and quality are the paramount goals of contract negotiation. And, there are some areas of contract negotiation, like clinical trial agreements, where time is of the essence. When solving or mitigating medical ailments, not to mention the human subject protocol dimension, it behooves the contract negotiators on all sides to reach agreement quickly so that the medical research can go forward. This requires effective and timely communication.

Conclusions Regarding the UIDP and TN

How does TN interact with communication? First, TN represents the action component of the UIDP, to provide concrete incremental improvements to the entire relationship. The forum (discussant) component of the UIDP is equally necessary in a broader context.

Communication remains critical to the UIDP and TN. This is a common sense conclusion, but if it is that easy, why hasn't communication been more effective? An analogy to the world of divorce law seems appropriate. As a former divorce attorney, I can testify to the importance of tending to the entire relationship, not just discrete aspects of it. This is equally true of university-industry collaboration. It is my conclusion that the UIDP forum and TN will play integral roles in the continual strengthening of communication among and between university and industry partners.

Conclusion

The importance of the *Laws of Communication* to university research administration in general and specifically to university-industry partnerships is evident. In a decentralized environment such as university research administration, it is clear that communication is critically important to the research enterprise at the personal (faculty, staff, administration) and institutional levels. If there is no consistent and clear communication both up and down, within the vertical structure that is university research administration, personal and institutional productivity suffers in the area of research grants.

The University-Industry Demonstration Partnership was created partially because communication among and within higher education and industrial partners was less than optimal, leading to concerns about American research competitiveness. More concise and effective communication is a clear need for improved productivity on the personal and institutional level.

CHAPTER 14
LAWS OF COMMUNICATION IN THE HEALTHCARE INDUSTRY

Carolyn M. DeLeon

In the healthcare industry, communication is critical for obtaining high levels of organizational performance, including quality patient care and patient safety. Healthcare industry leaders, particularly those in acute care hospitals, must acquire the ability to step outside of the silo-department mentality and into a highly interconnected, communicative environment in order to achieve high levels of employee, departmental, and organizational performance. The outcomes of achieving these high levels of performance are employee, patient, and physician satisfaction; overall high quality patient care and patient safety; and achieving the hospital's business objectives, whether the hospital is public or private, non-profit or for-profit.

Department managers and organizational leaders in acute care hospitals can use the principles of Schuttler's *Laws of Communication* to identify the location of their current levels of communication in relation to employee, departmental, and organizational performance. The communication models can aid in identifying strategies based on departmental goals, in alignment with the overall organizational goals, to achieve the next level of performance and sustain high levels of performance in the future.

Many of the communication systems used within a hospital are in place because of the 24/7 operation, the wide range of careers and educational levels from housekeeping to post-graduate degreed specialists, and the unique organizational design of the hospital, which requires multiple communication methods.

Within hospitals, information is communicated in multiple ways: a cascading flow that runs vertically, horizontally, and diagonally.

Vertical communication occurs from the top down or from the manager to the followers and from the bottom up or from the followers to the manager (Hersey, Blanchard, & Johnson, 2001). Horizontal communication occurs between employees, departments, and departmental managers. Diagonal communication occurs between and across multiple departments. Diagonal communication is seen in committees, task force teams, and cross-functional project teams (Shortell & Kaluzny, 2000).

Organizational Communication

The following segments present an overview of organizational communication in a hospital setting. Examples are taken specifically from an acute care hospital, illustrating how the *Laws of Communication* can be successfully implemented in the healthcare industry.

Several dynamics occur when the *Laws of Communication* are operating successfully at the hospital from the director and manager level. First, in an acute care hospital, when departmental managers communicate effectively, not only intra-departmentally but also inter-departmentally, they help to eliminate the silo effect typically seen in many hospitals. Second, effective cross-departmental communication improves the overall organizational performance in patient flow, patient satisfaction, and physician satisfaction.

Law of Communication Model #1

Example 1

This first segment addresses the principles of the first *Law of Communication* and its related models at the director and managerial levels. This segment provides examples of how two different acute care hospital managers, one inpatient and one outpatient, lead and communicate and the resulting employee, patient, and physician satisfaction measures. At the department level, communication occurs vertically and horizontally from the leader to the followers, from the followers to the leader, and among departmental employees (Hersey et al., 2001).

The first department is a 44 bed, inpatient adult acute cardiovascular unit inclusive of a 14 bed progressive care unit (PCU). The manager of this department has 85 employees, two assistant managers, and one administrative assistant. The unit has a variety of patients with cardiac diagnoses and/or complications ranging from mild chest pain to open heart surgery.

In the PCU area, the unit primarily admits post-cardiac catheterization intervention patients who have had invasive procedures and will be sent home within 24 hours. The cardiovascular unit overall has a 24-hour patient turnover average rate of 85% and operates within California state-mandated nursing ratios of 4:1.

The department manager has been in this position for one year and has improved departmental and employee performance by bringing a different leadership and communication style that is representative of the first *Law of Communication*. The primary element evident in this manager's leadership and communication style is her disposition for *walking the talk*. This manager works alongside her nurses and will not ask her employees to do anything she would not do herself.

This manager does not simply articulate the core values of her department in patient care and leadership: she models them on a daily basis. The manager maintains an open door policy and takes the time to listen to her employees about any issue they want to discuss, whether it is professional conversation about patient care, the hospital, the unit, or personal conversation about family, friends, and personal interests.

By walking the talk of her values in leadership and communication, this manager has created a trusting environment with committed employees. Under her leadership, the department vacancy rate has dropped from 16.9% to 6.8%.

This manager also demonstrates an element from the second *Law of Communication* in her effective feedback and feed-forward. Previous leaders in the unit led with a micro-management, one-way communication style, resulting in poor employee morale, high turnover rates, and poor physician satisfaction scores. As a result of this new leader engaging the employees and physicians and communicating effectively in both feedback and feed-forward mechanisms, department morale has greatly improved, and employees and physicians have a clear sense of purpose and direction. Organizational and departmental information is continually disseminated to employees and physicians, giving both groups a continual sense of organizational and departmental direction.

This manager offers feedback to employees in the form of coaching and mentoring through effective performance management. Purposeful and meaningful feedback is given immediately to employees, creating a mutually trusting, non-hierarchically driven relationship. Physicians and patients provide feedback regarding departmental performance in monthly patient satisfaction surveys and yearly physician satisfaction surveys.

The manager of this department is actively involved in the growth and development of her employees. She continually engages her employees and challenges them to learn. She provides an energizing, interactive environment by empowering her employees to take on individual projects that improve departmental performance. By engaging the employees to be innovative and creative in solving departmental problems, she has created a motivational, empowering atmosphere in which employees strive to reach departmental and organizational business goals. Celebrating the successes of reaching their goals is a core philosophy of the unit.

Having a hospital manager lead and communicate using the principles of the first *Law of Communication* has resulted in current year employee satisfaction and engagement scores at the top levels of performance, both within the hospital and across the 175 hospitals represented in the corporate organization. Patient satisfaction levels now reside in the 1st quartile performance, and current year physician satisfaction scores report an 80% response rate of *satisfied* or *very satisfied.*

Example 2

The second department is an outpatient Mammography Center. This department is a full-service breast center offering screening and diagnostic mammography, diagnostic ultrasound, and x-ray core biopsies. It is a provider-based department of an acute care hospital located two miles from the main campus in a freestanding medical office building.

The organizational structure of the department consists of one director who reports to the Chief Operating Officer/Chief Medical Officer in the hospital, 29 employees, and partners with a radiology group to provide services for the patients, including a referral base of over 200 physicians. The department provides services to approximately 25,000 patients annually.

The director of the department has served for 10 years in this position. The leadership style and communication strategies that she has implemented over the course of her tenure have resulted in a high performing department in the areas of employee, patient, and physician satisfaction.

Specific characteristics that the department director uses include elements Schuttler describes as residing in the *green zone* of the first Law's communication model. The leader demonstrates a strong desire to foster open dialogue among her staff and physicians. Her philosophy is to share good *and* bad news with her team of employees and physicians, and she has the leadership integrity to walk through both the good *and* the bad times with her team. She makes the effort to keep open dialogue and two-way communication with other departmental directors, managers, and key stakeholders to facilitate team collaboration and negate the silo effect.

The second element that she incorporates into her department is a feedback and feed forward communication style. The department director feeds-forward to her staff:

1. Communication regarding organizational issues,

2. The hospital vision and mission, and

3. How they fit into the overall strategic business plan, all of which help the organization reach its business goals.

Feedback communication from patients is always delivered in a constructive way and framed as an opportunity to improve and excel to higher levels of customer satisfaction. As a result of customer feedback, the manager allows the employees to champion any change efforts that create a highly motivational atmosphere and positive morale. Change efforts also allow employees to take on both leading and following roles.

The third element the department director demonstrates in her leadership and communication style is the role of a coach and mentor. As an effective coach and mentor, she consistently upholds a philosophy of giving meaningful and objective feedback. The director holds in high priority the critical nature of performance management and providing immediate constructive feedback to both employees and physicians.

She coaches and mentors throughout the year, not just at annual evaluation periods. This practice has resulted in high performing employees who continually bring innovative ideas to staff and committee meetings. The employees are empowered to implement their ideas and drive their innovative ideas to completion.

Ultimately, through using the elements in the first *Law of Communication* model, such as open dialogue, coaching and mentoring, meaningful objective feedback, walking the talk, and becoming actively involved with all stakeholders, this department director has achieved high performing departmental employee and physician satisfaction results.

The current year's employee satisfaction scores are at the top level of percentage performance for the individual hospital and across the larger organization of 175 hospitals. Patient satisfaction for 3 consecutive years has remained within 1st and high 2nd quartile performance. Finally, physician satisfaction ranked in the 90th percentile within the radiology group.

The hospital received the Blue Cross of California Designated Center of Expertise for Coronary Bypass Graft Award and the Outstanding Achievement Award from the American College of Surgeons (ACoS) Commission on Cancer for cancer care services. This designation was due, in part, to two of the outcomes of effective and successful leadership and communication strategies at the departmental level as represented by the first *Law of Communication.* When a hospital consistently maintains high-performing departments across disciplines, all of the individual high performing departments collectively merge into a high performing organization.

Law of Communication Model #2

The second segment addresses the principles of the second *Law of Communication*—how hospital organizations communicate and the impact of this communication on overall organizational performance.

The Joint Commission on Accreditation of Healthcare Organizations (JCAHO) recognizes communication as an essential element in safe patient care and has named *caregiver communication* as one of the top national patient safety goals. Communication is a significant element in all the JCAHO standards, which include the following:

1. Provision of Care, Treatment and Services (PC).

2. Leadership Standards (LD).

3. Management of the Environment of Care (EC).

4. Management of Human Resources (HR).

5. Management of Information (IM).

6. Medical Staff (MS) (JCAHO, 2007).

Effective communication in healthcare organizations must be integrated into all aspects of hospital operations, hospital quality, and stakeholder groups, which include employees, physicians, patients, the Board of Trustees, and the community that the hospital serves. Within most healthcare organizational design structures, organizational leaders can develop and sustain communication strategies that are methodical (Maini & Morrel-Samuels, 2006) and that can be used consistently, ultimately improving and resulting in high levels of organizational performance.

To better articulate how the second *Law of Communication* is enacted, it is important to understand the organizational design of the hospital, as the design impacts the way communication is delivered and the effectiveness of communication strategies. Thus, continual feedback loops are critical within the design of hospital strategic communication systems because they provide a means for leaders to know where changes are required (Shortell & Kaluzny, 2000).

Examples of continual feedback loops can be patient comment cards or a Gallup electronic patient communication system that delivers patient comments back to hospital leadership within a 24-hour time frame. Other examples include feedback from employee, patient, and physician satisfaction surveys.

Employee advisory groups (EAGs) are another feedback loop strategy. EAGs, led by a human resources executive or other chief hospital executive, consist of a group of employees from a variety of disciplines and departments within the hospital who meet regularly to address frontline issues and discuss performance improvement ideas in various areas of the hospital. This practice provides a venue for employees to have a voice and for communication to loop back directly to the senior leadership team of the hospital.

Communication Strategies: Hospital A

Healthcare facilities use both formal and informal communication strategies to accomplish organizational goals and objectives. The following examples describe the formal and informal communication strategies used by the hospital described in this chapter and the resulting organizational performance its leaders have achieved by using these communication strategies. They are examples of the second *Law of Communication*, and both demonstrate data-driven organizational results.

Formal Communication Strategies

As noted, Hospital A is part of a larger organizational corporation that includes 175 hospitals, and it is part of a division that is inclusive of nine other hospitals in the Western United States. Effective and purposeful communication is accomplished through multiple venues in a hospital setting, including, but not limited to:

1. Clearly articulating and living the vision and mission of the hospital.

2. Cascading communication methods and learning experiences.

3. Promoting venues for two way communication.

4. Providing electronic informational updates.

5. Calling departmental staff meetings.

6. Creating and maintaining newsletters.

7. Designing new employee hospital orientation.

Using multiple venues for organizational communication is an important strategy for operating in the *green zone* within Schuttler's *Laws of Communication* model.

Communicating the hospital's vision, mission, strategic goals, and objectives to all employees helps them to understand that each individual or department, when working toward the same goal, creates motion that drives the organization toward meeting these goals. Open communication also gives employees a broader awareness of how their daily work helps to fulfill the hospital's mission.

By using various positive communication styles and strategies, hospital leaders can enable their followers to see, hear, touch, feel, and taste the vision (Kouzes & Posner, 2002). By bringing life to the vision of the organization, leaders begin to ignite passion in their followers for the mission of their hospital, creating a highly compassionate, customer-focused environment of patient care.

When a hospital organization has highly effective vertical, horizontal, and diagonal communication systems and strategies, the organization will likely experience success in organizational initiatives and regulatory performance measures. The communicative characteristics and strategies of the organization should facilitate organizational effectiveness rather than impede high performance (Ginter, Swayne, & Duncan, 2002).

The first example of the second *Law of Communication* stems from the senior leadership perspective of Hospital A and the impact of the senior leadership communication strategies on organizational performance. On an annual basis, the hospital's senior leadership team meets with the Board of Trustees to review the organization's vision and mission and to determine the hospital's strategic business goals and direction. Goals and objectives are developed as a team, and the vision, mission, strategic goals, and objectives are then communicated to the management team of the hospital and then to the employees through employee forum meetings and departmental staff meetings.

Continual updates on organizational progress toward goals and objectives are accomplished throughout the year in formal committee meetings that are inclusive of many hospital stakeholders. Continual updates to employees and physicians are also accomplished throughout the year, not only through on-going employee forums, medical staff forums, departmental staff meetings, electronic updates, and medical staff newsletters, but also through celebrations that occur when the hospital reaches any of its organizational goals.

The hospital joins together in celebration, and employees are rewarded for their part in helping the hospital to reach its goals. Different celebratory activities are used, including ice cream bars delivered by the senior leadership team to every employee on all three shifts, departmental catered meals for all three shifts, and summertime hospital barbeques.

The second example of this *Law of Communication* is the hospital's rapid response stroke task force. This task force is a high performing organizational team that uses a communication system inclusive of vertical, horizontal, and diagonal communication strategies to promote a *green zone* culture of self-improvement, corporate citizenship, and strategic focus. The stroke task force in this hospital over the years has developed solid communication strategies and teamwork between hospital leadership, hospital employees, physicians, and the community Emergency Medical Response (EMS) team.

As a result, the hospital is one of the first five hospitals nationally to achieve the JCAHO certification as a Primary Stroke Center. This nationally recognized stroke program, and the campaign it has engendered, has also resulted in recognized global implications, a nationally recognized stroke task force team, and a proud, trusting environment within the organization. Communication strategies have fostered the growth and development of a community organization to educate consumers about strokes and advocate for enhanced stroke care.

A third example of the second *Law of Communication* in Hospital A is a high-performing Quality Standards Committee. The Quality Standards Committee is comprised of multiple disciplines within the hospital that are representative of and responsible for JCAHO standards being met and maintained. This committee promotes the *green zone* elements in the communication model, a culture of continuous self-improvement, and strategic focus on patient safety within the hospital.

Using a formal diagonal communication system, the committee's results have been highly successful, as indicated on JCAHO surveys year after year. This communication style of continuous self-improvement and strategic focus has served to maintain a high performing quality team, create cycles of refinement for quality standards, and enable full accreditation from the first unannounced JCAHO survey.

Other examples of formal communication strategies used by Hospital A are internal electronic communication, formal newsletters to physicians and departments, direct mailings to employee homes, and new incumbent communication through formal orientation processes, both at the organizational and departmental levels. These types of written communication strategies are seen as formal policies and procedures within the hospital.

Even though most employees of an organization will never read all policies and procedures in depth, for a culture of open communication they will need access to all the information. Additionally, during JCAHO surveys, surveyors do not expect employees to know every policy of the organization, but surveyors do look for employees' knowledge of where to find the information.

The senior leadership team of the hospital adopted a *mock survey team* in which representatives from the quality and nursing departments randomly choose departments to perform mock patient tracer surveys. The mock survey team will question employees about their knowledge of patients and of where to find critical information regarding hospital policies to determine if the hospital policy is in alignment with daily practice. The creation of this mock survey team internally resulted in a successful JCAHO tracer survey, with—as mentioned—the hospital eventually receiving full accreditation.

These examples, according to Schuttler's *Laws of Communication* model, indicate that with clear organizational communication strategies and systems and a clear sense of purpose, top-level organizational performance can be achieved, sustained, and eventually reach national recognition levels.

Informal Communication Strategies

Many informal communication strategies used by a hospital organization can demonstrate leadership visibility and model the values of the organization. Informal communication strategies are a subset to enforce the formal communication strategies in place. Informal communication is the ultimate result of interpersonal relationships (Shortell & Kaluzny, 2000).

One such mechanism is *leadership rounding*. The senior leadership team of Hospital A rotates weekly responsibility for employee rounds. During the week of rounds, the administrator on duty for that week will make rounds to all departments, both inpatient and outpatient, to engage with employees, to receive direct feedback, and to address in real time any issues employees are experiencing.

This type of planned but yet informal communication strategy supports the *Laws of Communication* model by making leaders visible in their modeling of the hospital's vision and mission. Also, the strategy gives the employees an opportunity for direct two-way communication with senior leadership. Importantly, one series of rounds is conducted on the night shift and one series of rounds is conducted on a weekend day, giving employees in all shifts the opportunity to speak directly with senior leaders.

These informal communication strategies help build trust with the senior leaders through visibility and presence. This strong relationship was evidenced in the results of a current employee satisfaction and engagement survey. Within their open comments, employees expressed appreciation for the visibility of senior leadership.

Another type of informal communication with the patient and family stakeholder population is administrative rounding on patient floors. The senior leadership team approaches different inpatient departments and engages with patients and families to inquire about the care they are receiving and to ask if there is anything else they might need. This creates a continuous, open communicative environment for patients, families, nurses, and leaders of the hospital.

Open communication is another type of informal communication strategy the hospital uses for gathering input for improvement from multiple sources. The hospital's senior leadership and management team have a philosophy of open communication for receiving performance improvement suggestions and innovative ideas from employees, patients, visitors, physicians, volunteers, and the community.

Having an open communication philosophy has been highly effective in adopting best practices from sister hospitals within the organization and in the organization's continued ability to adopt best practices. As such, the hospital is able to adapt quickly to changing environments while continuing to meet business needs and providing high quality patient care.

Results of ongoing formal and informal organizational communication and celebration are seen not only in high overall organizational performance, but also in patient satisfaction scores residing in the 1st and high 2nd quartile ranges and multiple inpatient and outpatient departments in the 1st quartile exclusively. Current scores indicate physicians' satisfaction with the hospital administration's communication to be well above national norms and improving. A recent employee engagement survey indicated that overall employee satisfaction levels are on the rise and that some of the top performing areas of the organization address culture and recognition.

Summary

Communication in healthcare is essential to growing and sustaining high performing organizations. The communication strategies and characteristics represented in the *green zone* of the *Laws of Communication* result in high performance. Departmental managers have used communication strategies that resulted in high performing outcomes. Hospital A operated with communication strategies in the green zone, and the resulting performance levels earned national recognition and solid JCAHO performance.

Most hospital organizations are not fully operating in the *green zone* of the *Laws of Communication*. The healthcare industry at large can use these *Laws* to evaluate and identify where both the hospital managers and the organization are operating, all towards the goal of implementing new ways of communicating and leading to the next level of performance.

Hospital managers and senior leadership may find that certain arenas of communication within different areas of the hospital are operating at different levels. Some may be red, some may be yellow, and others green. Thus, the key to successful overall organizational performance is to identify and use communication strategies and styles that are meaningful to employees and other key stakeholders. The ultimate goal is that all functional areas operate in the *green zone* and sustain high levels of organizational performance in order to promote a continuous environment of growth and learning.

CHAPTER 15
LAWS OF COMMUNICATION: APPLICATIONS FOR THE NURSE-PATIENT RELATIONSHIP

Kelley Waugh

Every communication touches social norms, ways of thinking about relating to others, feelings, values, and ideas that are unique, rich, and complex. Consider, for example, the communication between a nurse and a patient. To operate consistently in the *green zone*, a nurse must understand the role of communication in each relationship and note that the language, spontaneity, and message employed in conversation will depend on the patient's needs. Understanding a few simple aspects of nurse-patient communication can help nurses direct this communication toward more positive ends. These laws make the relationship safe for the patient through behavior regarding confidentiality, level of involvement, and competency.

How nurses perceive certain *Laws of Communication* and their ability to adhere to these laws has a profound effect on the success of interpersonal communication in the nurse-patient relationship. Patients invite nurses into the innermost spheres of their lives, almost without question, in the context of the nurse-patient relationship. The nurse functions as a trusted confidant, educational resource, and sounding board. In times of stress, patients trust that the nurse will help them understand their situation and regain control of it.

Communication is a process through which the nurse can establish a human-to-human relationship and fulfill the purpose of nursing. Through application of simple *Laws of Communication*, the nurse can assist the patient and families to prevent and cope with the experience of illness and suffering, thus staying in the *green zone*. Nurses need to understand that this communication process includes complex cognitive, behavioral, and cultural factors. This understanding, along with the following techniques, will augment nurses' skills and their interactions with patients. The result is that both nurse and patient can more effectively cope with the demands placed upon them.

In the following sections, I describe four laws in terms of the *types* of communication nurses employ when working with patients:

1. Spoken language
2. Non-verbal / body language
3. Therapeutic communication
4. Active listening

Within the description of each type of communication, I also discuss strategies for remaining in the *green zone*. It should be noted that none of these communication types exist in isolation from the other three. Communication with patients involves a complex array of verbal and non-verbal behaviors for the purpose of sharing information. As such, within the nurse-patient relationship, any exchange between them carries a message that can change the way in which both parties receive and interpret information.

Law Number One: Spoken Communication of Language

Everyone uses language as a tool to generate ideas, share experiences with others, and validate the meaning of perceptions about the world. Without the use of communication, people would be severely limited in their ability to classify and order information in ways that can be understood by themselves and by others.

The meaning of spoken words, or language, extends far beyond that of just saying words. The interpretation of the meaning of language may vary according to the person's background, gender, and experiences. One can easily step into the *yellow* or *red zone* when assuming that spoken communication has the same meaning for everyone, especially in terms of the nurse-patient relationship. Spoken communication is useful only to the extent that it accurately reflects the experience it is designed to portray.

There are two levels of meaning in the spoken communication of language. Both are influenced by culture. Leininger (1991) portrayed culture as a factor that influences healthcare, communication, and practices directly related to the patient's health and well-being. The interaction among these factors takes place in a wide variety of nursing communication. The nurse-patient relationship frequently acts as an interpersonal bridge between systems, with the nurse providing the communication needed to negotiate and accommodate the patient and family requests without compromising care.

Denotation in communication, as part of verbal communication, refers to the generalized meaning assigned to a word, whereas *connotation* points to a more personalized meaning of the word. As a nurse, one should be aware that many patients' communications convey only a part of the intended meaning. Nurses should never assume that the meaning of the message is the same for the sender and the receiver until mutual understanding is verified. The following are some ideas to consider when using spoken language as communication and attempting to operate in the *green zone*:

- How does the patient's culture have a bearing on our communication?
- How does the patient's gender have a bearing on our communication?
- Am I using slang and/or jargon? Can I restate ideas in a more common way?

Metacommunication

Metacommunication is a broad term used to describe all of the factors that influence how a message is received. People communicate not only information, but also messages about how that information is to be interpreted. This ancillary information is known as metacommunication. Metacommunication messages may be hidden within verbal or non-verbal communication.

In a professional relationship, verbal and non-verbal components of communication are intimately related. When the verbal message is incongruent with the visual image, it is important to help the patient understand and assimilate the discrepancy so that content can be dealt with directly. The nurse non-verbally communicates acceptance, interest, and respect for the client through eye contact, body posture, head nodding, and frequent smiling. Additionally, studies have found that nurses who touch their patients, speak softly, and employ non-verbal communication have been perceived both positively, as caring, and negatively, as controlling (Mulaik, Megenity, Cannon, et al., 1991).

Vocalization

Also involved in spoken communication is *vocalization*, or the oral delivery of the verbal message, expressed through tone of voice and inflection, sighing, or crying. This component of spoken communication is important for the nurse to understand as it impacts how the verbal message is likely to be interpreted. For example, the nurse might say, "I would like to hear more about how you are feeling" in a voice that sounds rushed or harsh. This message is more than likely to be misinterpreted by the patient. When the tone of voice does not fit the words, the message is less easily understood and is likely to be discounted, falling into the *yellow* or *red zone.*

Rules and Boundaries

In the *green zone* of spoken communication, comments are descriptive rather than judgmental. Each person's role, abilities, and boundaries are clearly recognizable by all participants. When the purpose of the relationship no longer requires constant interaction, the nurse and patient should terminate the process. This factor is important to remember because some patients and nurses would like to allow a satisfying relationship to extend beyond goal achievement. To do so can compromise the law of communication and cause the nurse-patient relationship to enter the *yellow* or *red zone*. In order to avoid this problem, the nurse needs to remain focused on the patients' current healthcare needs and goals and support them.

Law Number Two: Non-Verbal Communication

In nursing, non-verbal communication includes facial expressions, eye movements, body movements, posture, gestures, and the use of space. This type of communication is commonly referred to as body language. Whereas spoken words are intended to direct the content of communication, the message can become altered by the emotion conveyed through body language, particularly facial expressions. As such, even subtle non-verbal communication can affect the vast majority of nurse-to-patient communication.

Generally, non-verbal expressions of communication are considered useful for social communication and can be more reliable than their verbal counterparts, but to be effective, non-verbal behavior should be consistent with and reinforce the verbal message. A great example would be that of a registered nurse who smiles as she tells her manager that her assignment is more than she can handle—with this non-verbal gesture, she negates the seriousness of her message.

Body Cues and Facial Expression

In nursing, posture, rhythm of movement, and gestures accompanying a verbal message are non-verbal behaviors associated with the overall process of communication. Body stance may convey a message about the nurse or even the family of the patient. For example, speaking while directly facing a person conveys more confidence than turning one's body at an angle. A slumped head-down posture and slow movements give an impression of lassitude or low self-esteem whereas an erect posture and decisive movements suggest confidence and self-control. Rapid, diffuse, agitated body movements often indicate anxiety. Vigorous, direct actions can suggest confidence and purpose. More force with less focused direction in body movements might symbolize anger.

Eye contact, especially when nurse-patient focused, and facial expressions appear to be important in signaling feelings. Throughout life, people respond to the expressive qualities of another's face, often without even being aware, and research suggests that people who make direct eye contact while talking or listening create a sense of confidence and credibility. Facial expressions are equally important to getting messages across. They connect the words presented in the message to the internal dialogue of the speaker. Facial expressions either reinforce or modify the message the listener hears. If the verbal message is inconsistent with the non-verbal expression of the message, the non-verbal expression is generally perceived as being more trustworthy. One study (Mehrabian, 1971) on this topic simulated the impact of words, vocalization, and facial expression on the receiver, and the findings indicated that non-verbal content far outweighed the power of actual words.

Law Number Three: Therapeutic Communication

To operate in the *green zone*, registered nurses use the method of therapeutic communication—a goal-directed, focused dialogue between the nurse and the patient specially designed to meet the needs of the patient. This process involves the exchange of ideas, feelings, and attitudes related to the desired healthcare outcomes. The physical environment in which therapeutic communication takes place may be a hospital, the patient's home, a community health center, or a nursing home. Therapeutic communication takes place within an interpersonal environment that, in addition to the patient and the nurse, can also include the healthcare team and family.

Therapeutic communication directly related to nursing develops in a conversational format. It is a complementary process in which every participant must be actively engaged. For effective therapeutic communication to continue, the nurse must be prepared to answer the patient's questions and respond appropriately. This means the nurse must be open-minded and waiting to receive the message. Careful attention to the patient's body language and how to answer the message enhances the chance of open therapeutic communication. Once the message is received, the nurse can then choose the most appropriate response for the patient.

In nursing, therapeutic communication between nurse and patient has a serious purpose. Through therapeutic communication, the patient can learn about his or her illness and how to cope with it. Therapeutic communication comforts dying patients and assures living patients that someone is there to be with them and ease their suffering. It can make the illness bearable by reinforcing the natural healing powers of the patient.

Purpose of Therapeutic Communication

Ruesch (1961), the originator of therapeutic communication, notes that "the aim of therapeutic communication is to improve the patient's ability to function alone, with another, and in groups" (p. 32). Specific advantages of therapeutic communication between nurse and patient include the following:

- Therapeutic communication is a critical factor in helping patients reassess priorities.
- Therapeutic communication is an opportunity for patients and their families to explore new information about themselves.
- Therapeutic communication is an interpersonal experience of discovering meaning in current life circumstances.
- Therapeutic communication is an avenue for the discovery of new possibilities to achieve well-being.

Therapeutic communication is a mutual process, with both participants seeking to understand each other's position and support the goals of the relationship. Still, it is not a completely reciprocal process in the sense that both nurse and patient can expect their needs to be met through the communication. The nurse's feelings, attitudes, values, and behavior all show through in therapeutic communication and are indirect contributors to the success of the relationship. Intimate details of the nurse's life experience, except as they might facilitate the relationship, are deliberately excluded from the communication.

Characteristics of Therapeutic Communication

Therapeutic communication is more than the transfer of information or ideas from one person to another. Emphasis is placed on reaching realistic solutions to the patient's healthcare problems and needs. Discussions occur within the context of a clear definition of the values, purposes, and goals directly related to the needs of the patient. The nurse must always ask these questions:

- What is the purpose or objective of sharing information or asking this question?
- What are the main points to be shared, and in what order?

Adhering to relationship goals is an art requiring conscious effort and considerable practice. The patient's needs dictate a sense of timing and sensitivity and a coordination of interpersonal skills to meet the demands of each situation and each patient.

Law Number Four: Active Listening

For nurses, active listening is the process whereby a person hears a message, decodes its meaning, and conveys an understanding about the meaning. In the communication process, active listening is as important as talking. Although other means provide valuable information in a patient assessment, they are not a substitute for active listening and face-to-face contact with the patient.

Listening differs from hearing. Many times, a nurse can listen for 90 seconds and completely hear the message the patient is saying. This rapid transfer of information is achieved through active listening and is essential in nurse-patient relationships. The meaning derived from the communication, however, may be altered if two separate people, with different values, expectations, and/or experiences, hear the conversation. For this reason, validation and self-awareness are important for this communication to continue operating in the *green zone.*

To develop shared meanings, active listening requires nurses to think critically about choosing responses that will aid in keeping communications in the *green zone.* Active listening includes a recollection of the previous laws by paying close attention to non-verbal cues, body posture, gestures, and culture. Nurses listen for changes in tone, pauses in the conversation, and our own intuition about the communication. They also remember previous communication with the patient, as well as communication from physicians and families to assist with active listening techniques.

A simple way for the nurse to develop active listening skills is to begin to listen to oneself and ask a set of crucial questions:

- How do I transmit messages?
- How do I decode a patient's message?
- What type of feedback am I offering?
- What about my eye contact and non-verbal cues?

Active listening responses have other benefits in the development of nurse-patient relationships. It provides evidence of the nurse's recognition and validation of the humanness of the patient. When a nurse listens to the patient and tries to understand and respond to the patient's fears, feelings, and ideas, the person feels validated. Confirming a patient's worth can be as important as understanding a diagnosis when promoting, maintaining, and restoring his or her health.

Strategies for Listening Responses

Nurses who listen and tune into the non-verbal cues of the patient's message are more likely able to support the patient's goals and outcomes. In nursing, feedback in the form of listening shows that the nurse is interested in processing the information and remembering important facts about the patient in an accurate data assessment. The nurse uses words and touch as listening responses to encourage further disclosure, to convey understanding, and to provide immediate feedback to the patient related to their needs and health problems.

Appropriately used verbal cues, clarification, restatement, paraphrasing, reflection, silence, and touch are examples of *skilled* communication strategies the nurse can use to elicit a complete database. Clarification is used to obtain more information when data are incomplete. Restatement is appropriate when a particular part of the content is needed. Paraphrasing addresses the content or cognitive component of the communication, and summarization integrates the content and feeling parts of the message by rephrasing two or more parts of the message. All of these techniques are intertwined and overlapping.

Summary

When communication slips into the *yellow* or *red zones*, the nurse-patient relationship suffers immensely, but careful communication can enhance interaction between the nurse and patient and allow the communication to remain in the *green zone.* Effective communication will fit the purpose of the nurse-patient relationship, with its ultimate focus on the healthcare needs and goals of the patient. With consistent attention to the four main aspects of nurse-patient communication—spoken language, non-verbal cues, therapeutic communication, and active listening—greater levels of healthcare service can be achieved every day.

CHAPTER 16
COMMUNICATION, LEADERSHIP, AND PERFORMANCE IN AN EDUCATIONAL SETTING

Kelly Preston Anderson

Schuttler's *Laws of Communication*, with their associated attributes and outcomes, can be readily observed in numerous organizations, including private educational settings. In this chapter, the *Laws of Communication* will be applied to an educational organization that provides religious education to youth and young adults in settings throughout the world. A principal who oversees between 3 and 30 teachers leads each faculty member. As such, the need for communication is consistently evident.

Law of Communication #1

The first *Law of Communication* addresses how supervisors communicate with subordinates and how that communication style correlates with employee performance. Fifteen years of experience working for the previously noted educational organization has provided ample opportunities to observe communication between organizational leaders and faculty.

Law #1—Red Zone Observations

One characteristic of employee performance in the *red zone* is that employees do only what is required. The policy manual for this religious organization states that teachers are to arrive at work at least one half hour before classes begin and remain in the workplace for at least one half hour after the final class concludes. Additionally, teachers are to work at least 40 hours each week.

Over the years, some supervisors have frequently observed that their employees fail to meet these minimum standards of performance, yet in some locations, every employee willingly meets these minimum standards and gladly extends extra efforts. Within one faculty that falls into the latter category, the principal was usually the one to unlock the doors in the morning and to lock the doors in the afternoon. No one ever questioned if he was fulfilling his required time because it was obvious that he did. On the other hand, the leaders of faculty who were struggling with this policy would often arrive at work shortly before the students and would regularly be the first out the door at the end of the day.

Because their employees did not follow policy, the less effective principals in this example needed to demonstrate constant focus on the policy, with frequent reminders for faculty. They demonstrated myopia with the belief that everyone, except for themselves, needed to strictly adhere to that policy. The subordinate faculty believed their leaders were trying to control their every move and would often mock the principals outside of their presence. Faculty who were subordinate to more effective leaders would praise the principals both in and out of their presence and were fully committed to giving whatever effort was required to assist in meeting goals and objectives.

Law #1—Yellow Zone Observations

During the summer vacation months, this organization sponsors teacher training meetings to help the teachers either increase their knowledge of the curriculum or refine their teaching skills. These meetings are held in various geographic locations on a weekly basis and are designed to be attended by approximately 40 teachers. Unfortunately, there are typically only 8-10 teachers in attendance, including those assigned to provide the training.

During the spring of each year, the principals of each faculty meet together to plan these summer training meetings. At one of these meetings, the area supervisor, who provided leadership for 20 faculty, asked for input regarding the last round of meetings held the previous summer. Each of the principals in attendance spoke about how these meetings were wonderful and effective. After a moment, the area supervisor turned to ask the opinion of one newcomer who had remained silent. He then responded by asking why, if these meetings were so wonderful and effective, only about 25% of the teachers actually attend them. He suggested that something needed to be done to improve these meetings and make teachers actually want to attend.

Everyone in the room sat in stunned silence. Because it was this principal's first time attending one of these meetings, he was not aware that everyone typically delivered the answers that the area supervisor wanted to hear, rather than being honest and attempting to improve past practices. The area supervisor looked directly at this new principal, voiced his opinion that last year's meetings were a success, and abruptly moved to the next item on the agenda.

This scenario demonstrates characteristics of an organization operating in the *yellow zone*. First, employees were expected to attend these summer training meetings; however, very few actually did. Although teachers were required to attend the meetings, there was no record of attendance and, thus, no accountability. From this, an organizational culture developed among the teachers of doing whatever they wanted, including not attending the meetings. Likewise, their leaders did not adequately correlate the organizational performance standards with the area supervisor's desired goals. The teachers were invited to the meetings without being shown the larger vision and purpose of the training.

A few changes in communication patterns could greatly improve this scenario and bring the organization into the *green zone*. First, the area supervisor needs to be open to accepting constructive criticism regarding the organization's programs. Many leaders become so intertwined with the organizations they lead that they believe any criticism of the organization is a direct criticism of them. By allowing open dialogue, the area supervisor could have gained honest insight from the teachers as to what topics should be covered in the training meetings.

The principals also could have made changes in order to make the process more effective. Too often, subordinates will voice their criticisms and true feelings as long as their superiors are not present. But, as soon as their superiors are present, their views are often tainted with forced optimism. In a culture, such as this example, where it is widely known that the supervisor wants only positive comments, the subordinates must band together and voice their opinions in a polite manner in order for the superior to see a realistic viewpoint. When middle managers commiserate with their subordinates but then do not pass along those views to their superiors, it creates a culture of mistrust between the middle managers and their subordinates.

Law #1—Green Zone Observations

Lest anyone believe this educational organization constantly flounders in the *yellow* and *red zones*, there are countless examples of leaders and employees from this organization operating in the *green zone*.

High performing faculty are led by people who are comfortable receiving suggestions and eager to implement any idea that will lead to greater success—regardless of whether it was their idea or not. One such principal leads a faculty of six, and together they teach a student body of nearly 1,000 students. This person's success stems from a variety of practices he employs at work and also one overriding personal characteristic.

First, the personal characteristic that makes all of this possible is this man's level of self-confidence. He is not threatened when someone else's idea is adopted over his own. Instead, he will rally others in support of the new idea and help everyone enjoy greater success as a result of their collective efforts. He realizes that someone else's success does not take away from his own worth and value as a person or as a leader. His direct reports and peers acknowledge this trait and recognize his desire to help each of them develop and succeed in their own pursuits.

Another practice that contributes to the success of this team is their regularly held faculty meetings. Many others dread faculty meetings, but this team actually views the meeting as a highlight of each week. There are many reasons why these meetings are so successful. First, each member of the faculty comes to the meeting prepared to share information on a particular topic, such as the corporate policy manual, a teaching technique, or a motivational experience from the classroom. In this way, each member is actively contributing to the success of the team, rather than attending as a passive participant.

Another aspect of these meetings that lead to their success is their regularity and the strict time limit to which they are held. Most team members hold sporadic faculty meetings, so faculty members are always wondering if they *have to* attend a meeting this week or not. These teachers will often plan other obligations that make their attendance at faculty meeting—if it is held—impossible. Teachers who have open lines of communication with their superiors know that meetings will be held every week and that they have specific starting and ending times. Through these communications, the principal shows respect for the time of his subordinates and does not keep them from their other obligations.

This example of respect from superior to subordinate demonstrates a sense of humility, and it assures the subordinates that they will be treated fairly. Having this assurance, subordinates can then openly discuss and resolve any concerns or issues they may experience, instead of discussing these issues at the water cooler and allowing them to fester.

Law of Communication #2

The second *Law of Communication* deals less with the communication between individuals within an organization and more with the communication throughout the entire organization. Again, observations from an educational setting will be used to illustrate examples of this law in each of the three zones of performance.

Law #2—Red Zone Observations

One characteristic of the *red zone* is that communication occurs only one way, from top to bottom. A danger of this one-way communication is that leaders often become out of touch with reality—in this case, what a teacher actually confronts everyday in the classroom. Most administrators in the field of education started as teachers in a classroom, but by the time they reach the age of retirement from an administrative position, they may not have taught in a classroom for decades.

A perfect example occurred in the mid-1990s in this educational organization. In 1996, the head of informational technology spoke about the future use of computers within the organization. He outlined a plan that would have a computer on each teacher's desk within a couple of years. Two years came and went, and no teachers received a computer or heard anything more about this plan. When asked about the status of this plan, the head of the IT department stated that the plan had been abandoned, and they now had no intentions of purchasing computers for the teachers. He said that one of the upper-level leaders put an end to the plan by stating he could not understand why a teacher would possibly need a computer. Shock and disappointment was felt throughout the organization.

One of the teachers asked the head of the IT department if this upper-level leader even knew how to use a computer. He responded that this leader had two computers—a desktop and a laptop—and that he used them constantly. Unfortunately, because he had been in administrative roles since the late 1970s, he honestly could not understand why a teacher would need a computer. He viewed them as purely administrative tools because that is how he had always used his computers. The point is that this administrator was not a bad man—he was just out of touch with the frontline of the organization. When he had left the classroom to take an administrative position, the new technology of that period consisted of mimeograph machines and chalkboards.

Since this time, the educational organization has improved greatly in this realm. Each teacher has a laptop computer and other technological tools for teaching, and the administration also frequently invites feedback through online surveys about what tools are needed to enhance classroom instruction.

Law #2—Yellow Zone Observations

There are instances where this organization is operating from within the *yellow zone*. It should be noted, however, that, similar to Schuttler's example of the nuclear power plant, some aspects of this religious educational organization are not open for discussion—matters of doctrine and beliefs. Still, *yellow zone* performance, in general, can limit this organization from reaching its full potential.

One characteristic of *yellow zone* performance is that the organization allows past successes to block the path of future improvement and innovation. Numerous employees—both administrators and teachers—hesitate to find fault with this educational organization because it is also a religious organization. They believe that criticism would be tantamount to denying the faith and entering a state of personal apostasy.

A few years ago, a group of teachers were pursuing a master's degree in the same program and cohort. An assignment for one of these classes required the teachers to plan a fictitious school. Two members of the group wanted to complete the project by creating a school exactly as the educational organization was currently organized because they did not feel they could rightly suggest changing anything. The other two members of the group voiced contrary opinions. They believed that seeking improvement was never wrong.

Not all employees of this organization are opposed to seeking improvement. In 2001, an area supervisor arranged a field trip for all principals to visit a local Air Force base. Upon their arrival, they were taken to a hangar to see an F-16. Their guide explained to them that when the F-16 was first made in 1976, it was the greatest fighter jet in the world. However, despite being the greatest fighter jet in the world, the F-16 had undergone thousands of modifications and improvements over the years. The guide further explained that none of these modifications took away from the well-deserved title of the greatest fighter jet in the world—it only further secured the F-16's claim to that title.

Organizations performing in the *yellow zone* may resist improvement efforts, and they might also limit the full development of their employees. A recent example of this *yellow zone* performance involves an employee who attained a doctorate degree in leadership studies. His dissertation was named the top-selling dissertation of 2005 worldwide. While some might think any organization would proudly proclaim that achievement, there was no recognition of this award from within the organization. Colleagues within the organization have openly wondered about the lack of recognition or utilization of this teacher in a leadership position and question why the organization would not want to capitalize on the opportunity.

Law #2—Green Zone Observations

As with Law #1, there are many examples of *green zone* performance within this educational organization. One principal within the organization has operated in the *green zone* throughout his career. This man did not wield his authority as a hammer above his subordinates' heads, but rather used his authority as an opportunity to provide greater service to those he was asked to lead. Every morning, before classes began, this principal would visit the teachers individually and ask what he could do to help them that day.

Many teachers were initially perplexed by this offer and would tell him that they did not need the help, but he would then explain that his duty as a principal was to assist each teacher in performing the job more effectively every day. When teachers understood his desire to serve, they would then give him something to do that could alleviate their stress and allow them to perform their teaching tasks with greater effectiveness.

This attitude of service, rather than one of superiority, created an environment of trust that infected the entire group. Each member of the faculty would vigilantly look for ways to help each other succeed, and this attitude did not stop with the punching of a time clock at the end of the day. This desire to serve permeated each teacher's life to the point that nobody could rest until they had helped someone else that day.

Conclusion

All organizations have their moments or their areas of operation where they regularly operate in the *green zone*. The essence of creating a more successful organizational culture and improving communication is to be attentive in maintaining these areas of proficiency. Organizations must also be open to change and correction so that they might migrate from the *red* and *yellow zones* into the *green zone*.

CHAPTER 17 COMMUNITY FOUNDATIONS AND THE LAWS OF COMMUNICATION

Julia East

Schuttler's *Laws of Communication*, which stress the importance of effective communication, aptly apply to community foundations. Unlike some industries in which organizational audiences can be narrowly defined, community foundations must successfully communicate with a wide array of people and organizations, such as volunteer boards, donors, nonprofit organizations, for-profit businesses, grantmaking organizations, professional advisors (attorneys, trust officers, accountants, and family wealth managers), elected officials, community leaders, the media, and the community at large. This diverse constituent base requires community foundations to provide excellent communication.

Community foundations are public, non-profit, non-sectarian, philanthropic organizations that are repositories of endowed funds. These funds promote the health, growth, and longevity of a particular geographic area, such as a city, county, region, or state. Frederick Harris Goff, a Cleveland, Ohio banker and lawyer, established the first community foundation in 1914 when he created the Cleveland Foundation. By 2006, there were approximately 1,175 community foundations in 46 countries. Of those, over 700 were in the United States (Council on Foundations, 2007).

Ranging in asset size from $100,000 to several billion dollars (Gast, 2006), the majority of community foundations focuses on one city or county and has assets of under $10 million (Foundation Center, 2007). With $44.8 billion in combined assets, U.S. community foundations represent only 1% of assets available for granting, yet they account for more than 10% of total annual grants, providing $3.6 billion in assistance in 2006 alone (Council on Foundations).

While a common thread runs through all community foundations, each is unique and is a reflection of the community it serves. For example, a community foundation located in a small, rural, economically depressed area may be primarily focused on providing assistance to agencies promoting economic growth or nonprofit organizations that provide human services. A community foundation in a thriving coastal tourist community may be primarily focused on ensuring that the environment remains pristine with abundant cultural attractions for tourists. Because foundations are always focused on the community they serve and represent, their work may shift as their communities and the needs of their communities change. Still, effective communication practices are essential for the success of a community foundation, regardless of its size, location, or focus.

The remainder of this essay is divided into two parts that correspond with Schuttler's two *Laws of Communication*. The first section applies *Law of Communication #1* to the internal relationships of community foundations. Section two delves into the external communications of community foundations and their relevance to *Law of Communication #2*.

Internal Communication

Schuttler's *Law of Communication #1* applies to effective communication between leaders and employees. This section reviews the quality of internal relationships with examples of effective (the *green zone*) and ineffective (the *yellow zone* and *red zone*) communication behaviors.

The Board

For a community foundation, a board of volunteers is the governing body and has the legal and fiduciary responsibility for the foundation. The board is charged with creating the investment, operational, fund development, and grantmaking policies; developing the mission, direction, and strategic plan; hiring, supporting, and evaluating the CEO; and general oversight of the community foundation (Gast, 2006). It has one employee—the CEO, President, or Executive Director—whose job it is to manage the day-to-day operations of the organization within the policies, procedures, goals, and priorities established by the board and to initiate strategic planning (Business Roundtable, 2002). The CEO is also expected to take the lead in identifying new ideas, programs, and markets (Adams et al., 2003) and serve as the public liaison and spokesperson for the community foundation.

The board's responsibility is to clearly communicate the mission, strategy, direction, expectations, and priorities of the community foundation to the CEO. The board chair is the primary spokesperson for the board in the board/CEO relationship. Thus, effective communication between the board chair and CEO is crucial to a productive working relationship. One challenge in this relationship is that the board chair typically changes every year or two.

Enthusiastic board chairs often desire to leave their mark on the organization and, thus, make subtle, or not so subtle, changes to the priorities, direction, and strategies of the foundation. Such tendency for change can place community foundations in the *red zone*, but this tendency can be offset with clear direction and focus via the creation of a strategic plan. Community foundations with comprehensive strategic plans spend their time working to implement, review, and revise the plan. Effectively communicating the strategic plan will work to decrease frequent directional shifts and avoid the *red zone*.

The Staff

The CEO is responsible for ensuring that the mission, strategy, direction, expectations, and priorities of the community foundation are communicated to, and implemented by, community foundation staff. Three primary functional areas within a community foundation include asset development, asset management, and granting/community leadership. Alignment of these functional areas within the mission, strategy, and priorities identified by the board is essential to creating a positive impact in the community and maintaining the overall health of the foundation. As an example, a community foundation may identify affordable housing as a critical issue and establish a five-year plan to research the issue, develop a plan, establish measurement tools, and implement the plan.

The asset management area of the foundation will determine the investment strategy for assets earmarked for this initiative. If the CEO has not effectively communicated the importance and timing of the affordable housing initiative, the asset management employees will not be able to implement *green zone* behaviors, such as revaluating and modifying the investment plan.

In addition to the asset management area of the community foundation, all three functional areas will be affected by the housing initiative. The asset development area may shift its focus to securing unrestricted funds or field of interest funds specific to housing or affordable housing issues. This effort may include a general communication plan to raise awareness of the issue of affordable housing.

The foundation may also develop targeted messages to donor advised fund holders to encourage them to support the community foundation's efforts. If the CEO has not clearly communicated the affordable housing priority to the asset development employees, they may take the *yellow zone* approach of "anything goes" and seek fund types that will not assist the foundation in reaching the goal.

Likewise, priorities within the grants/community leadership area may also shift. This area of the community foundation may need to reevaluate the current granting process and determine that a significant portion of the grant money available will be used specifically for the affordable housing initiative. For the first year of the initiative, available grant money might be used for research and plan development. For the second and third years, grant money might be used for convening activities. For the fourth and fifth years, the foundation might provide significant grants to organizations for targeted projects with a positive impact on affordable housing. If the CEO has not clearly communicated the affordable housing priority to the grantmaking/community leadership area of the foundation, those employees may fall victim to *red zone* behaviors of group think or doing only what is required.

This example illustrates the critical nature of effective communication and feedback between a community foundation CEO and staff. Well-communicated changes in organizational priorities allow employees in all functional areas of the community foundation to re-evaluate process, procedures, and area-specific goals. This type of communication also empowers employees to make the necessary modifications to work together to meet the new objectives. *Green zone* behavior is only possible if the CEO is openly and interactively communicating the priorities established by the board to the employees.

Minefields

Healthy and effective community foundations have clearly defined roles and responsibilities for the board and the CEO. It is essential to ensure that board members and the CEO understand the reporting lines and the lines of communication within the organization. While the CEO is hired and monitored by the board, it is not realistic for the CEO to receive directives from multiple board members. Theoretically, the board chair is the final voice of authority for the CEO, though often the chair will defer to the knowledge of other board members for particular functional areas within the foundation. This may create a situation where the CEO is receiving conflicting directions from multiple board members. This *red zone* behavior can be avoided by clearly delineating the primary board member who will be responsible for providing direction for each area within the community foundation. For example, the board chair may appoint the chair for the finance committee to work with the CEO on any adjustments that must be made to the foundation's investments or finances between board meetings.

Definitive reporting relationships and lines of communication between the board and staff are also critical. Many board members form close working relationships with staff members. This is especially true between lead staff members for particular functional areas and the chairs of related committees. While this working relationship can be effective, it must also be closely monitored to ensure that staff members know from whom to accept directions—the board member or the CEO.

Even the most informed board members do not know the daily demands and timeframe expectations for staff members. It is the responsibility of the CEO to set these expectations and monitor staff performance. Board members should not be directing staff activities or making direct requests of staff members. Such directives can leave a staff member floundering in the *yellow zone*, trying to determine which request has the highest priority and how to deal with conflicting requests.

Boards and CEOs should take care in synchronizing organizational goals and performance measurements. For example, a community foundation may have two primary goals for a given period of time. One goal may be capacity building for area nonprofits to increase their sustainability, while the other goal may be to affect positive change in homelessness through grantmaking and community leadership activities. These goals will guide the activities of the staff during that specified period of time. If at the end of that time period the foundation measures success by the number of funds held and the amount of assets under management, the employees' evaluations will potentially reflect underperformance because the activities they would have undertaken for fund and asset development would be very different from the activities used to meet current organizational goals. This mismatch between stated organizational goals and performance goals places the community foundation in the *yellow zone*. *Green zone* behavior requires the foundation to clearly define how staff performance will be measured and to align organizational goals with staff activities and performance.

Summary

Using *Law of Communication #1*, leaders of community foundations can assess the level of internal communication effectiveness. This assessment can provide community foundation boards and CEOs with action steps to bring the community foundations out of *red* and *yellow zone* behaviors and into the more productive *green zone*.

External Communication

Community foundations are complex organizations that adopt a myriad of roles within the community. These roles include builders and stewards of permanent community resources; grantmakers; service providers to nonprofit organizations; service providers to donors; conveners, catalysts, and collaborators; and promoters of philanthropy (Gast, 2006). To accomplish their varied roles, community foundations must successfully communicate with a wide array of people and organizations.

A foundation's external constituents may include donors, nonprofit organizations, for-profit businesses, grantmaking organizations, professional advisors (attorneys, trust officers, accountants, and family wealth managers), elected officials, community leaders, the media, and the community at large. Thus, community foundations must provide excellent communication to be effective and productive.

Gathering Funds

Of all their functions, first and foremost community foundations build permanent community resources through endowed funds (Gast, 2006). Donors may establish a number of different types of endowed funds, either during their lifetimes or through their estate plans. Each giving vehicle has a somewhat standard agreement form for ease in processing, but community foundations should avoid *red zone* behavior by guarding against strict adherence to standard agreements.

Green zone foundations will have fund agreement frameworks and identified parameters within which they can provide donors flexibility. Because of increased accessibility to information, donors are becoming more and more sophisticated in their philanthropic goals and strategies. Thus, community foundations need to provide flexibility in order to meet donors' needs. But, too much flexibility and lack of fund agreement frameworks, working parameters, and gift acceptance policies also put community foundations in peril of *yellow zone* behavior. Well-crafted and communicated policies allow foundations the flexibility to meet donors' needs without creating overly burdensome procedures or cost-prohibitive fund types.

Though many types of endowed funds make up community foundations, two fund types are of greatest significance—unrestricted and field of interest. As the names indicate, these funds have the fewest donor restrictions and, thus, provide foundations with maximum flexibility to meet the changing needs of their communities, a *green zone* behavior. Yet, unrestricted and field of interest funds are also the least likely fund types to be established because most donors like to specify how their gifts will be used.

Community foundations need less restrictive funds in order to maximize organizational performance and meet unforeseen community needs. For example, community foundations with ample unrestricted funds will better serve areas that suffer a natural disaster, providing immediate funding to relief aid and rebuilding. Community foundations that educate their donors on the importance of less restrictive funds to the long-term health and vitality of their communities will undoubtedly have more assets for effectively meeting current and future needs. By effectively communicating with their donors, these foundations will be operating to their fullest capacity and making the greatest positive impact.

Distributing Funds

Community foundations are commonly thought of as grantmakers. Nonprofit organizations, for example, look to their local community foundations to provide much-needed financial resources. In order for the nonprofits and the community foundations to have successful grantee/grantor relationships, the foundations must communicate their strategic focus.

When grant request criteria is disseminated clearly and concisely, organizations seeking grants can then determine if their requests will fall within the foundation's current priorities and parameters and apply, or not apply, accordingly. When these organizations understand funding parameters and required documentation, valuable staff time can be saved for both the granting and grant seeking organizations. Otherwise, the community foundations may fall into the *yellow zone*, resulting in redundant work and concerned customers.

The granting demands on community foundations far exceed granting resources. It is important for all community foundations to have a clearly defined mission and a strong sense of identity because a lack of corporate identity can create instability in organizational integrity (Rossouw & van Vuuren, 2003). Without clearly defined and communicated policies and directions, community foundations can become reactive firefighters and, thus, migrate into the *yellow zone*. Sometimes referred to as "the sprinkle effect," small grants are given to a multitude of organizations with relatively insignificant community impact. Strategically focused community foundations with multiple vehicles for accomplishing their missions are able to operate in the *green zone* and achieve their goals to make significantly positive improvements in their communities.

Convening Community Leaders

Because of their nonpartisan nature, community foundations are in a unique position to be visible community leaders, conveners, and catalysts for change. By living their missions and strategically focusing on corporate citizenship, *green zone* community foundations are able to build trust and unite multiple organizations. No other organization is so naturally able to bring together for-profit businesses, nonprofit organizations, governmental entities, community leaders, elected officials, private citizens, and the media to discuss, plan for, and address community needs.

Green zone community foundations can also have an impact on public policy regarding critical issues within their geographic areas. Foundations are in a unique position to see the needs of their communities from many perspectives, and they build support for much-needed policy changes by educating citizens as well as local, state, and federal elected officials.

The unique position of community foundations provides them with a global perspective that few others in a community can attain. Perhaps one of the greatest services a foundation can provide is connecting philanthropic individuals with community needs. Still, foundations can become mired in the *red zone* when enforcing by-the-book behavior, or they may fall into the *yellow zone* when not using their expertise to its fullest extent. In both cases, they will miss vital opportunities to connect members of the community for the greater good.

Green zone community foundations process the information they receive from various constituents and recognize the global implications of this knowledge. They combine their global knowledge with their technical and functional expertise, and they take a visible role by helping others in the community understand the issues and become part of the solution.

Under a Microscope

The ineffective leadership and communication of unethical businesses, such as Enron and WorldCom, have had an enormous impact on the way business is conducted, but not just in the for-profit world. Greater scrutiny has been focused on the nonprofit world as well, and the lens has particularly focused on foundations because of the longevity of endowed funds. As previously stated, community foundations in the United States have over $44.8 billion in endowed funds (Council on Foundations, 2007).

The nonprofit sector is a uniquely American construct (Gardner, 1990). The comment, “America loves nonprofits. They represent what is best about our country: generosity, compassion, vision, and the eternal optimism that we can solve our most serious problems” (Berry, 2003), highlights the importance of nonprofit organizations in the United States.

Nonprofit organizations offer a way to address social issues without governmental intervention, thus reducing dependency on the government and increasing community self-reliance (Wuthrow, 2002). Some even believe that nonprofit organizations are important to democracy because they provide nongovernmental ways to accomplish social gains, thus making citizens freer (Frumkin, 2002). These sentiments illustrate the importance of nonprofit organizations in providing essential services that help make up the very fabric of American culture.

Community foundations in the United States provide 10% of annual grants to nonprofit organizations, amounting to $3.6 billion in assistance in 2006 alone (Council on Foundations, 2007). Vital services critical to the core of American society would be lost if the funding stream from community foundations were to vanish. Yet, there are indications that state and federal elected officials do not understand the unique assistance of community foundations in sustaining essential services to the American public. Funding of these services would fall to governmental entities if the current level of community foundation support were curtailed due to legislative changes.

Thus, in order for community foundations to fulfill their missions, they must exhibit *green zone* behaviors including visibility, being strategically focused, and communicating with elected officials about their vital role in the well-being of United States citizens. They need to help their elected officials understand the potential negative impact on their communities if improper legislation restricting community foundation activities is enacted.

Summary

Community foundations are complex organizations that perform multiple roles. Their external constituents include donors, nonprofit organizations, for-profit businesses, grantmaking organizations, professional advisors, elected officials, community leaders, the media, and the community at large. Effective communication with these external partners is critical to creating and sustaining healthy, strong, growing communities. Using *Law of Communication #2*, leaders of community foundations can assess the level of external communication effectiveness. This assessment can assist community foundations in identifying *red* and *yellow zone* behaviors and, thus, position the organization to move into the *green zone*.

Conclusion

Community foundations play a key role in sustaining their communities. To fully reach their potential, they must implement effective communication strategies and practices, both internally and externally. In 2006, United States community foundations held $44.8 billion in assets and provided more than $3.6 billion in grants in that single year (Council on Foundations, 2007). With these figures in mind, it is clear that community foundations provide vital services that are critical to the core of American society. If these foundations were to slip into the *red* and *yellow zones* of communication, their effects would diminish, and governmental entities would feel pressure to fill the role previously taken by the foundations.

Still, the importance of community foundations goes far beyond endowed fund stewards and grantmakers. Because of their nonpartisan nature, community foundations are in a unique position to be visible community leaders, conveners, and catalysts for change. Their unique 360-degree view of their communities provides them with a global perspective that few others have. Thus, community foundations can act as conveners, connecting individuals and organizations. They can use their global knowledge, technical expertise, and functional experience to help community members understand pressing issues and work together to create strategies for stronger, healthier, more viable communities. But, community foundations cannot be conveners and catalysts without effective communication practices.

Schuttler's *Laws of Communication* provide a tool by which community foundations can assess their communication effectiveness. Using *Law of Communication #1*, community foundation leaders can review their organization's internal communication effectiveness. Using *Law of Communication #2*, leaders of community foundations can determine how effectively they are communicating with their external constituents. Identification of *red* and *yellow zone* practices, internally and/or externally, can provide the basis upon which the community foundations can build more effective practices. Community foundations in the *green zone* will be higher performing and, therefore, a greater asset to their communities.

CHAPTER 18
THE LAWS OF COMMUNICATION IN AN ORDER FULFILLMENT ORGANIZATION

Alice Gobeille

Order fulfillment is the e-commerce answer to virtual manufacturing. Companies engaging e-commerce websites compete with department stores, but offer the convenience of ordering from a home computer. Call centers are plagued with "where is my order" calls from multitudes of consumers every year because consumers are expecting fast-paced, 24-hour order fulfillment service. As such, the order fulfillment organization must have a flexible workforce with excellent communication to realize a profit. Goris, Vaught, and Pettit (2000) studied the effects of leadership direction on job performance, and the study identified a positive correlation between communication and job performance and satisfaction. As communication improves, job performance and satisfaction also improve.

In this assessment of the *Laws of Communication*, an order fulfillment organization located in Duncan, South Carolina, and referred to as "Duncan," is examined for evidence of a correlation between communication and performance. First, the supervisor staff will be evaluated for their ability to communicate with their subordinates against Schuttler's proposed *Law of Communication #1*: *Failure of supervisors to effectively communicate with subordinates results in poor employee performance.* Then, the executive leadership team will be examined according to the *Law of Communication #2*: *Failure of the organization to effectively communicate within results in poor organizational performance.* Last, a summary of the failures and successes of the supervisors and executive team will be reviewed to identify communication improvements that could possibly transition the organization from a *red* or *yellow zone*, where performance deficits are common, to a *green zone*, where a creative and motivational atmosphere promotes exceptional employee and organizational performance.

Introduction to the Duncan Order Fulfillment Organization

South Carolina is an optimal choice location for many distribution companies due to the central location to the United States population on the Eastern seaboard. Order distribution from Duncan, for example, can reach 70% of the U.S. population within two days by using the ground shipping service level for many small parcel companies, including UPS, FedEx, and DHL. The U.S. Postal Service serves as the preferred shipping solution for products requiring flat type shippers, like letter-sized envelopes, due to the speed of delivery in the postal mail stream.

Due to these options, Duncan offers a variety of shipping solutions for companies competing to deliver exquisite order fulfillment service to their millions of consumers. The Duncan total supply chain services and order fulfillment solutions appeal to the computer software and electronic hardware companies who currently make up the largest client base for e-commerce. Due to the increasing cost and delay of shipping products cross country, orders that were formally shipped out of California's Silicon Valley were relocated to the East Coast, where they could be produced and fulfilled in a location closer to the customer base.

Speed of delivery is only half of the solution for Duncan clients. Duncan must also provide the low cost solution for procuring the individual components and assembling the software and hardware kits in preparation for consumer orders. Multiple warehouse sites under one leadership team offer the flexible order fulfillment solution needed to be a low cost provider. Services are distributed throughout three buildings within one mile of each other. The approximate annual sales revenue for 2006 was $55M. Employee head count ranges between 450 employees in non-peak season and 1000 employees during peak season. Warehouse space is approximately 600,000 square feet.

The Duncan executive leadership team reports to a vice president who reports directly to the North America Chief Operating Officer at a West Coast headquarters location. The leadership team at Duncan is comprised of seven directors who have responsibilities for different aspects of the business. The executive leadership team reporting to the Vice President of Operations is comprised of the directors of operations, supply chain, quality, finance, logistics, client services, and engineering. The directors lead departmental teams, with managers and supervisors, floor leads, and individual contributors reporting to them. The entire operation follows a lean management model to manage and guide the work of hundreds of staff to accomplish the goals of shipping orders at the lowest price, to the right location, at the right time, in the fastest mode possible, while delivering the highest level of excellence in their product quality and service.

The first assessment for the Duncan team examines three supervisors who appear to use different modes of communication. They will be evaluated using the *Law of Communication #1*. In the second assessment, three different functional departments that provide services to other departments will be evaluated using the *Law of Communication #2*.

Assessment of Three Leaders' Communication and Employee Performance

Three supervisors will be evaluated for their ability to communicate with their subordinates according to the *Law of Communication #1*: *Failure of supervisors to effectively communicate with subordinates results in poor employee performance*. These supervisors oversee work and staff in the shipping, warehouse, and operations areas. All have several factors in common: they are located in the same building, they report to the same Operations Director, and they provide services to the same customer client. Some of the differences between these supervisors include age and gender, years of service at Duncan, educational accomplishments, and number of employees reporting to them. The purpose of this assessment is to evaluate the supervisors' communication styles with their employees, to categorize them into the various stages of *Law of Communication #1*, and to suggest opportunities to improve their communication and, thus, improve productivity and efficiency within their departmental staff.

Case #1: Leadership in the Shipping Department

The Shipping Department processes a range of hardware orders daily, consisting of small parcel and truck shipments that range from a few hundred orders in the non-peak season to a few thousand orders in the peak season. The orders have multiple products with multiple units going to different locations. The orders are shipped directly to retail stores, consumers, and retail distribution locations. The Shipping Department has the fewest employees, only eight, as compared to the warehouse and operations departments.

The stress level is greatly increased when the orders are flowing at a high demand, as compared to slow days when orders are fewer and easier to manage. The small parcel shipping companies and freight forwarders have different pick-up appointments throughout the day. The small parcel companies, like UPS and FedEx, have multiple pick-up times per day. The objective of the Shipping Department is to have the orders packed by shipping service level, palletized, and ready for shipment for the appointed pick-up times.

The employees' behaviors reveal much about their supervisor's communication style. One obvious behavior is the employees' passive loyalty to their supervisor. On one occasion, there were two job postings for positions in the Quality Department, which would be a promotion and pay increase for the employees in shipping. Interestingly, all employees in the Shipping Department bid on the two open positions, and all were interviewed before the job was posted externally. However, the overabundance of job applications from the Shipping Department led the hiring Quality Director to wonder what has happening in the Shipping Department.

When the director asked the shipping employees why they bid on the job posting, they did not respond that they wanted to come to Quality Department; rather, they indicated that they were looking for a position outside their current department. Still, only one applicant spoke negatively of the current shipping supervisor while being interviewed. Most interviewees avoided giving a direct response that shed poor light on their supervisor, though no one spoke in favor of the supervisor either. This type of passive loyalty demonstrates employee behavior found in the *red zone* of the employee performance continuum.

Some Shipping Department employees choose to terminate their employment with Duncan. In fact, compared with other departments, the Shipping Department has a much higher employee turnover rate (*red* and *yellow zone* attributes), which negatively affects employee productivity and efficiency. A constant influx of new personnel results in constant training and orientation, and employees are often engaged in training for most of their tenure, never coming to full productivity. In addition, the Shipping Department has reported an employee theft, which was captured on closed circuit video surveillance.

The shipping supervisor's poor communication skills promote employee behavior traits resembling the *red zone* of the *Law of Communication #1*. The observed behaviors—passive loyalty, self-termination, and employee theft—are all symptoms of this poor leadership communication, and new communication techniques are needed to change the current trends in this department. The shipping supervisor can drive change in his department by creating an environment that breeds trust, productivity, and employee satisfaction.

Case #2: Leadership in the Warehouse

The Duncan warehouse is 300,000 square feet. The Warehouse Manager has responsibility over the receiving operations and inventory control for the multiple clients serviced in the same building. The Warehouse Department has 12 employees with an office at the back of the building near the receiving docks. All warehouse personnel are drivers for material handling equipment and are paid at a higher level than the shipping and operations personnel.

In addition, the employees in the Warehouse Department have various duties based on the service they provide to the operations department. The receiving personnel perform and record the inspection of supplier receipts. The inventory control personnel perform daily cycle counts (total count of an inventory sku) and index audits (verification that a sku is in the correct location) and research inventory sku or location discrepancies as needed to keep the physical inventory and the SAP operating system inventory levels matching.

Firefighting behaviors and departmental process complexity promote employee traits resembling the *yellow zone* of the *Law of Communication #1*. For example, the employees in the department are internally competitive with each other. Though warehouse employees are required to execute daily tasks, they are often not held accountable for their mistakes, and they fall into the blame game as opposed to finding solutions for the prevention of errors.

The leadership behaviors of the Warehouse Manager resemble the *yellow zone* of the *Law of Communication #1*. The daily norm for the department includes assigning resources for firefighting. The priority placed on the investigation of lost and found inventory resembles the high stress atmosphere of an emergency operation, such as getting a building fire under control. There is no systematic approach to triaging the lost inventory.

In most cases, the inventory was temporarily misplaced and had no impact on production. Too much focus on lost and found activity causes mistrust and suspicion among employees who seek to identify a scapegoat. All drivers can make inventory errors, and regardless of who is at fault, the witch hunt creates a culture of mistrust. Rather than exerting time and energy on faultfinding, employees would better serve the organization by focusing on the prevention of inventory errors.

Competition within the Warehouse Department is evident, as each driver is cautious of error while fulfilling his or her responsibilities. The fear of making an error and having that error publicized during an inventory investigation causes stress between departmental employees. The employees are conscious of their work and give their full attention to their immediate tasks. Employees receive positive publicity for found inventory errors, but the result is intra-departmental competition.

The root cause of an error needs to be identified, but this is difficult to do without exposing human error. Scales and counting machines are sometimes to blame, but the function of counting and storing inventory is extremely manual, and the opportunity for error exists mainly in the human part of the activity. Although no one wants to be the recipient of the *blame game*, all warehouse employees continue to play the game because the Warehouse Supervisor's leadership behaviors resemble the *yellow zone* of the *Laws of Communication*. Departmental leadership focused on solutions through open communication could improve the departmental culture and create a stronger team atmosphere.

Case #3: Leadership in the Operations Department

The operations manager promotes healthy leader and follower relationships resembling the *green zone* of the *Law of Communication #1*. The operations department displays several attributes of a high performing organization. Employees are empowered to cooperate directly with each other to solve operational issues, and they use innovative and creative solutions for continual improvement. As a result of open dialog in a trusting environment, the employees understand the organization's business goals, and everyone has a universal commitment to customer satisfaction and organizational success.

Employees in the operations department are continually reminded of their duty to serve the customer. The operations manager supports and stimulates employees' empowerment through leadership communication activities. The manager is actively involved in leading daily department meetings and encouraging employees to do whatever they need to do to ensure that they meet the production schedule without compromising the quality of their work. The manager preaches the concept of *quality first* to all employees in order to build pride in their workmanship, and he empowers the employees to initiate change in the process, to improve operational efficiencies and product quality.

The operations department has a culture built upon open dialog and trust (*green zone*). The leads within the department and the assembly employees are encouraged to share their ideas and suggestions with the department manager and supervisors. The manager's open door policy is welcoming to employees who seek a small audience with management, and employees enjoy the opportunity to share their ideas. Employees are publicly rewarded when their suggestions generate improvement. When an error is found, focus is turned to the solution and not the error itself. The daily meetings create a level of trust and camaraderie in the department that makes exposing problems less stressful. This culture of trust breeds loyalty in the department between leaders and subordinates.

The Operations Manager consciously designed a departmental culture based on universal commitment to customer satisfaction and organizational success. He has also kept a keen focus on operational metrics of productivity and on-time performance. Business goals are communicated within the department and updated frequently upon departmental success in reaching target goals. Everyone in the department has a clear understanding of how his or her contribution affects the overall business goals. The combined leadership focus on continual improvement and customer satisfaction has created departmental momentum to exceed the goals for Operations metrics.

The examination of the *Law of Communication #1* included assessing the employee leadership and culture created by the departmental leaders for three departments. The Shipping Supervisor's poor communication behaviors promote employee behavior traits resembling the *red zone*, and new communication techniques would be needed to change the current trends in the Shipping Department. The Warehouse Supervisor's leadership behaviors most closely resemble the *yellow zone*.

Departmental leadership can focus on finding solutions through open communication in order to improve the departmental culture and create a stronger team atmosphere. All departments can learn from internal benchmarking activities based on the *green zone* leadership behaviors of the Operations Manager, who is focused on continual improvement and customer satisfaction and has created departmental momentum to exceed the goals for the Operations metrics.

Departmental leadership behaviors of the organization must be assessed for overall improvement opportunities. In addition, organizational leadership and communication can be assessed according to *Law of Communication #2*. Gaining organizational alignment through departmental supervisors is partially effective. An organization must also align overall leadership and effectively communicate with all support functions.

Assessment of Duncan Organizational Communication and Organizational Performance

Three Duncan executive leadership teams are reviewed according to behaviors described in the *Law of Communication #2: Failure of the organization to effectively communicate within, results in poor organizational performance.* Within this assessment, *red*, *yellow*, and *green zones* of effective communication are examined. Organizational communication between the Client Services Department and the rest of the organization demonstrates some traits of *red zone* behavior, and communication between the Human Resources Department and the departments they service resembles traits of *yellow zone* behavior. However, communication between the Planning Department and the organization resembles traits of *green zone* behavior. Though each department may portray some leadership behaviors in all three zones, they demonstrate the majority of their communication behavior characteristics in the one particular zone mentioned.

Case #1: Leadership in Client Services

The Client Services Department consists of a director and several account managers. The account managers are the customer interface between the organization and the operational business. They are also responsible for the financial performance of the business account. The organizational communication between the Client Services team and the rest of the organization resembles observable traits of the *red zone* of the *Law of Communication #2*.

The leadership in this department has undergone several changes that have damaged the communication flow from the Client Services team to the organization. For example, the incumbent director has yet to establish good communication relationships with the leaders on the operational side of the company. This one-way communication resembles a giving of direct orders, a communication style that the operations group resents. As such, the Client Services team and the Operations team lack the zealous cooperation needed to sustain customer satisfaction and promote organizational performance.

The Client Services Department's main mode of communication is one-way conversation via email. The department's focus on account management is understandable, but communicating the needs of the customer should not be force-fed to other departments. For example, when a customer reports an external product or shipment failure, the account managers assume fault with the Operations team. As such, they email a long list of damage control tasks to the Operations team to correct the error. This one-way mode of communication seem to assume fault with the Operations team and is in direct opposition to the culture of open communication that exists in the Operations Department.

The direct approach used by the Client Services team is often met with passive resistance. Department leaders do not want to feel blamed for a customer complaint, and they do not want to be told what to do by someone outside the department. The Client Services team expects other departments to be reactive and firefight when customer issues are exposed, but departments that are blamed for customer issues prefer that the issue be communicated with as much fact as possible to aid in an investigation. The lists sent by the Client Services team are often vague in details of the issue and rich in reactive instructions. Department leaders prefer to identify root cause before determining the course of action. Thus, Client Services could better service the other departments if they focused more on fact gathering and less on prescribing instructions for damage control.

If mutual respect existed between Client Services and the different departments, then the blame game would not exist. As it would be, Client Services is notorious for accepting fault for a reported issue on behalf of Duncan, and then they shift this blame to the department where the issue is thought to originate. Lack of mutual respect and cooperation inhibits a company from reaching full potential. Client Services does not treat the departments they support with respect; therefore, the department is not respected in return. Client Services needs to understand their mutual dependency with each department to sustain customer satisfaction and promote organizational performance.

Case #2: Leadership in Human Resources

The Human Resources Department services the employees in the three Duncan facilities, supports hiring activities, and enforces company policy for all departments. The communication between the Human Resources Department and the departments they service resembles traits of the *yellow zone* of *Law of Communication #2*. The Human Resources Director was recently promoted to the position from another location, and his support personnel have less than one year of employment with Duncan. Because of high turnover in this department, Duncan does not effectively direct employees' activities and or enforce policy. Human Services employees often communicate policy enforcement with mixed messages because they are not confident of the information they are communicating. As a result, the department frequently pushes back policy launch dates.

The Human Resources Department has lacked consistency for several years. There was over 100% turnover in the department personnel over the past year. Though the new employees in the department are Human Resources professionals, they lack the technical expertise to support the software management systems for payroll, performance evaluations, and benefit allocations. The departments supported by Human Resources have resorted to using internal experts in their own department to support the personnel management systems.

Under the leadership of the previous Human Resources Director, an employee transferred from the department and took the technical expertise of the payroll system with her. The new director has not tapped into the knowledge of the former employee in order to train the replacement employee. As a result, the new employee has experienced a greater learning curve than necessary and has resorted to trial and error to learn the existing systems.

Excessive turnover and new departmental leadership has created a lack of structure within the Human Services Department. In addition, Human Resources personnel are located only in one building, where all the support is focused. In two other Duncan buildings, where no Human Resources personnel are located, procedural support is lacking. Duncan employees in these two buildings can no longer count on Human Resources procedures used in the past, and departmental leaders must strive to self-support their employees. Though the new personnel in the Human Resources Department are eager and energetic about their work, department managers throughout the organization are skeptical of the department's new initiatives.

Recently, an employee manual was published by Duncan's parent company in an effort to add consistency in company policy. The Human Resources Department was given the responsibility to distribute this new manual and enforce the policies within it, but personnel's lack of familiarity with the policies hindered policy enforcement. As with system support, the responsibility for policy support was redirected to departmental managers, and the policy to award employees for perfect attendance, for example, was lost in the transition. Additionally, departmental leads received no criteria for rating attendance during the annual employee performance evaluation. As a result, departmental managers created their own scale for rating attendance.

Improved communication from the Human Resources Department to the supporting departments would improve organizational performance. The Human Resources Department needs to stabilize and reflect *green zone* characteristics. Then, the departments supported by Human Resources would not need to use internal experts for personnel management systems, and they could improve productivity by aligning resources to operational functions. The Human Resources personnel need to be available to employees in all buildings to improve the effectiveness of communication and organizational structure. Consistency in support will reduce the policy confusion and improve communication with the employee population.

Case #3: Leadership in Planning

The Planning Department led by the Director of Procurement provides the components, materials, and supplies for all departments in Duncan's three buildings. They also execute the materials planning for forecasted customer orders. The communication between the Planning Department and the organization resembles *green zone* behavior of the *Law of Communication #2*. The high performance team of the Planning Department effectively anticipates the needs of the Operations team and provides the necessary materials and supplies with flawless accuracy. The strategic focus of the team enables seamless execution of the materials planning function. The Planning Department promotes a culture of customer focus and meticulously adapts to the changing environment of customer requirements through innovative organizational improvements.

The flawless accuracy of the Planning Department is a testament to the leadership communication within the department, as well as cooperation with external customers and suppliers. The Director of Procurement leads by example in his quest to provide the needs of the customer on time, in full, every time. Data analysis and goal focused metrics drives the departmental focus to align with Duncan's strategic goals. Customers are strongly encouraged to provide updated forecasts each month and suppliers are measured on the ability to deliver to the customers' forecasts. Analysis of customer forecast accuracy and supplier scorecards fine-tune the department's ability to stay focused on meeting operational needs, thus delivering customer satisfaction.

The Planning Department's strategic focus enables seamless execution of the procurement processes. All departments are serviced with a just-in-time accuracy. The goals are to eliminate backorders and support on-time accuracy of customers' service level agreements. Leading and lagging metric indicators are used to maintain departmental focus, and inventory levels are set to minimum and maximum levels in SAP to support the high and low seasonal demands on production. Client service is supported through business review metrics for inventory turn ratios and inventory no movement reports. Supplier quality management is supported through supplier business reviews, supplier quality audits, and quarterly supplier scorecards. This heavy use of metrics in the Planning Department helps maintain strategic focus.

The Planning Department has a stable staff of highly competent and motivated people. The turnover is minimal, with most employees exceeding 4 years with the department. When a position opens within the department, the most skilled and trained employees apply. The buyer/planners meticulously adapt to the changing organizational environment when new customers are added to the customer base and when existing customers launch new products. The Planning employees are strongly encouraged to continue higher education and certifications for operations and inventory management, and the competency levels in the department are a direct reflection of the leadership for organizational communication.

Leadership and communication between the Planning Department and the supported organizational departments resemble the attribute traits of the *green zone* of *Law of Communication #2.* The Planning Department's flawless accuracy of the supply of inventory is a testament to the organizational communication within the department and the cooperation with external customers and suppliers. The strategic focus of the Planning Department enables seamless execution of the procurement processes by using planning and results metrics, and employee competency levels are a direct reflection of the leadership.

Organizational communication has a direct correlation to organizational performance. As such, the Duncan team can improve organizational performance by transitioning its *red* and *yellow* attributes toward *green zone* characteristics. First, several departments will need to undergo assessment, where the communication zone each area resembles most should be identified. The next step is to identify the green attributes each department is lacking and to develop a plan to move the organization toward the *green zone.*

Suggestions to Improve the Organization through Improved Communications

According to the *Laws of Communication*, correlation between communication and performance means that improved leadership communication can promote improved employee performance. Likewise, improved organizational communication can promote an improvement in organizational performance.

Improved Leadership Communication

Improved leadership communication can improve employee performance. The Shipping Supervisor and Warehouse Manager would need to realign themselves with the work staff by actively interacting with employees at the work level. Similar to the Operations Manager, they too would need to open dialog with the employees and develop a coaching and mentoring relationship with them. The results in employee performance would yield innovative problem solving skills. Additionally, the relationships between workers would improve and a mutual respect would develop between the leaders and departmental employees and between each employee and other employees. The leaders would create a motivational atmosphere that promotes positive change and attains business goals.

Improved Organizational Communication

Improved communication between the Client Services and Human Resources teams to the organization's departments could improve overall operational performance. Similar to the Planning Department, the leaders of the Client Services and Human Resources Departments would need to establish visibility with the other organizational leaders and open communicative dialog about strategic goals and initiatives with the departmental managers.

The services provided by the Client Services and Human Resources teams would need to take on a seamless global appearance to the organization departments to deliver services with little to no impact to operational efficiencies. The overall organizational performance would result in a cycle of refinement that achieves organizational goals and maintains customer focus. The Client Services and Human Resources teams would need to seamlessly interface with the operational teams to achieve a combined organizational high performance team that adapts to the changing environments of the organization and exceeds organizational performance goals.

Conclusion

A correlation between communication and performance means that improved leadership communication can promote improved employee performance. Likewise, improved organizational communication can promote an improvement in organizational performance. The communication failures and successes of the organization's supervisors and executive teams help identify communication improvements that could possibly transition the organization from operating in the *red* or *yellow zones* to the *green zone*, where a creative and motivational atmosphere promotes exceptional employee performance. Promoting the organizational attributes of the *green zone* can generate the performance necessary for organizational growth.

CHAPTER 19
NAVIGATING ORGANIZATIONAL COMPLEXITIES: LAWS OF COMMUNICATION IN THE AVIATION INDUSTRY

Warren St. James

Schuttler's *Laws of Communication* apply to several, if not all, industries worldwide—including aviation. Aviation communication has been around for several centuries. In fact, one of the first forms of aviation can be found as far back as 300 B.C., when the Chinese used innovative ideas to design kites.

In modern times, despite economic hardships, the collaborative efforts of airline leaders, employees, and stakeholders continue to add innovation to the industry. This success can be easily attributed to good communication skills, as described by Schuttler's *Laws of Communication.* To understand and successfully navigate organizational complexities, leaders also need a toolbox full of communicative skills.

Using the acronym *POWER TOOLS*, I will outline a strategic plan to enhance organizational performance through effective communication.

P = People

An organization's performance depends largely on its people and their skills and abilities. In aviation history, for example, the Chinese and ancient Greeks helped pave the way for two Frenchmen who would design, develop, and initiate the first manned flight in an artificial device.

In modern times, the attributes of aviation employees assist them during irregular operations, when they are inundated with complaints from irate passengers. The promotion of customer service lends itself to innovation. The needs of passengers and the innovative ideas of employees continue to spur further upgrades in technology and customer services.

O = Organizational Efficiency

As the years passed, interest in air travel grew exponentially. As this occurred, safety became an ever-increasing concern, one that would inevitably slow down departures and arrivals and introduce passengers to schedule changes, crew rest times, and federal regulations. Because of heightened public interest in passenger security and well-being, aircraft designers were motivated to create a safer aircraft. Additionally, the Civilian Aeronautic Board (CAB) was established in 1938 to monitor routes, fares, and safety standards.

These consorted efforts helped increase the number of annual airline passengers from thousands to millions in just two decades. Airlines companies continue to seek new methods of organizational efficiency, with cutting-edge flight technology and innovative online ticket systems.

W = World Class Performance

Organizations need to understand communicative differences and incorporate these differences into core competencies. A global business practice supports the core competencies of the business, enhances distribution channels for management, increases brand equity, increases production processes, and influences mass customization production processes (Lawler, 2006). The Internet now serves as a global distribution channel where pricing actions/trends provide competitive edge over other businesses.

E = Ethnicity

When companies compete in a global marketplace, culture analyses will be vital for developing strong relationships with international partners. Training in cultural diversity is indispensable.

Researchers have proposed that businesses need to be more accepting of individual differences in order to remain competitive in the future.

When connecting world class performance with ethnicity, communication plays a major role in organizational success. When traveling internationally, passengers may find themselves confronted with extended wait times, immigration inquiries, and overall tighter security. Leadership communication must focus on these issues and diplomatically resolve them in a timely manner.

R = Return on Investment (ROI) Leads to Rewards

The intricacies of investment analysis, speed to market, and corporate profit vs. loss initiatives will be moot to the average employee if not communicated efficiently and effectively. Burns (1978) stated, "Transactional leadership occurs when one person takes the initiative in making contact with others for the purpose of an exchange of valued information" (p. 19). This collaboration should include fleet simplification, a leaner maintenance operation, and alliances with outsourced contract collaboration. Leaders can accomplish this influential transformation through coaching, timely performance evaluations, and teamwork.

T = Teamwork

Schuttler's *Laws of Communication* cannot work to enhance an organization's prosperity without effectively functioning teams, and organizational leaders should be an integral part of these teams. Blanchard (1999) stated, "Leadership is not something you do to people, it is something you do with people" (p. 140).

The initial challenge of effective teamwork is moving through the stages of team development, as conflict or *storming* will inevitably factor into the equation. Just as passengers have problems and concerns, airline employees and their accompanying leadership have issues as well. To help assist the traveling public, there must first be internal synergy and collaboration within the organization.

O = Operational Optimization

Operational efficiency, the evaluation of organizational processes for near perfection, should involve Six Sigma. The gist of Six Sigma is to scrutinize all processes, pinpoint where and why errors occur, analyze them, correct them, and plan for the future by putting measures in place to control the processes.

The Wright brothers were not privy to Six Sigma, but they understood the principles. For the most part, today's passengers do not understand the principles of Six Sigma either, but airline employees will be better equipped to deliver smooth services when operational optimization is in place.

O = Organizational Skills / Time Management

Good leadership requires vision, organization, and time management. Effective organizational leaders build strong employer/employee relationships by clearly communicating the organization's direction and specific benchmarks. Applying a philosophy of employee and stakeholder participation in the process will led to better decisions and better implementation (Lawler, 2006)—the theme of Schuttler's *Laws of Communication.*

L = Denounce Laissez-Faire Leadership

Scholars have consistently found laissez-faire leadership to be the least effective of leadership styles (as reflected in the *red* and *yellow zones*). Influential organizational leaders produce change by providing employees with a clear direction and the motivation to align toward that change. A reliable business solution, one that promotes sustainability and future growth, is created through collaboration and rigorous decision-making processes.

S = Synergy

Good leaders have the ability to bring people together within the organization. Through constant communication, employees are provided with encouragement and motivation to work together, through the phases of norming, storming, forming and performing, to create an internal synergy that supports organizational goals. An organization that truly listens to the needs of its customers and employees will be interested in developing upgrades and improved processes (*green zone* attributes).

Summary

The aviation industry has experienced remarkable progress and innovation throughout the centuries, but no organization is perfect, and even those that appear close to perfect should remain open to improvement. For the *Laws of Communication* to be effective and assist leaders in making valuable paradigm changes in organizational structure, collaborative interactions with employees must occur, and this process would not be complete without a leader's *POWER TOOLS*. In order for an industry to prosper, organizational leaders must implement ongoing evaluation procedures, welcoming the ideas of the entire organizational team.

CHAPTER 20
A CASE STUDY: THE FIFTH DISCIPLINE AND THE LAWS OF COMMUNICATION

Mark Esposito

The *Laws of Communication* can pinpoint communication disease within organizations. In order to demonstrate the application of these *Laws*, I will discuss my recent experience at an organization where I worked for a number of years. I left the organization as it struggled in between the *red* and *yellow zones*—unfortunately mostly in the *red zone*. According to the stoplight metaphor, the company operated within a mixture of the *red, yellow*, and *green zones*, all at different intensities and degrees. This inconsistency produced a sense of immobility among the employees and led, inevitably, to poor individual and organizational performance. But, one department was an exception, as it flourished and produced proportionally more than the others.

Interesting enough, I believe the *Laws of Communication* manifest themselves within any given spectrum and at any given time. But, when there are regular fluctuations between zones caused by organizational leaders, a lack of consistency is apparent and employee morale and performance suffer. Attaining consistency allows one to plan, adapt, and design a sound and systematic approach to greater levels of effectiveness and efficiency. When this can occur, the organization and its people prosper, and an agile learning organization comes to life.

I will analyze the applicative aspects of the *Laws of Communication*, while applying concepts deriving from Peter Senge (1992) in his book, *The Fifth Discipline*, to the workplace environment I have described. Several rules will be the taken as a benchmark for the application and demonstration of this case study.

Today's Problems Come from Yesterday's Solutions

Life in my prior place of employment was dictated mostly by the mode, pace, and tone that resulted from the organization's declining culture. The company has a clear identification with its past, history, and accomplishments. The most influential members have been onboard since the initial start-up when nothing had a name, no definition—just an inspirational vision. Today, there is a clear sense of misguided pride. The organization operates in the *red zone*, illustrated by the high frequency of employee discipline. The same group thinking that had at one time shaped the organization was now creating a troubling differentiation among members of the organization.

How the organization operates today is a clear example of what the *Laws* define as myopic area of operations. In fact, short-sighted conversations are anchored to past successful experiences rather than today's immediate concerns or future excellence. The organization's internal and external communication is controlling and selective, and the inadequacy of the senior leaders' tone can be unpleasant.

This organization, much like a family-started, owned, and operated business, struggles to differentiate between the business to business domain and the interpersonal, familiar domain. As a matter of coincidence, the origin of organizations in the western world was primarily based on the more traditional kinship model (patriarchal model). In modern times, larger corporations have gravely diluted and shifted from the kinship organizational model to a more competence-based model. Family businesses tend to interpret communication as an integrative component of who they are in the relationship, rather than closer to a more natural confrontation which would derive from a real communicative interchange.

Today's problems stem from the solutions to problems that occurred years ago during the organization's start-up phase. In short, leadership approaches and management practices have not kept pace with the organization's growth. What was once a small business, led and managed by a few, has grown to a medium-size business—only *still* led and managed by the same individuals and philosophies. What worked in a start-up no longer works after 10 years of growth—the senior leaders are victims of their own prosperity. Unfortunately, they may also be at fault in future failures.

The Harder You Push, the Harder the System Pushes Back

These senior leaders do not make any exceptions to the second rule of the *Fifth Discipline*. The complacency ruling the organization creates systems of inoperability within most departments. The level of inaccurate communication from senior management represses the lower levels in a consistent and equal manner. The only difference is that movement from the top does not do as much good as the bad that originates from the bottom. In a traditional pyramid structure, the foundation enjoys and exploits a wider base of resonance than anything falling down from the top.

Senior leaders believe that their *healthy* and *family-oriented* approach to communication is still effective, but it is resented and resisted by midlevel supervisors and front-line employees. Due to the lack of good leaders who can self-assess and lead by example, subordinates stopped going the *extra mile* (being self-directed) that at one time had resulted in the organization's successful beginnings. *Red zone* attributes are reflected in the tone of the intra-organizational communications, many of which are inconsiderate of the efforts and core values of the organization.

Employees work the minimum necessary hours and do only what they are told. If they can manage any of the assigned tasks outside of the organization, such as telecommuting, they do so to avoid having to come to work. Very few good employees want to participate in volunteer work, such as committee and team events, and skilled employees are seeking work elsewhere. This is not the outcome senior management wants, but it is what they have produced. Senge's second rule is demonstrated in that the harder senior leaders push, the harder the subordinates are pushed—in many instances to the point of complete disconnection. In a most unpredictable and tacit way, the same system of information sharing that made the organization a success is now a critical factor in their likely demise.

The Easy Way Out Usually Leads Back In

When thinking of Senge's third rule, I cannot help but smile. Maybe it's because the rule is so simple to understand but so deep in its application. Organizational naivety, lack of real and profound business understanding, amateurism, and the complete lack of decision-making sense may be some of the causes that explain this rule and its applicability within the realm of the organization. During the four years I worked in the aforementioned environment, I observed that when decisions needed to be made, short-sighted and short-term thought ruled the process. Much like the *yellow zone* suggests, *firefighting* occurred—problems were quickly addressed only to recur over time. No one wanted to take a long-term approach and perform a root cause analysis to solve the problem at its primary level.

This approach made for quick and easy decisions when they were needed, but the ultimate result was that this easy way out led to the return of the same problem over and over. Additionally, as the problem returned, it usually returned in greater severity than the time before. If the problem was a supplier-related issue, the supplier would charge more for rework or stop doing business all together. This organization and its people had learned a limited portfolio of possibilities, and every solution was derived from previously made, myopic decisions.

The Cure Could Be Worse Than the Disease

A wrong diagnosis made by an inexperienced doctor can lead to more side-effects and repercussions than the symptoms of the disease itself. When organizations are not doing root cause analyses when problems occur, employees tend to only fix symptoms. Thus, the problems keep arising, often with different symptoms. Such results can be demeaning to employees and costly in resources allocated.

When revenue was low and resources scarce for this organization, a great deal of pressure was placed on employees in many ways. The nature of the business resulted in an unequal distribution of responsibility for generating revenue, despite shared accountability throughout the organization. One example was reflected when the marketing department was quick to blame others for the lack of revenue instead of realizing their own impact on the problem. This situation was made worse when senior leaders decided to reduce employee provided benefits on site that were always provided "perks" for all concerned.

The communication conveyed directly or indirectly was at times abusive, unsupportive, accusatory, inconsistent with a real willingness to solve the problem, and above all, endangering (*red zone* behavior). A key instance of communication failure occurred when senior management decided to deny access to the coffee machine during non-meal times in a company-provided cafeteria. The leaders noticed employees frequently gathering around the coffee machine, and claimed that the consequent chatting was inappropriate to the organization's overall ambiance. The practical reason was that leaders did not want to spend the extra money for coffee as they always had done.

The cure in this case was worse than the disease. When senior leaders took away the minimal perk of providing free coffee, the employees became upset and began to see senior leaders as adversaries rather than individuals they should emulate. One result from this decision was that employees would now have to walk to a local retailer to purchase coffee and were actually away from work longer than they would have been otherwise.

In an attempt to reduce expenses, senior leaders failed to communicate the real concerns to employees, lied about the reason behind a policy decision, and lost respect from subordinates. The way senior leaders went about for making up for low revenue was much like the saying "don't cut off your nose to spite your face," suggesting that this was not a good approach to deal with low revenue. The intangible aspects of related cost to this approach were more than the cost of the coffee.

Faster is Slower

Another incident in the organization's history clearly recalls Senge's sixth rule in *The Fifth Discipline* as applied to the *Laws of Communication*. Organizational leaders announced a major change initiative but allowed no time for employees to adapt to the associated mandates. A new set of rules and practices, decided upon by only senior leaders with no input from others, was put in place to expedite the process of economic recovery. The rules and practices, much like the change to the availability of coffee in the above section, had not been discussed and were imposed at a pace that could not allow for open conversations and dialogue.

Employees reacted to the announcement in a skeptical and uninterested manner. Change was purposely slow, as employees were unwilling to change with no rationale or explanation for the change. Once again, senior leaders immobilized their own organization by acting insensibly fast (*yellow zone* behavior). It did not take them long to realize that the pace of tasks and duties in the organization had decelerated drastically after a few days from the original announcement. One area that becomes clear in both Schuttler and Senge's models is that organizational leaders must take accountability and responsibility for when and how they will implement change. Without a clear plan and without including stakeholders into a change initiative, success will be diminished and incur often adverse reactions from those involved.

You Can Have Your Cake and Eat It Too—But Not All at Once

Organizations tend to forget, quite easily, their primary mission in the business arena, and they tend to diminish the relevance of their visions by only adjusting to petty daily/weekly or annual budgets, which are sometimes simply dangling carrots for the stakeholders and/or shareholders. Granted, all aspects of business must be attended to, but organizations without a balance rarely remain in business long.

The senior leaders in my organization were quite loyal, seeking short-term financial growth via certain business arrogance. This was probably due to periods of substantial growth in the market that was due to an indirect consequence of good market momentum. After all, when the organization was first started, the market conditions were ideal and immediate growth occurred. Initial success means little without long-term continued success and continual growth. It is often said in business circles that "businesses are either growing or dying."

The frantic pace of the first few years was spent on the laurel and celebration of initial achievements. But during the past few years, a focus towards the future and how it could have been maintained and sustained did not occur. The capacity to adapt and preserve authenticity, while renewing and reinvigorating the ultimate purpose of the organization, needed to be expressed through communication at every level of the organization, including the strata from which it originated.

Organizational leaders did not share information well, and they were certainly not willing to apply an *Open Book Management* approach, causing resentment throughout the company (*yellow zone* behavior). Organizations that achieve long-term results extend the energy as far as possible within organizational branches so that new emphases can be produced and envisioned.

Summary

These examples provide evidence of areas in which the *Laws of Communication* could have been used to achieve excellence through strategic communication. The episodes listed represent a wide spectrum of common mistakes, most of them converted into real and recurring testimonies for the company's ineffective management. The organizational leaders and employees are all good people who are skilled in their professions, yet their myopic views and inability to self-reflect were what ultimately harmed the business they started.

The case itself develops a tri-dimensional analytical scheme in which situations offered coincide with the insights provided in the *Laws of Communication* and *The Fifth Discipline*. The insights from these models can combine to offer practical diagnostic tools for improving organization performance. The ability for senior leaders to assess not only organizational performance *and* their own contributions to that performance is at the heart of what Schuttler and Senge suggest in their work. To pinpoint organizational disease, leaders must be willing to make their organizations and themselves available for diagnosis before fatal outcomes result.

SECTION 4
Assessing Communication in Organizations

CHAPTER 21
EVALUATING THE COMMUNICATIVE STRUCTURES AND PATHWAYS

Michael J. Nanna

What is Communication?

Communication is touted as being the *sine qua non* of building and maintaining both healthy relationships and organizations. It is a word that is frequently bandied about as being vital to addressing employee concerns and for improving the overall functioning and health of an organization. But, effective communication, although easily stated, is probably the single most significant obstacle that an organization can confront.

Why is it that something that seems so simple is in actuality infinitely complex? One reason, perhaps, is that too often communication is taken for granted, at least superficially, as being straightforward. For example, a simple command such as, "please close the door," is easily understood and readily addressed with minimal confusion, provided that both the subject and object in this dyadic exchange speak the same language.

It seems noteworthy to point out that if the person on the receiving end of the command has even a minimal linguistic deficiency in the language in which the command was spoken, simply is not paying attention to the request, or has no interest in the request, what at first seemed simple has now become increasingly complex, if not impossible. And, this example is probably one of the simplest forms of linguistic communication, i.e. it is one directional, involves only two people, and consists of a single simple command. Complicating things even further is the fact that a great deal of communication is actually non-verbal in nature and often not direct.

What does it actually mean to communicate? Although the term "communication" is often thrown around liberally, what does it actually mean to communicate? What are the requirements that must be met, and how do we measure whether something has actually been effectively communicated? There is little doubt that what seems to be an uncomplicated process on the surface is in actuality anything but uncomplicated.

For example, using our above scenario, what would be the intended outcome if, while the person giving the verbal command (in this case to close the door) simultaneously signals using body language (e.g., a hand signal), that the person receiving the command in actuality should *not* close the door? What is really being communicated in this situation, and how is one to discern between the contradictory signals?

At the most basic level, communication is a directed attempt to (accurately) convey the multi-dimensional internal experience of one person via a two-dimensional medium (usually language) to another person. This is done in an attempt to evoke that same multi-dimensional experience within the individual or group of individuals on the receiving end. This is particularly true when we move beyond the simple command level of communication and enter into the arena of abstract concepts, complex constructs, and hypothetical future events. Even if we take the simplest communicative pathway, one between two individuals, and even if we can assume that the two individuals come from identical socio-economic, ethnic, and educational backgrounds, it is an exceptionally complex proposition; and one fraught with potential pitfalls of misunderstanding, misinterpretation, and even a complete lack of comprehension.

If we acknowledge the simple fact that many people come from different socio-economic, ethnic, and educational backgrounds—let alone professional or gender backgrounds—the probability of effective communication decreases exponentially. Then multiply the number of communicative pathways that exist within even the smallest of organizations and the complexity indeed becomes formidable. In truth, it is amazing that we are able to communicate even the most elementary concepts with any accuracy whatsoever given the underlying complexity of human language and communication in all of its forms, e.g. verbal and non-verbal.

Given this complexity, what can be done to facilitate effective communication, and what are the foundational requirements necessary for effective communication? How can people in relationships and across organizations effectively address the potentially unlimited number of pitfalls that lie in wait, ready to thwart even the best of intentions? These are not easy questions and have been the focus of countless psychological, sociological, and leadership studies over the years. What is more, the significance of these questions is taking on a greater level of importance as the world continues to shrink and as the number of multinational and cross-cultural cooperative efforts continues to increase both in scope and number.

Complicating the situation even more is that not everyone has the same innate capacity for effective communication (e.g., language deficiencies, etc.) and in other cases people are simply not receptive to, or interested in, what has been communicated. Personality conflicts or poor morale among employees may leave people feeling disempowered, dissociated, and as a result, less receptive to hearing what others have to say, thus further inhibiting communication before it even has a chance to start.

Here we tend to get at pre-existing structural, cultural, and personality issues. For example, the simple scenario outlined above represents an optimal situation where all parties involved in the communicative pathway are trying to, or are at least open to, communicating with one another—a situation that is often not the case. In particularly toxic environments, attempts at communication often result in nothing but static.

Human relations are indeed complicated and rife with contradiction. Competing agendas, family and domestic issues, emotional or psychological problems, health issues, low job satisfaction, lack of confidence, improper training, lack of respect for senior leaders, and personality conflicts all work to further impede and even exacerbate an already tenuous situation. Still, even with all of these potential impediments, the need to communicate is very real and is absolutely necessary for the successful functioning of personal relationships, families, businesses, schools, and society as a whole.

Characteristics of Good Communication

Given what seem to be insurmountable obstacles, what can be done to increase the probability of effective communication occurring within organizations that are relatively healthy, and what can be done to implement more effective communicative and, hopefully, transformative strategies within organizations that are not? Schuttler identified two essential laws of communication that are necessary for developing and maintaining healthy organizations. He further identifies essential benchmarks and qualities relevant to high performing organizations and describes them as being both precursors to, and qualities of, healthy organizations. At the foundation of these healthy qualities is communication. Of particular importance are how supervisors communicate with subordinates and how the organization as a whole communicates with all employees and stakeholders. I suggest that how employees communicate with one another be added as an additional factor, which can be equally important.

The primary characteristics associated with what Schuttler identifies as being "best in class businesses," i.e., businesses that function at a very high level, include the following:

1. Open and renewed communication
2. Corporate citizenship
3. Continuous improvement
4. Customer-focused
5. Trustful environment

6. Feedback is regular and constantly sought
7. Visible leaders
8. Shared strategic focus
9. Vision and mission lived
10. Low absenteeism
11. Little confusion
12. Active customer participation
13. Multiple vehicles of communication
14. Seamless influence
15. High morale
16. Entrepreneurial spirit
17. Two-way communications
18. Clear focus on priorities

Fundamentally, these characteristics represent the sum total of the relationships that exist between people within an organization. Indeed, relationships are the ultimate building blocks upon which an organization is built, managed, and ultimately maintained. Unfortunately, cultivating and maintaining good relationships can be difficult, because if we examine relationships in more detail we see that underlying any good relationship is an ability to effectively communicate. It is a circular relationship in that the seeds of one quality yield the fruit of the other and vice versa.

Closer examination of the list suggests that these qualities are not one-dimensional, but instead can be broken down into (at least) two separate categories. For the purposes of this chapter, I have broken down the qualities identified by Schuttler into two major categories: 1) qualities that can be classified as attributes (i.e., qualities that are more structural in nature) and 2) qualities that can be classified as functional (i.e., qualities that are more process oriented). This is an important distinction because both attributes and functional qualities are necessary characteristics that most likely work in a synergistic manner within most, if not all, healthy organizations and relationships.

For the purposes of this chapter, it is helpful to think of attributes as being foundational qualities that provide a fertile structure upon and within which functional qualities have a *better chance* of taking root and ultimately propagating. As with most things in life, a strong foundation is essential to, and even pre-requisite for, proper and healthy functioning and stability. For example, if we take a healthy seed and plant it in soil lacking in the necessary attributes (e.g., sufficient levels of nitrogen and oxygen, moisture, etc.) the seed simply will not germinate. At best, the seed will remain dormant and may eventually decompose over time.

Consequently, having a strong foundation that lacks appropriate functional qualities will most likely lead to stagnation. For example, a healthy seed that is planted in fertile soil will still not germinate, and certainly will not flourish, without sufficient and appropriate levels of water and, after sprouting, sunlight. Even the "simple" act of seed germination is in actuality not so simple when the necessary attributes and functional precursors are lacking.

Taking this example a step further, once the initial attributes and subsequent functional qualities have been established, i.e., those needed to sprout and initially grow our seed, the resulting sprout still requires regular watering, sunshine, and nutrients if it is to grow into a mature and self-sustaining plant. Even then, a mature plant still needs regular watering and exposure to sunlight. Likewise, cultivating or reinforcing healthy behaviors and relationships within an organization is not a static process and represents only one-half of the process. Subsequent steps must be taken to ensure that a healthy dynamic, once established, is maintained.

It seems important to note that attributes and functional qualities are not mutually exclusive, and that there is most likely a great deal of overlap between them. Nonetheless, there appears to be an apparent delineation worth noting. For example, the characteristics identified by Schuttler might be broken down as follows:

Table 21.1. General Attributes and Functional Qualities

General Attributes	Functional Qualities
Corporate citizenship	Open and renewed communications
Continuous improvement	Feedback regular and constantly sought
Customer-focused	Active customer participation
Trustful environment	Two-way communications
Visible leaders	
Shared strategic focus	
Vision and mission lived	
Low absenteeism	
Little confusion	
Multiple vehicles of communication	
Seamless influence	
High morale	
Entrepreneurial spirit	
Clear focus on priorities	

Notice that a majority of these qualities have been identified as attributes. Attributes can be thought of as representing structural components and foundational qualities, which are essential to the healthy and productive functioning of an organization, and which serve as prerequisites for more functional qualities. Functional qualities, on the other hand, can be thought of as dynamic processes that occur across an organization—i.e., they are the glue that holds everything together.

Remember, though, that it is a cooperative and two-way relationship in that the existence of strong functional qualities helps to establish strong attributes. Conceptualizing the characteristics identified by Schuttler this way will ultimately help to provide a framework for identifying and evaluating communicative gaps that exist within an organization, which is the first step toward helping the organization to improve by closing the gap between what is needed within the organization and what is currently in place.

I mentioned previously that both attributes and functional qualities are interdependent and are most likely dependent on having good interpersonal relationships within an organization—specifically, quality relationships between individuals within a department and between departments themselves. Having good relationships allows for an open exchange of ideas, concepts, and strategies.

Show me a friend, and there is nothing we cannot accomplish together. Show me my enemy, and there is nothing we can accomplish. If we dig deeper, we may find that there are other prerequisite qualities at a more micro level such as:

1. The ability and qualifications of individual employees,

2. The ability and qualifications of supervisors,

3. Job satisfaction among employees and supervisors, and

4. Individual motivation.

Having identified some of the qualities associated with healthy organizations, what is the best way to evaluate an organization in order to determine whether or not, or to what degree, these attributes and functional qualities exist? Next, how do we define, operationalize, and ultimately measure their presence or absence? Even more important, how does an institution effectively use the information obtained through a detailed and honest self-evaluation to actually effectuate real change?

There is, of course, no single or even simple answer. Complicating this reality is the fact that there is, in actuality, no single set of attributes and functional qualities that must exist within any particular organization. The truth is that organizations are diverse, with each having their own sets of needs; however, the preceding list of attributes and functional qualities can serve as a set of general guidelines that are fundamental to *most* healthy organizations, and may serve as an initial starting point toward developing and implementing a comprehensive self-evaluation.

Steps Toward Evaluating and Assessing Communication

The first step toward improvement or change is to undertake an honest and detailed self-analysis and evaluation of the organization in order to identify the absence (or degree of presence) of the essential attributes and functional qualities and to identify the primary communicative pathways that exist both within and between departments and across the organization—at all levels. Careful and honest assessment at any level—whether at the personal or institutional level—is often a painful and scary process, and resistance can be expected at almost every level. If not handled appropriately, resistance can lead to further internal discord.

Then again, initial conflict and resistance, if managed correctly, can lead to positive changes and a new organizational synthesis. That is why the first step in any self-assessment or evaluation initiative is to formulate a well thought-out strategy for dealing with resistance and conflict *prior* to initiating the process, and to also acknowledge that a great deal of flexibility needs to be built in to the plan. More than likely, an assessment will need to be done at both the micro (employee-to-employee and employee-to-supervisor) and macro (president and senior administrators to middle managers and front-line workers) levels. In fact, careful identification of both attributes and communicative pathways at both the micro and macro levels is necessary for identifying the gaps that exist in an organization's functional processes.

Although presenting a detailed and specific evaluation plan and assessment process for all organizations is well beyond the scope of this chapter, there are several benefits associated with doing so that are worth pointing out. For example, undertaking an honest organizational assessment and evaluation can be a first step toward helping an organization to achieve the following:

1. Establish and implement a formative review process for all functions and services offered.

2. Insure continuous improvement of service delivery and organizational operation.

3. Provide the organization with a clear and comprehensive picture regarding the impact of its services, both internally and externally.

4. Provide alternative criteria for making decisions regarding resource allocation and for judging overall organizational effectiveness.

Prior to achieving these goals, fundamental steps must be taken in order to lay the foundation for proper evaluation and toward developing a comprehensive organizational evaluation plan. First, a careful review of the organization's mission must be undertaken to ensure that the mission of the organization reflects both the ethos and intended goals the organization seeks to accomplish. Second, a set of measurable objectives that are tied directly to the organizational mission should be identified with each department identifying its own set of goals and objectives, which are likewise directly in line with the organization's goals and objectives. And, finally, a set of intended measures needs to be specified.

There are no magic bullets, but developing a well thought out evaluation plan can help an organization with the following:

1. Increase awareness of the consequences and impact of its services.

2. Improve planning and resource allocation at all levels of the organization.

3. Provide more accurate information to employees and customers.

4. Assist marketing departments toward building effective strategies during times of increased competition.

5. Demonstrate success and overall effectiveness of meeting the organization's goals and objectives.

6. Encourage overall organizational improvement.

7. Recruit appropriate staff and senior-level executives.

8. Serve internal and external clients by accurately conveying what can be expected.

9. Promote organizational accountability.

Below are several recommended steps toward developing and implementing a comprehensive self-evaluation to determine the absence of, or degree of presence of, both key attributes and functional qualities that have been identified as leading to a best practice business:

1. Establish a timeline for the initial self-evaluation.

2. Complete an inventory of the organization's operative statements of mission, goals, and objectives and identify the primary organizational purpose.

3. Ensure that the mission statement reflects, in specific terms, the primary organizational purpose.

4. Develop a set of primary organizational goals and ensure alignment with the organizational mission statement.

5. Set measurable objectives and goals; ensure that they are in alignment with the organization's mission statement.

6. Develop a conceptual assessment matrix for each department, including a set of key measurable indicators.

7. Set a timeline for the self-evaluation and target dates for measuring key indicators.

8. Specify a hierarchical set of goals at both the organizational and departmental levels.

9. Take an inventory of evaluation processes and self-monitoring activities that are already in place.

10. Evaluate how well existing strategies are working (or not working).

11. Conduct an honest evaluation of both strengths and weaknesses at both the organizational and departmental levels.

12. Evaluate how existing data is currently being analyzed.

13. Identify areas to be measured.

14. Decide how results are to be processed and effectively utilized.

Summary

Evaluating the communicative structures and pathways within an organization is an essential step toward identifying existing problems and instituting effective change strategies within that organization. Lack of effective communication frequently underlies many organizational problems, as communication is a fundamental building block for promoting quality relationships, which in turn provide the foundation for establishing healthy organizational attributes and functional qualities that are integral components of healthy organizations and best-in-practice businesses.

Of course, before any solutions can be implemented at an organizational level, an honest and comprehensive evaluation of the existing culture, organizational structures, and communicative structures currently in place must be undertaken. Communication plays a foundational but difficult role within organizations. Establishing a general framework for developing and implementing a comprehensive self-evaluation plan is a fundamental precursor to further and more detailed analysis of an organization, including the implementation of surveys, focus groups, as well as other evaluative tools.

CHAPTER 22
THE RED ZONE: ANALYZING AND ASSESSING HOSPITAL LEADERS' COMMUNICATION FAILURES

Ruby Rouse

The popular television series *CSI: Crime Scene Investigation* uses forensic science to examine physical evidence inadvertently left behind when crimes are committed. Over the course of the show, viewers often witness autopsies, postmortem examinations of evidence designed to determine the cause of a person's death. These detailed procedures illustrate how retroactively examining information helps assess what went wrong.

Using a similar paradigm of introspection, Jeffrey Sonnefeld, Professor and Senior Associate Dean at Yale School of Management, and Andrew Ward (2007), Management Faculty at the University of Georgia, suggest leaders should regularly perform failure autopsies to learn from leadership mistakes. "It seems strange," they argue, "that the intricacies of failure are not examined with the same intense scrutiny that we invest in dissecting the sources of success" (p. 60).

Interestingly, the *Laws of Communication* use an intuitive framework for conducting "autopsies" of leaders' communication behaviors. Schuttler presents a stoplight metaphor to classify leaders' communicative behaviors as operating in *green*, *yellow*, or *red zones*. *Green zone* behavior reflects effective leader strategies that promote appropriate employee performance. *Yellow zone* behavior signals leaders to exercise caution, while *red zone* behaviors warn of immediate and significant danger to the organization.

Red zone behaviors are especially problematic in healthcare because poor employee performance may endanger patient safety and lives. Applying *Law of Communication #1*, this chapter suggests that ineffective leader communication aggravates problems with employee performance. In particular, two failure autopsies of hospital leaders are conducted in order to demonstrate the need to formally assess whether organizations operate in the *red zone*.

Spiraling Out of Control

According to the *Law of Communication #1*, leaders operating from the *red zone* typically display three ineffective communication behaviors. The *Law* suggests such supervisors tend to be myopic, nearsighted, and often narrow-minded individuals who are blind to the long-term consequences of short-term decisions. Equally frustrating for *red zone* employees, micromanagement behavior occurs when supervisors constantly look over workers' shoulders, trying to control every aspect of employee behavior. Little, if any, freedom is granted to the employee; instead, workers are directed to do as they are told. Finally, often struggling to improve performance, *red zone* supervisors frequently change strategic directions—allowing little opportunity for employees to adjust to new approaches.

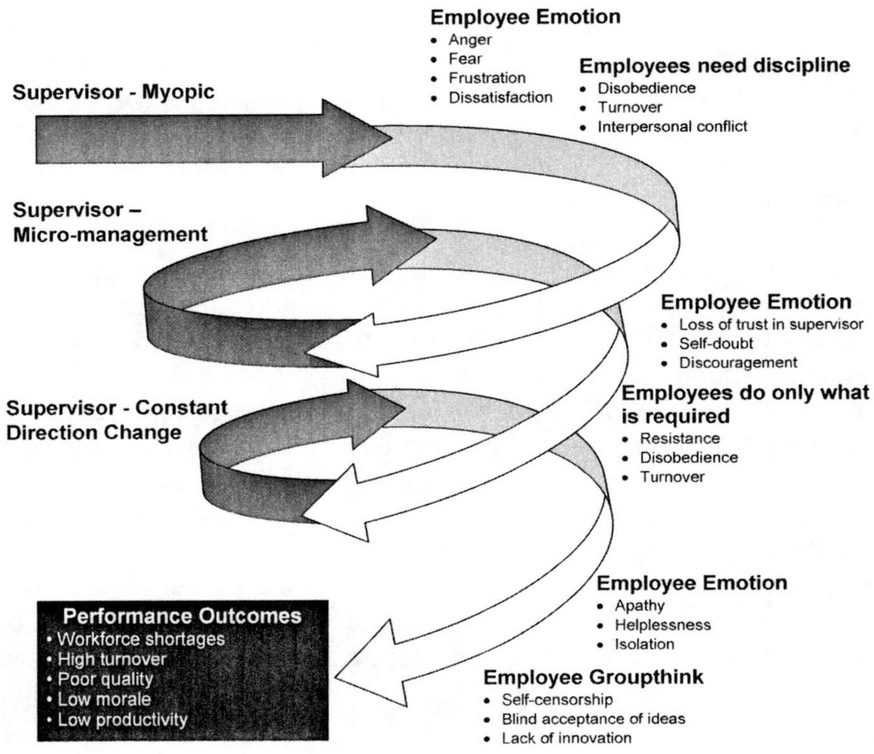

Figure 22.1. Downward performance spiral of the red zone

Figure 22.1 suggests the *red zone* is neither linear nor static. Rather, it represents a communicative progression where, if unchecked, employee performance suffers in a downward spiral. The left side of Figure 22.1, shown in dark gray, diagrams problematic supervisor behaviors, and the right side, shown in light gray, illustrates employees' emotional and behavioral responses to supervisors' actions. For instance, when a red zone supervisor displays myopic behavior, employees, perceiving the action to be shortsighted, may become angry or frustrated—leading to worker disobedience. In response, supervisors may attempt to control noncompliance by micromanaging employees. Such restrictive behavior may then cause workers to do only what is required. Attempting to adapt, supervisors may then decide to change strategic directions, resulting in employee apathy and groupthink. Overall, Figure 22.1 suggests the *red zone* is an interactive, dyadic process where both supervisor and employee influence organizational performance.

In order to illustrate the interactive and progressive nature of the process, this chapter conducts two failure autopsies on the behavior of actual *red zone* hospital leaders. Both cases illustrate how supervisors' myopia, micromanagement, and direction change behavior adversely influence both employee and organizational outcomes.

Failure Autopsy #1: Chopping Off Your Nose to Spite Your Face

In December of 1993, a Joint Commission on the Accreditation of Healthcare Organizations (JCAHO) guideline urged all hospitals to adopt a smoke-free policy (Associated Press, 2005). Designed to protect patient safety, more than 96% of hospitals in the United States reported complying with the standard by 1994 (Fee & Brown, 2004). When implementing the policy, most hospitals elected to ban smoking in all facilities, with the hospital's building functioning as a smoke-free zone. Publicly applauded as a much needed part of an industry-wide ban on smoking in public places, policymakers claimed the ban had the added benefit of encouraging healthcare workers to stop smoking.

Whereas the guideline appeared well-aligned with the long-term health objectives of both patients and providers, the short-term realities of the policy quickly caused new problems for hospital leaders. Nationwide, about 28% of licensed practical nurses (LPNs) and 15% of registered nurses (RNs) smoke (American Nurses Association, n.d.). In 2005, the policy affected about 33,000 employees in one Ohio-based organization alone (Smoking Health Care Workers Not Wanted, 2005). Nicotine-addicted healthcare providers struggled as they tried to quit smoking. Some succeeded; however, many did not. Whereas the smoke-free directive was designed to protect public health, it had the unintended effect of making smokers feel angry, unappreciated, and dissatisfied with their new work conditions.

Soon hospital leaders began to feel the long-term consequences of enforcing the smoking ban. Dealing with increasing shortages of qualified workers, local leaders faced a difficult choice. Should they enforce the national smoke-free policy or possibly risk losing experienced employees? Confronting harsh workforce realities, several hospitals, particularly smaller ones, changed directions. Some hospital leaders developed “smoking huts” outside of medical facilities (Associated Press, 2005); others allowed employees to privately smoke in their cars. Others did not enforce the smoking ban at all.

In one mid-size hospital in the central United States, these myopic compromises initially seemed to work. However, over time the bending of the organization’s policy by local leaders resulted in unintended negative consequences. Employees, smokers, and nonsmokers alike quickly learned that local supervisors, who felt their staffing concerns were ignored by corporate management, openly disobeyed the smoke-free policy.

As a result, many employees began doubting the credibility and integrity of the hospital’s corporate leadership. Mimicking local managers’ disregard for the policy, employee discontent spiraled into behavioral consequences. Despite the clarity of the ban, workers smoked in bathrooms and stairwells. Others circumvented the regulation by taking smoking breaks in their cars or going off site. “After the smoking policy was put in place,” one local manager joked, “I kept overhearing people say they were ‘going to church.’ Then I figured out the neighboring church’s parking lot was the new unofficial smoking area, since employees were no longer allowed to smoke on campus” (P. Autumn, personal communication, March 23, 2008).

In a seemingly unrelated situation, the hospital’s local performance improvement director noticed a rise in the number of patient falls a few months after the smoking ban was implemented. After collecting and analyzing trend data, it was determined that the vast majority of patient falls occurred during the shifts of employees who smoked. Because these employees were no longer able to take a quick cigarette break, smokers retreated to their cars or went off campus to smoke. In an ironic twist of fate, the smoking ban, originally intended to improve hospital safety, inadvertently harmed patients when smoking employees left patients unattended for longer periods.

Eventually, the hospital's corporate leadership learned of local supervisors' disregard of the smoking policy. No longer trusting local managers to enforce the regulation, corporate supervisors took the matter into their own hands. Micromanaging the process, the organization's vice president of human resources, a woman with an unyielding reputation, scheduled a site visit and personally issued a stern directive revoking previously established smoking areas. Employees were explicitly instructed they were no longer allowed to smoke anywhere on campus—not even in their cars.

The consequences of national leadership's dogmatic adherence to the smoking ban were swift. Despite the urging of local managers, one of the hospital's best employees resigned the morning after the new smoking directive. Within an hour of quitting, the worker secured a job at a competing hospital with a "smoke hut" for staff. Other employees followed suit.

As detailed in Table 22.1, this communication autopsy revealed the hospital leaders' handling of the smoke-free directive was a failure at both the corporate and local level. The initial national policy, while well-intended, was myopic. Whereas it was clinically sound, corporate leaders failed to adequately consider the long-term effects on employee staffing and morale.

Table 22.1. Failure Autopsy of a Red Zone Hospital's Smoking Ban Policy

Smoking Ban Policy's Purpose	Leader Communication	Employee Outcomes	Organizational Performance Outcomes
Improve patient and employee health and safety	Myopic: Failure of national leadership to recognize long-term loss of employees due to the smoking ban. Micromanagement: Failure of national leadership to understand nurse managers' workforce shortage concerns. Constant directional change: Failure to stay the course; frequently revised smoking policies.	Need discipline: Employees disobeyed the policy by smoking in bathrooms and stairwells; local managers looked the other way rather than risk losing valued employees who smoked. Do only what is required: Hospital staff circumvented the policy by taking smoking breaks in their cars or offsite.	Workforce shortages Increased workload for non-smoking employees who must cover for smoking employees on longer breaks Inadequate patient supervision Poor quality care Increased patient falls Increased medical errors Reliance on less experienced caregivers Increased litigation and malpractice

Attempting to minimize resistance from valued employees who smoked, local managers changed directions, offering smoking employees choices other than termination. Yet, when national leadership learned of the lack of enforcement of the directive, they micromanaged the process. Clamping down on local managers as well as employees who continued to smoke, senior leadership lost significant credibility and trust, local managers felt betrayed, and many experienced employees left the hospital. In retrospect, this case demonstrated how the organization's corporate leadership "chopped off" the local staff's "nose" to spite local managers who disregarded the smoking ban. In the end, the organization's long-term desire to protect public health ultimately resulted in damaging employees' trust as well as endangering patient safety.

Failure Autopsy #2: The Emperor Has No Clothes

A second failure autopsy examined the communication of physician leaders at a small for-profit hospital in a Midwestern region of the United States. Leveraging the success of prominent specialists in the area, the healthcare facility contracted with approximately 10 "moneymaker" physicians to generate revenue. Guaranteed an annual salary of about $650,000, the doctors also earned 50% of all income generated from hospital services provided to their patients. Designed to be a *win-win* situation for both the physician and hospital, the collaborative agreement encouraged prominent physicians to regularly bring business into the organization.

One physician who averaged about 70 to 80 patients a day clearly was a profitable moneymaker for the small hospital. A brilliant physician, beloved by his patients, the doctor understood the importance of his contribution to the hospital's financial performance. Sharply focused on profitability, he had no tolerance for staff inefficiencies, even when the nurses were shorthanded.

Oblivious to the needs of other doctors' patients or the staff's heavy workload, the physician was notorious for shouting profanities at nurses in front of patients, family members, doctors, and other hospital employees. His myopic view of patient care centered exclusively on his personal needs. Impatient with the performance of the hospital staff, he called a meeting with all the nurses to explain a new procedure to help moneymakers move more efficiently through morning rounds.

Micromanaging the staff's routine, he explained that each morning, before his arrival, the staff was expected to have a fresh pot of coffee prepared. Additionally, they should have a chilled Gatorade for him each morning. In order to keep moneymakers happy, he explained, the staff should have donuts and fresh fruit available each morning. Furthermore, a qualified nurse should always be at his side, so he never had to request assistance while in the hospital. In addition, attending nurses should always have clean tissues available, in case he should need one when interacting with patients.

Stunned nurses sat in silence as the doctor, blind to the absurdity of his requests, detailed how their activities should revolve around his personal needs. The next day the story of the staff meeting spread like wildfire through the hospital. Outraged by the arrogance of the physician's requests, overworked nurses complained they were not waitresses; they had significantly more pressing things to do than cater to the whims of an egotistical doctor.

Fearful of belligerent encounters with the moneymaker, early morning staff quickly learned to disappear from the nurse station before he arrived. Infuriated at the lack of attentiveness of the staff, the doctor forcefully protested to hospital leadership. In an effort to pacify the moneymaker, the hospital agreed to hire three nurses, handpicked by the demanding physician from his prior organization. These individuals would be dedicated to catering to his needs while he worked in the hospital.

However, in order to recruit the desired nurses, hospital leaders were forced to bend salary and work responsibility policies at the hospital. The moneymaker's LPNs, who only had one year of formal training, received a salary equivalent to the hospital's RNs, with 10 years of nurse experience. Similarly, the moneymaker's RN was granted significantly more money than RNs at the hospital. When nurses complained of the inconsistent pay, they were told nothing could be done. Senior management, preoccupied with profitability, refused to address the salary or workload concerns of the staff nurses.

Exasperated with the situation, the next morning a group of 12 nurses working the moneymaker's morning shift wore *head waitress* labels stuck on their nametags as a humorous protest to the administration's support of the doctor's demands. Reinforcing their position that the moneymaker was blind to the nurses' opinion about their new menial duties, the arrogant physician never noticed the nametags.

As detailed in Table 22.2, the moneymaker analysis reveals how even a single leader can cause a downward spiral throughout an organization. His narrow, egotistical focus devalued the contribution of hardworking staff nurses. His micromanagement, almost to the point of absurdity, caused significant anger, frustration, and stress throughout the hospital.

Table 22.2. Failure Autopsy of a Red Zone Hospital's Moneymaker Policy

Moneymaker Policy's Purpose	Leader Communication	Employee Outcomes	Organizational Performance Outcomes
Generate hospital income: Key physicians receive $650,000 annual salary, plus 50% of hospital revenue generated by the doctors' patients.	Myopic: Failure of corporate leadership to recognize the long-term consequences of demeaning and devaluing the contribution of hospital staff nurses.	Need discipline: Nursing staff vigorously complain to nurse supervisors about the inappropriate personal requests made by moneymaker physicians; nurses file complaints with the HR department regarding inconsistent salaries and work requirements.	Increased interpersonal conflict between staff nurses, hospital management, and moneymaking physicians
			Increased complaints of discrimination and harassment
Maintain positive relationships with high income-generating physicians of the hospital.	Micromanagement: Failure of the physician leader to recognize the inappropriateness of his profanity and personal demands.		Nurse stress and burnout
			Less time with patients
			Staff nurse turnover

	Constant directional change: Failure of hospital leadership to maintain salary and workload policies by consenting to higher pay for the moneymaker physician's nurses.	Do only what is required: Hospital staff disappear from the nurse station before the arrival of confrontational moneymakers, avoiding the new requirement to cater to non-clinical requests by physicians.	Reduced profit margin for the hospital, as a result of the additional cost of highly-paid moneymaker nurses.
		Groupthink: Disillusioned by hospital leaders' unwillingness to address their concerns, a group of staff nurses stage a brief protest by wearing head waitress stickers on their uniforms.	

Nevertheless, fearing the loss of revenue generated by the physician, senior management sacrificed their integrity by abruptly changing workload and salary policies. In turn, employee morale was significantly undermined. Much like the villagers in the children's fable who were afraid to say the emperor was wearing no clothes, the hospital leaders in this situation refused to point out the absurdity of the doctor's requests, which were clearly seen as laughable by the organization's community.

Turning On the Light

This chapter's failure autopsies illustrate how healthcare leaders are often unaware of the consequences of their actions. In order to stop a downward spiral, *red zone* organizations must first be able to objectively assess their supervisors' communication. Only after identifying problematic behavior can intervention strategies be developed.

A *red zone* assessment tool, based on Schuttler's typology, is located in Table 22.3. A convenient sample of employees (n = 87) representing various industries was used to evaluate the reliability of four *Laws of Communication* dimensions: frequency of communication, supervisor behavior, employee behavior, and organizational performance.

Table 22.3. Law of Communication #1—Red Zone Assessment

Red Zone Dimension/Item Phrasing	Cronbach's Alpha
Frequency of communication (n = 76)	.88
Informal feedback (i.e., face-to-face, telephone, email, etc.).	
Positive, encouraging feedback that helps improve employee performance.	
Timely feedback delivered at an appropriate time and place that helps improve employee performance.	
Supervisor behavior (n = 69)	

	Myopic	.89
	Supervisors are shortsighted in their planning.	
*	Supervisors carefully consider both short and long-term consequences before making any changes.	
	Micromanage	.93
	Supervisors micromanage employees.	
	Supervisors look over employees' shoulders to monitor their work.	
	Constant direction change	.75
	Supervisors are inconsistent with their expectations.	
	Supervisors frequently change strategic directions.	
	Supervisors regularly change policies and procedures before any one method or process can become routine.	

	Employee behavior ($n = 67$)	
	Need discipline	.89
	Employees lack discipline.	
	Employees disregard policies and procedures.	
	Do only what is required	.78
	Employees do only what they are told to do.	
	Employees do only what is required.	
	Groupthink	.89
*	Employees feel free to openly disagree with supervisors.	
*	Employees feel free to say what they think.	
	Organizational performance outcomes ($n = 67$)	
	Productivity	.89
	Employee productivity is low.	
*	Employee productivity is high.	
	Turnover	.79
	Talented employees seek employment outside the company.	
*	Employees have no desire to leave the organization.	

	Interpersonal relationships	.85
*	Employees trust their supervisors.	
*	Employee morale is high.	
Overall Cronbach's alpha		**.89**

* Reverse scored

The frequency of communication items asked participants to indicate how often they receive various types of communication (*never*, *rarely*, *sometimes*, *often*, *very often*). In contrast, the organizational performance, supervisor and employee behavior items asked respondents to indicate their level of agreement (*strongly disagree*, *disagree*, *uncertain*, *agree*, *strongly agree*) with a series of statements. Several items were reverse scored, phrased in an opposite direction, in order to verify that subjects were reading the questions, rather than choosing the same response for all items. As shown in Table 22.3, each sub-scale was found to be sufficiently reliable, with an overall Cronbach's alpha of .89. Estimated to take less than five minutes to complete, the 22-item assessment offers organizations an efficient and reliable method of evaluating whether their leaders are in the *red zone*.

Summary

Organizations that operate in a *red zone* risk spiraling out of control. As shown in the two failure autopsies analyzed in this chapter, myopic planning, micromanaging, and/or constant changes in direction complicate managers' ability to work with employees. Reacting to their supervisors, employees' emotional responses prompt behavioral changes that often hurt organizational performance.

As with crime scene investigation, systematic examination of evidence is a necessary first step when attempting to unravel organizational challenges. Just as forensic detectives use reliable instruments when collecting fingerprint and blood samples, organizational leaders must apply similar precision when collecting data about supervisor and employee communication.

Using Schuttler's *red zone* typology as a theoretical framework, this chapter developed and tested a *red zone* assessment to help organizations "turn on the light" so they can see what is happening between supervisors and workers. As detailed in this chapter's failure autopsies, *red zone* supervisors are often unaware of their behavior. In order to develop improvement strategies, organizations must be willing to take the time to stop and put their process under the microscope.

CHAPTER 23
MALCOLM BALDRIGE CRITERIA IN A CLINICAL LABORATORY SETTING

Karen Fong

The Malcolm Baldrige Award

The United States Congress enacted the Baldrige National Quality Award on August 20, 1987[1] to directly combat growing competition from foreign countries. The award originally related to quality in our manufactured products, yet as the award process has evolved, it has grown into other areas including small business, non-profits, education, and healthcare. Over the last few decades, the Baldrige award has become the premier U.S. award for quality.

The Baldrige program has developed its healthcare criteria, in particular, based on these core values and concepts:

- Visionary leadership
- Patient-focused excellence
- Organizational and personal learning
- Valuing staff and partners
- Agility
- Focus on the future
- Managing for innovation
- Management by fact

---

[1] The Malcolm Baldrige National Quality Improvement Act of 1987 - Public Law 100-107

- Social responsibility and community health
- Focus on results and creating value
- Systems perspective

Successful implementation of these core values and concepts indicates a company that is able to adapt to the quickly changing environment of healthcare with a distinct focus on patient care. In the competitive world of healthcare, with shrinking insurance reimbursement and increasingly expensive modalities of care, these organizational traits are becoming necessary for survival.

The Baldrige Quality Award has an extensive list of criteria that examiners must review to determine if an organization is successful. Two criteria in the Baldrige award process are communication and organizational performance. These particular areas examine how well the leadership promotes, communicates, and empowers all staff throughout the organization.[2] How honest is the communication between leadership and staff employees? For healthcare, an honest and open line of communication is necessary to maintain patient safety and well-being.

What is a Clinical Laboratory?

A clinical laboratory is where healthcare professionals analyze or test a sample by order of a physician. Most people have had the experience of leaving a sample of blood or urine in the doctor's office. The sample is sent to the laboratory where it is analyzed. Most people understand the glucose and cholesterol tests. The glucose test determines how much sugar is in a person's body and is of particular interest to people with diabetes. The cholesterol test provides findings in regards to the level of "bad" fat that one's arteries.

---

[2] 2006 Leadership Criteria, 1.1b in *HealthCare Criteria for Performance Excellence*

The Clinical Laboratory and Vital Communication

One of the most important areas of communication between the laboratory and the patient caregiver (either an RN or physician) is communicating when a test result is near *critical value*. The term critical value is applied to a result that is either too high or too low to properly sustain life. In this situation, communication is vital to patient safety. In fact, the communication is so important that regulatory agencies dictate how the critical value is to be communicated.

The critical value must be given to the caregiver and the date/time is recorded. In addition, the caregiver must *read back* the information to ensure that the correct test result and value has been received. Next, the caregiver, if a nurse, must document that he or she has communicated the result to the physician, and then record what the physician has ordered as a response to the critical result.

An example of a critical value is a glucose result that is too high or too low, which could signal serious complications for a patient, including death. Let's say that you find someone who is unconscious, and you know that this person is diabetic. You hurriedly call an ambulance. Once on the scene, the ambulance personnel perform a finger stick glucose test and find that the glucose is too low. They then give the person some sugar in an intravenous drip. Once the patient is at the hospital, the hospital will draw a blood sample to re-test for glucose. If the result is still critical–either too high or too low—the laboratory will call in that result to the emergency room staff so that they can begin to get the patient's glucose level under control.

Communication in a hospital environment is not always critical, but when it involves patient well-being, it is always important. A common problem at a hospital is the simple matter of releasing patient test results in a timely manner so that the patient can be discharged to go home. Most hospitals strive to discharge a patient by a predetermined time, so if the laboratory staff knows the physician is awaiting test results, they will make a concerted effort to prioritize those samples. Unfortunately, this discharge information is not always communicated, and often, despite a laboratory's best efforts, the test results are not released in a timely manner. This scenario is an example of how simple communication between the laboratory staff and physician can impact the well-being of a patient.

Communication and Operational Impact

In the above example, the delay of a simple test result can delay a patient's discharge from the hospital. How does this situation impact the operations of the hospital? If the physician cannot discharge the patient in a timely manner, then the cleaning of the patient's room is also delayed. And, if the patient's room cannot be cleaned in a timely manner, then a new patient awaiting hospital admission is also delayed. In today's hospital environment, bed rotation is similar to *just-in-time* philosophy; it is not unusual for patients to remain in a hospital's emergency room or a "pending" area while waiting for rooms to be cleaned.

A simple item like a test result can impact the operational flow of the entire hospital. The physician is unhappy because his or her decision for the patient is delayed. The patient is unhappy because the patient would like to go home. Patients who are waiting for admission want to get treatment and rest. All of these factors make the timeliness of the morning test result a quality indicator in clinical laboratories. Hospitals track turnaround times for morning laboratory tests with the benchmark goal of 90-95% completion by a set time, for example, 7 a.m. each morning.

Communication and Empowerment

Is all communication life and death? Thankfully, it is not. A simple cholesterol test result with a value of 400 mg/dL tells the physician and patient that the cholesterol level is too high. Given this information, the patient strives to exercise and change his or her diet to lower the cholesterol value to the preferred range of less than 200 mg/dL.

This scenario is an example of simple communication that serves to *empower* the recipient to enact a desired result. If the patient changes his or her diet, increases exercise, and the cholesterol level still does not decrease, then the physician will likely prescribe medication. Still, a patient may receive information that the cholesterol level is too high, but he or she will choose to do nothing. Does this mean that the patient is no longer empowered? No. He or she has been given knowledge and, thus, has been empowered to make a decision, but this decision will vary based on the patient's lifestyle and various other factors. Inaction is still a decision, and it is often one made with knowledge of the possible consequences.

Communication in the Context of Baldrige Criteria

As stated earlier, test results can immediately impact the operational flow of a hospital and a patient's health status. In addition, patient-focused communication empowers the various individuals who receive health information to make informed decisions. Now that you have an understanding of a clinical laboratory and how it operates, provided is an example of communication in the larger context of the Baldrige criteria.

One of the Baldrige criteria for communication is to ask, "How do senior leaders communicate with, empower, and motivate all staff throughout the organization?" Communication, empowerment, and motivation are tough tasks within any organization. In the clinical lab, the challenge is even tougher. Why? The clinical laboratory staff tends to be comprised of introverted professionals. They are often skilled in what they do, but not very expressive about it. Generally, introverts like to work with "things" (e.g., test tubes and instruments) and not necessarily with people. The challenges of communicating with a staff that is predominantly introverted can be at times difficult but it can be done successfully with the refined communication processes and refined techniques of empowerment and ownership.

Successful Example of Communication, Empowerment, and Motivation

Many processes are non-negotiable in a clinical laboratory setting, but sometimes there is room for creativity. In one particular facility, a dedicated group of employees had already been working well together when federal law required them to add several new tests to their daily workflow. Adding these new tasks posed a significant challenge, but the staff was already familiar with the new tests and the federal government had provided a timeline for implementation. Still, no specific instructions were provided regarding the workflow process, and management decided that staff could determine this new process.

The staff collaborated on the new workflow process and, in the end, was efficient and effective at implementing a sound and systematic plan. In addition, they believed management had respected their experience and empowered them to do what was necessary. This respect was a great motivator for the staff. They were able to take ownership of the process and enact the necessary changes to ensure all requirements were met. This example is reflective of *green zone* supervisor and subordinate performance attributes. Supervisors trusted and respected employees, thus innovation and creativity were high amongst employees. These employees were self-directed and found ownership in their work.

Unsuccessful Example of Communication, Empowerment, and Motivation

Not all attempts at effective communication lead to a success story. In a different clinical laboratory setting, similar changes were also communicated and, again, the staff was empowered to adjust their processes to best fit these changes. Unfortunately, the response from staff was non-existent. They did not engage in support of their organization or the overall facility. All parameters of changes were explained to them, but when they were asked to provide input, none came.

The manager learned a great lesson. Even when approaching the same problem, the same solution is not always effective. Why? The culture of this particular facility was such that staff blamed management for every problem, rather than taking personal ownership or initiative. Within this culture, it was difficult to negotiate long-term solutions because the staff would find faults in every solution that was proposed. When the manager asked the staff to propose a solution, no solution emerged. Attempts at various forms of communication (one-on-one, group, mediations through HR, etc.) did not resolve the situation. In this case, it is unfortunate that staff members perpetuated their own unhappiness and then continued to complain about it.

This example reflects *red zone* attributes where employees do exactly what they are told and not much more. The manager did not move beyond telling and prescribing how the employees could work and the results were unfortunate. Often *red zone* attributes can shift to better *yellow zone* attributes if supervisors would ask for help and encourage employees who have poor attitudes to contribute to the problem-solving situation.

Communication and Inspections

As one would expect, clinical laboratories are inspected on a periodic basis by a variety of regulatory agencies. These inspections are usually mandatory and unannounced. The inspector's challenge is to communicate the intent of the regulations and determine if the facility has fulfilled the requirements. The challenge for the facility under inspection is to communicate how the facility fulfills the requirements.

Communication during an inspection is crucial to the long-term success of an organization, especially a medical laboratory. If the inspection does not go well, the facility may lose its accreditation status after several poor inspections. Losing accreditation status ultimately impacts on the success of the entire organization. If a facility loses accreditation, government reimbursements for patient care may decline, which impacts the financial status of the facility.

The success or failure of an inspection hinges on the communication between the inspector and the facility under inspection. All inspections take into account a set of requirements that the facility must fulfill. The goal is to find objective evidence that demonstrates the facility is fulfilling the requirements. In this regard, communication is not difficult. It becomes a matter of "show and tell." Still, communication can become difficult when a requirement is not fulfilled as expected and the inspector is looking for "something else."

How communication is managed is crucial to the success of the inspection. The facility must communicate how they have fulfilled the requirement, how they are going to change their practice to fulfill the requirement, or possibly that they have no idea of how to fulfill the requirement. In order to be most effective, this type of communication should be earnest and constructive, void of heightened emotion.

What is the Application?

Earlier, the core values and concepts of the healthcare Baldrige criteria were listed. Inherent in these values is that leaders must communicate with employees (*green zone*). For an organization to be successful, the executive management must communicate their vision and their expectations to the staff at a level that staff will comprehend. For example, while a *dashboard* can provide executive management with a good overview of where the company stands, to a staff member it may not mean anything. Staff personnel must know what specific steps each individual can take to ensure that their department and their co-workers embody the vision and values of the hospital.

For the clinical laboratory, staff may develop a heightened awareness of the need to test morning samples and release the results before 7 a.m. Likewise, medical professionals can aim to have successful encounters with each of their patients, even if they are unable to obtain a blood sample at every visit. A successful encounter would occur when the patient understands why the professional could not get the sample, what this means to the patient, and how the professional will try again to fulfill the physician's test order.

At one facility, if the individual collecting the sample misses and has to try more than once to get a blood sample, the patient is given a gift card to the hospital gift shop or cafeteria. While these tactics do not always work, the purpose is to make something positive out of a negative situation.

In the clinical laboratory, the following examples are positive Baldrige indicators:

- Successful phlebotomy (i.e., a blood sample is obtained)
- Minimization of repeat blood collections due to sample collection problems
- Successful communication with nursing staff for all critical values (i.e., 100% compliance with the critical value read back policy)
- Successful completion of the morning tests by 7 AM 90% of the time
- 95% patient satisfaction with the laboratory
- 95% physician satisfaction with the laboratory

Many areas can be examined, including the physicians' satisfaction with laboratory services, but the bulk of the given examples relate to effective communication. Quite simply, without excellent communication, the Baldrige criteria cannot be fulfilled.

The Laws of Communication in the Clinical Laboratory

Schuttler describes the *Laws of Communication* using a stoplight metaphor. Can these laws be applied to the clinical laboratory setting? Absolutely! Management and communication are universal in their application regardless of the industry.

The Law of Communication #1: Failure of supervisors to effectively communicate with subordinates results in poor employee performance.

The Red Zone

Using the stoplight metaphor, the manager who communicates in the *red zone* uses discipline as a means to keep the department "in check." There is no consistency in direction, and the relationship can be adversarial. The best employees leave for another facility, and the employees left behind are demoralized.

In one laboratory setting, a new manager lacked the background knowledge or experience to effectively run the laboratory. He could have gathered his senior staff and best technical people for weekly or bi-weekly meetings to discuss important issues within the department. Instead, the new manager chose to make all departmental decisions without consultation and, in particular, discouraged any effort by technical staff to take initiative. His attitude was "I'm the director, and I make the decisions."

The consequences of this manager's choice came to the forefront when a new instrument was being installed in the laboratory. Normally, a manager would gather key players to establish a project plan and determine job assignments and timelines to bring the instrument within regulatory guidelines in the shortest time possible. Instead, the manager did not communicate with the employees and offered them no direction.

The project floundered, and eventually the laboratory accrued additional implementation costs because of the delay. When the manager did discuss this situation with one technical staff member, he expressed the sentiment that he thought senior technical staff "would take care of it." The senior technical staff was astonished at this expectation because their initiative had previously been squelched. The inexperienced manager had created a situation where employees had become demoralized and unproductive. It was truly a *red zone* situation.

The Yellow Zone

Schuttler states that an organization is operating in the *yellow zone* when processes are poorly communicated and management is constantly in "firefighting" mode.

A laboratory's management could find itself in this zone if a manager has poorly communicated a change in a process. One manager decided to change a step in a laboratory process when a test result was released that should not have been. Unfortunately, this manager did not think through the change and realize that, while workable on the day shift, the new plan could not work on the overnight shift. A technical staff person informed him that the proposal could not work, but the manager released the revised process without further consultation.

When the night staff received notice of the change, they were incredulous. They asked, "How can we do this? This is an unworkable proposal." Because of these restrictions, the manager's plan was only partially implemented, but all members of the technical staff were afraid to report the news to the manager, and he erroneously assumed that he had solved the problem. Instead, he had created only a partial solution and lots of confusion.

The Green Zone

The *green zone* is an ideal state from which to operate, but these situations are unfortunately rather rare. An organization will typically oscillate between the *green* and *yellow zones* or have a mixture of both, depending on the department within the organization.

One facility consistently communicated highly important financial figures, including "bottom line" and budget information, with the management staff (in another chapter of this book, Box refers to this as *Open Book Management*). The staff was able to apply this information to their areas of expertise and work to enable change. Within one particular laboratory, management discussed reimbursement costs from insurance companies and the federal government, and it was discovered that the coding for a previous test had been incorrect.

The result was that reimbursement for the test would drop by two-thirds. As such, the laboratory staff collaborated and decided to change its testing methodology to where the quality of test results would remain the same but at a lower cost. *Green zone* employee performance attributes were realized as a result of how supervisors treated and respected their subordinates.

This laboratory facility avoided financial loss because they were operating within the *green zone*. Financial information was conveyed to technical staff, which had the knowledge and expertise to implement a testing methodology with increased cost effectiveness. If this information had not been communicated, the change would not have occurred.

The Law of Communication #2: Failure of the organization to effectively communicate within results in poor organizational performance.

The Red Zone

Communication is more than just words; it is also body language. The inexperienced lab manager described in the previous *red zone* example not only had poor verbal communication skills. He also had poor body language, especially in meetings. In one particular senior staff meeting, four to five senior staff members were present in the room with this manager, each representing a section of operation within the laboratory. For whatever reason during this meeting, the manager only spoke and made eye contact with one individual. What message did this action convey to the rest of the staff who were present at the meeting? They assumed that only one person had the manager's trust and respect. The rest of the staff were present physically, but their opinions and viewpoints did not seem to matter to this manager.

The Yellow Zone

From within the *yellow zone*, policies are in constant re-work, and the organization is in constant flux.

Within one facility, the president kept changing her mind about policies and processes. Then, she would get frustrated that no projects were ever completed and that management level personnel were in constant turnover. The president eventually brought in a performance management consultant to determine what was wrong with the management personnel and why the organization could not complete its goals, and the consultant had the unfortunate task of informing the president that *she* was the problem. The president hired a executive mentor to help her improve her consistency, but the effects on the organization are still ongoing.

The Green Zone

Organizations operating from within the *green zone* know that open communication is the best kind.

At a hospital facility, a new president was hired. He was young and energetic, and he did something that had never been done at that facility. In his meetings with management staff, he included not only the manager of each department, but also the section managers of each area of the laboratory. While the meetings did fill an auditorium, all management staff within the laboratory heard the same message from the same person.

There was no "filtration" in the communication process. In addition, the president stated the same information, on a less frequent basis, to the entire hospital staff when he would hold "town hall meetings." He would also rotate his workdays and shifts so that he could be personally available to all staff at any time to answer questions about the hospital's goals and mission.

If the hospital were having financial trouble, he would openly discuss it and ask for input from the hospital staff because they worked most intimately with the patients. While some employees viewed the president's actions with skepticism, most employees felt that the president was accessible and would sincerely listen to their concerns. The hospital leader used multiple vehicles to communicate a consistent message—*green zone* attributes.

Summary

Communication, whether with employees or customers, is the cornerstone of any business. And, because clear and effective communication is vital to the success of business, Schuttler advises that management must "communicate, communicate, and then communicate just a bit more," regardless of the industry type. The Malcolm Baldrige criteria also value communication and, in particular, point to the effectiveness of communication from senior management in order to determine if the facility "walks the talk." Whether you believe your organization is ready to take on the Baldrige challenge or just wish to be more successful in your business, communication is truly essential for success.

SECTION 5
Conclusion

CHAPTER 24
COMMUNICATING EFFECTIVELY IS A LEARNED SKILL

Richard Schuttler

The *Laws of Communication,* much like any laws that govern, can be used to provide order and discipline. The stoplight metaphor offers opportunities to gain a sense of where one is—whether that is oneself or one's organization. An understanding of one's strengths and opportunities for improvement is necessary to make the transition into the *yellow* and *green zones*.

Chapter 1 presented *The Law of Attraction,* which suggests that we "attract or get what we think about." *The Law of Cause and Effect* suggests that "for each cause there is an effect that influences something else." This chapter will incorporate these laws to provide a how-to approach so that "performance can be correlated to how one communicates" individually as well as collectively. If organizational leaders plan and communicate purposely, they can easily cause performance to increase.

This chapter is divided into two sections that provide starting points to improve communications. These starting points are approached from two vantage points: first the individual and second the organization. The vantage point from the individual is also rooted in two views: the supervisor to the subordinate and the subordinate to the supervisor. The second vantage point is from the organization as an entity to its employees as well as its other stakeholders.

Organizational opportunities for improvement, such as problems and processes, can easily be maximized without large sums of money or expensive consultants. The only requirements are time and the willingness by employees at all levels to make a difference. Employees can decide to do things differently today and tomorrow, and every day thereafter if a motivational atmosphere is created and cultivated. For example, for a supervisor to employ "multiple vehicles of communication" one merely needs to talk to employees, send out related emails, hold team meetings, provide posters in a break area, encourage participation, and be visible while communicating a consistent message, and all these things cost absolutely nothing!

Organizational senior leaders can determine if they want to conduct a third-party organizational communications assessment. An assessment is a sound and systematic approach to truly gaining a snapshot in time of how an organization and its employees communicate and the effect on employee performance. An assessment quickly identifies disparities and then identifies a plan of action to follow through and move toward the *yellow* and *green zones*. The old adage of "plan your work and then work your plan" is a simple yet practical method for any change effort that will need to occur.

The 21 supplemental chapters provide multiple practical perspectives that have worked for others. Each presents best practices worthy of emulating or considering as benchmarks that can be adapted by you and your organization. What follows are simple steps to bring back to the workplace.

Vantage Point: Supervisor and Subordinate

Regardless of their level in the hierarchy, supervisors should be the first to improve relationships. Part of a supervisor's responsibility is to develop a workplace culture conducive to accomplishing work in the most effective and efficient manner. Supervisors do not need to be a best friend to each worker, but they should take the initiative to speak with each worker individually. They should also speak with all workers as a team in team meetings.

Conversely, micromanagers may think that without their strict observation and guidance, employees cannot do well on their own. What actually happens is that employees fail to live up to their own full potential because they were not mentored or trained well. Instead of being innovative and developing their own solutions to problems, micromanaged employees simply do what they are told.

Leaders who operate in the *yellow zone* are exceeding their micromanager counterparts but still falling short of their potential. Their employees will likely fail to take ownership of the processes, which greatly inhibits the team from maximizing opportunities for innovation. Only when leaders are open to ideas and aim to maximize their employees' potential are they truly engaging the full potential of their employees and teams.

The Law of Cause and Effect and the Law of Attraction in Action

When *The Law of Cause and Effect* is combined with *The Law of Attraction*, a supervisor can define the desired work atmosphere and ask workers to help achieve that atmosphere. For example, if a supervisor is changing policy guidance on a regular basis, it is probably due to processes that are neither efficient nor effective. By putting together a team of employees to determine the cause and effect of having to change guidance frequently, process improvement can begin. As processes are improved and decision-making becomes consistent over time, the work atmosphere improves, morale often increases, and workers begin talking with one another about other processes that can also be improved. This is *The Law of Cause and Effect* in action.

The Law of Cause and Effect suggests that for every cause there is an effect, and this relationship can easily be displayed in a *Cause and Effect Diagram*. Kaoru Ishikawa conceived *The Cause and Effect Diagram* in Japan during the mid-1900s when quality improvement methods were beginning to rise in popularity. To achieve higher quality standards, Ishikawa designed the cause and effect diagram to help isolate areas that needed to be improved. The diagram was also known as a "fishbone" diagram because the standard diagram, before being filled in, resembles the skeleton of a fish.

The Law of Cause and Effect is based upon simple concepts, and it is easy to educate employees in its use. It is a sound, systematic approach adopted by several world-class organizations. When used properly, the cause and effective diagram helps to solve problems by isolating root causes from symptoms. The philosophy is designed to reduce a cause to its lowest possible concern, similar to the series of steps one might go through when an automobile does not start. It is either a problem with equipment (battery, starter), the materials (gas, oil), method (process to start), or person (knowledge of how to start the car). *The Law of Cause and Effect* sheds light on why effects are good or not so good, and it is a simple tool for all to learn.

Performance Management

Supervisors should communicate regularly with subordinates. But, it is especially important for a supervisor to communicate with a subordinate during a performance review. These reviews are critical, and they need to be timely. Those supervisors who are not timely in providing performance reviews are simply not taking their accountability and responsibilities as seriously as they should. Employees want and need to know how their supervisor assesses their work.

In many instances, annual pay raises are based on the annual performance review. If a supervisor does not conduct the annual review on time, deserving pay raises may not be provided on time. This reflects poorly on the supervisor's ability to adequately communicate and care for those for whom they are accountable. Supervisors who want to operate in the *green zone* can provide meaningful and objective feedback by designing their own process to deliver accurate and timely performance evaluations for each subordinate when due—never late.

Semi-annual reviews communicate how workers are doing at meeting the annual performance goals and expectations of the jobs they are hired to perform. If only an annual performance appraisal is provided, and no semi-annual review, workers are often left not knowing what to expect, and they may experience stress from not knowing how their performance will be judged. Taking care of employees means communicating to them about their performance.

As a supervisor, providing semi-annual and annual performance reviews on time yielded my best workplace team. These reviews were coupled with short, 15-minute quarterly counseling sessions. The quarterly counseling sessions began with statements from the workers. They were encouraged to relate their accomplishments from within the three month timeframe and describe two or three strengths as well as two or three opportunities for improvement. During this meeting, we discussed each area of their performance, the placed the form in their employee file. This system was easy, quick, and communicated concern for the employees.

Based on these quarterly reviews, employees often looked for opportunities for improvement early in the year and turned them into strengths by the time their annual reviews were due. Their actions reflected initiative and desire for professional and personal growth. Their improvements helped to build confidence in the workplace, as workers made progress in areas that were not only unique to themselves, but also important to the collective team. This item alone helped achieve employee performance in the *green zone* by facilitating a motivational atmosphere.

Whatever the method, performance management must be fair and timely for all. Informal dialogs throughout reporting periods are also helpful to build relationships and gain trust. Workers want to learn, and should know, how their supervisors perceive their performance. It is difficult for employees to grow and become more accountable if they are not told what is expected or how they are doing in the work they are assigned.

For employees to communicate freely with their supervisors, they need to feel that they have been treated fairly and that they can trust their supervisors. When meaningful and objective feedback is provided on a regular basis, employees are more willing to make recommendations for improvement and offer creativity and innovation to the workplace. Regular interactive dialogs from supervisor to employee are required first to allow for workers to be willing to communicate up the organization structure.

Everyone has a responsibility to become better communicators, but leaders have more responsibility to educate themselves as to how to communicate properly because of their chosen profession to lead. Effective communication does not come easily, especially during times of frustration. Practice and awareness of personal communication shortcomings are a necessity.

Vantage Point: Organization to Employees

An organization as an entity communicates to employees and stakeholders via mission, vision, philosophy statements, as well as policies and procedures. An organization's design communicates how it will function and to what degree employees are involved in day-to-day operations. An organizational culture reflects collective morale and welfare. The most senior leaders are responsible and accountable for each of these areas. The type of talent that is hired either aligns well or does not align well with that of the culture. And, at times, the culture is such where senior executives are replaced to rebuild and realign a culture that is conducive for growth and sustainability.

Mission, Vision, and Philosophy

Organizational leaders are accountable for communicating their mission, vision, and work philosophy to employees as well as other stakeholders. In particular, supervisors need to live their organization's mission, vision, and philosophy daily, as they set the example for all other employees to emulate. Organizational leaders must all agree to support policies and procedures. When concerns need to be expressed, this dialog should occur behind closed doors, not in front of other employees.

Leaders are responsible for visioning. They must create an organizational vision so clearly articulated that others can transform it from concept to reality. This is not to suggest that leaders can simply relinquish their ideas to others. Leaders need to assume accountability for their vision and involve others who control organizational resources. They are responsible for creating excitement for their ideas throughout the organization. To do so, they must communicate their insights, intentions, and expectations for the future.

Innovative and creative leaders are those who can see a better future than what the organization is experiencing, regardless of how successful they are or are not at the moment. These leaders do not see problems—they see future opportunities and challenges. World class businesses have leaders that are innovative in how they view the future, and the greatest leaders are able to invoke passion and actions in others. Leaders who can communicate their vision create the motivational atmosphere for others to be inspired.

Leaders are responsible for communicating the philosophy for how customers, suppliers, and all stakeholders will be treated. A leader sets expectations and then creates the organization's culture and tone. Leaders will be judged through their daily interactions with those in and outside the organization. Businesses in many ways act as a family unit. Children will learn how to treat others by imitating their parents and by observing their actions. In many instances, employees emulate their leaders in the same manner as children emulate their parents.

Workers need to hear consistency in what is spoken, written, or implied throughout the organization. Rumors can quickly run rampant through an organization and hurt morale, cause a lack of trust, and cause good workers to do less or quit. Employees just want to know the truth. Good or bad news, financial trouble, failing industry, it does not matter—employees need to know the truth about what is going on around them. People can deal with and overcome concerns and problematic areas if they know the scope and potential impact.

Walk the Talk comes from the notion that leaders will *do as they say* and set a positive example. Vice-Presidents, Department Heads, and Division Leaders need to have a consistent message. Success in senior positions comes from developing teams that are innovative, creative, and energetic. Poor or inconsistent communications will result in employees who are fearful, uncertain about their future, and resentful.

Self-Directed Work Teams

One of the best ways an organization can improve how employees communicate is to provide them more opportunities to collaborate. Movement through the *yellow zone* to the *green zone* occurs when organizational leaders purposely create a culture to allow employees to work together for the common good of all concerned. Increased employee productivity comes when employees are able to work together in a manner that is supportive and encouraging. Workplace teams have been known to increase communication at, and through, all levels of an organization as well as with stakeholders who are suppliers and to customers and end users.

Increasing productivity and reducing the costs of doing business do not just happen by putting five employees in a conference room every Tuesday afternoon for an hour and telling them to fix problems or improve processes. World class businesses, such as those applying for the American Society for Quality International Team Excellence Award (http://wcqi.asq.org/team-competition/participants.html), know how to implement teams to efficiently plan and develop both problem solving methods and improvement projects based on customer needs and expectations.

Achieving success through teamwork can and should be easy, but what makes it that way is a basic structure for empowering employees to work together. Positive and measurable results should be obtained each time a team is chartered. A simple yet efficient structure with minimal training can be employed in an organization of any size.

Customers and stakeholders are demanding the highest levels of service while expecting lower prices. Corporate leaders are concerned with increasing profits and maximizing resources. Both of these objectives help an organization to thrive, and results decrease costs for customers and add value to the product or service.

As Self-Directed Work Teams (SDWT) are empowered, these two corporate goals should always be kept in mind:

- How to generate revenue producing a return on investment
- How to save money and other limited valuable resources

Teamwork can promote cooperation and open communication across departments and across other organizational boundaries to include the supply chain. One person may have good insight and may be able to affect certain changes, but teamwork provides several options and opinions that can create change and increase stakeholder satisfaction on a much broader scale. When change needs to occur across departments, cross-functional teamwork lends itself to the accomplishment of this task. When everyone in an organization works together toward a mutual mission, everyone involved will feel like an owner of the change effort and do their best to make the quest successful. Teamwork is contagious, and customers like dealing with successful organizations.

Workplace Team Structure

Organizations with self-directed workplace teams commonly adopt a simple three-tiered approach. The top tier consists of the senior-level management group commonly referred to as the *Executive Steering Committee*, the second tier *Management Board*, and the third tier *Self-Directed Work Teams*.

The Executive Steering Committee (ESC) is usually chaired by the Chief Executive Officer (or the equivalent) and consists of senior level management in the organization (Vice-Presidents or Department Heads). The rationale for these leaders on the steering committee is that they direct and control organizational resources (budget, employees, and capital). The committee's responsibilities and functions consist primarily of the following:

- Implementing and developing the management philosophy in the organization
- Leading transformation
- Instilling the quality philosophy
- Developing the organization's long- and short-term strategic plans
- Providing the external customer focus
- Chartering management boards to translate customer requirements into quality products and services

The ESC will then charter a Management Board. A Management Board (MB) consists of cross-functional process owners or department managers. This group of departmental managers has a better understanding of day-to-day operations than ESC members, and often acts as the conduit from senior level executives to front-line workers. The MB's responsibilities and functions consist primarily of the following:

- Planning for change
- Introducing a sense of ownership in workers by encouraging participation in customer-focused teams
- Developing a plan for improvement aimed at the needs of the customer
- Chartering self-directed work teams to fix problems and to improve processes

Management boards, in turn, charter self-directed work teams (SDWT). These teams consist of employees who operate and manage specific processes and are often those who communicate directly with the customer base. The responsibilities of SDWTs are collecting data, identifying impediments and problems, removing special causes not inherent in a process design, and helping to establish process capability that will ultimately provide customer satisfaction.

The measures taken by chartered SDWTs are to identify critical processes within a significant process, to stabilize them, and to continually improve their process (or to find new ways to meet customers' needs). The integrated team approach strives to optimize resources and to improve continually in order to meet customers' needs today and in the future.

Under this integrated systematic philosophy, organizational leaders at all levels understand what teams are in place and what the purpose of each team is. Communicating in this team-like environment can be uncomplicated and manageable—everyone is connected.

This three-tiered approach allows for maximum communication opportunities from senior-level leadership to the front-line workers involved with customers and other stakeholders. When communication responsibilities are established for each team member in each tier, one point of contact—or *link*—in of the three tiers can actively ensure that the tier is aware of progress as well as impediments.

Two Types of Teams

Self Directed Work Teams are designed to identify and fix problems or to improve existing products or services. Problem solving teams are usually assigned to address specific problems by finding and eliminating these problems' root causes. These teams also provide training for improved processes, develop the standard operating procedures to be maintained, and design metrics and measurements to follow up on new process implementation.

Improvement teams either enrich an existing product, service, or process or they develop and install a new product, service, or process. With improvement teams, the root causes of problems may not be known or available. Often an improvement team is designed to improve a process by reducing cycle time or reducing the costs of doing business. In any circumstance, the rationale, role, and purpose of any improvement team should be explained to all employees who might be affected by the changes the team makes or recommends.

All SDWTs, regardless of their function, should have measurable and defined outcomes, a common goal or goals, and the appropriate team skills to enable success. In the beginning, a team should include a team facilitator who can provide dynamic and just-in-time training to keep the team efficient and effective. This facilitator will work closely with the team leader to ensure the reason the team was charter is achieved.

Teams need to determine what the current situation is and what the ideal future situation might be. An analysis of data may be required to identify possible improvements or root causes. Often, working with customers to gauge their concerns requires the skill of articulation. That is, a team should be able to communicate clearly and unambiguously. The ability to clearly communicate is required at all levels in every organization.

When there is untimely communication, lack of direction, unclear goals, and a lack of leadership presence, employees become frustrated because the consistency of purpose is not clear. Often there is enough communication between the employees to keep it out of the *red zone*, but when information is inconsistent, fragmented, and usually inaccurate, even those with the best intentions will slide into the *red zone*. Also, promising employees quickly move on to other positions with clear challenges and goals under a different leader, usually in another company. The *Laws of Communication* can and should be used to train senior leaders, midlevel leaders and managers, and all other employees. The *Laws* provide governing rules and clear-cut lines between danger (*red zone*), risk (*yellow zone*), and success (*green zone*).

Conclusion

The *Laws of Communication* reviewed the importance of effective communication in the workplace and the direct correlation effective communication has on increased performance within the organization. The effectiveness of the communication between leaders and their direct reports determines the level of success the team will achieve. The more effective the communication, the more successful the team will be. Consequently, poor communication leads to assumptions that often result in frustrated workers and poor performance.

The concepts provided in the *Laws of Communication* and in the supplemental chapters suggest examples of three different zones (red, yellow, and green) that correlate performance based on the communication between leaders and employees. In the *red zone*, team morale, communication, and performance are low. The team does not work well together, and turnover is high. In the *yellow zone*, communication is better than in the *red zone*, and the team has some success but also has some failures and struggles with maintaining consistency. In the *green zone*, team morale, communication, and performance are high. The team works well together, and employees want to work in this environment.

One perspective that holds true from the *Laws of Communication* and from the authors of the 21 supplemental chapters is the suggestion that communicating effectively comes from well-developed relationships. Without trust and respect, no matter what is communicated, it will not be received well. The fundamental aspects of workplace communications have far less to do with grand mission statements, ideal market conditions, desires to serve a customer, or the need for one's professional advancement than how one person treats another, as well as how an organization's culture is aligned.

To move from the *red zone* into the *yellow zone*, or from the *yellow zone* into the *green zone*, requires leaders who are able to cultivate relationships that create an atmosphere of trust where all employees are able to safely, without fear or stress, communicate up and down the organization's structure. Cultivating a culture of unity calls for continual efforts by all concerned to make today better than yesterday and tomorrow better than today. Organizations would benefit greatly if they offered the teachings of the *Laws of Communication* to their managers and leaders, as an understanding of how leadership and communication affect employee performance is essential for success.

REFERENCES

Adams, R., Magoteaux, S., Matz, V., Stiefel-Francis, C., & Westerheide, J. (2003). *The board member's guide: Making a difference on your board and in your community.* Columbus, OH: The Academy for Leadership and Governance.

American Hotel & Lodging Association (AHLA) (2007a). *Lodging industry profile.* Retrieved on December 16, 2007 from http://www.ahla.com/products_info_center_lip_2007.asp.

American Hotel & Lodging Association (AHLA) (2007b). *Top 50 hotel companies.* Retrieved on December 16, 2007 from http://www.ahla.com/products_info_center_top50.asp.

American Nurses Association, Inc. (n.d.). *Nurses and smoking: It's a union issue.* Retrieved on March 19, 2008 from http://nursingworld.org/DocumentVault/TobaccoFreeNurses/NursesandSmokingItsaUnionIssue.aspx.

Associated Press (2005). *Hospitals ban smoking everywhere on campus.* Retrieved on March 9, 2008 from http://www.wqad.com/Global/story.asp?S=3427319.

Berry, J. M. & Arons, D. F. (2003). *A voice for nonprofits.* Washington, D.C.: The Brookings Institute.

Blanchard, K. (1999). *The Heart of a Leader.* Tulsa, OK: Honor Books.

Buhler, P. M. (1999, February). Managing in the 90s: Opening up management communication: Learning from open book management. *Supervision,* 16-18.

Burns, J. M. (1978). *Leadership.* New York: Harper & Row.

Business Roundtable (2002). *Principles of corporate governance.* Retrieved on August 29, 2007 from http://www.businessroundtable.org/pdf/704.pdf#search='The%20Business%20Roundtable%20Principles%20of%20Corporate%20Governance.

Case, J. (1998, May). HR learns how to open the books. *Human Resources Magazine*, 71.

Casey, J. J. (2004). Developing harmonious university-industry partnerships. *Dayton Law Review, 30,* 251-52.

Chambers, N. (1997, July). Ownership gets big; ownership culture. *American Management Association Management Review*, 5.

Christenson, C. (1997). *The Innovator's Dilemma*. Boston: Harvard Business School Press.

Cooke, R. (1996, February). The value of an open book. *Credit Union Management*, 32-33.

Council on Foundations (2007). *Fact sheet. Community Foundations*. Retrieved on August 29, 2007 from http://www.cof.org/Members/content.cfm?Item Number=1281.

Covey, S. R. (2005). *The 8th Habit: From Effectiveness to Greatness*. New York: Free Press.

Dalton, J. C. (1999a, March). Between the lines the hard truth about open-book management. *CFO,* 58-64.

Dalton, J. C. (1999b, March). Salaries still a sacred cow, *CFO,* 61.

Fee, E., & Brown, T. M. (2004). Hospital smoking bans and their impact [Electronic version]. *American Journal of Public Health, 94*(2), 185.

Foundation Center (2007). *Key facts about community foundations*. Retrieved on August 29, 2007 from http://foundationcenter.org/gainknowledge/research/pdf/keyfacts_corp_2007.pdf.

Frumkin, P. (2002). *On Being Nonprofit: A Conceptual and Policy Primer*. Cambridge, MA: Harvard University Press.

Gast, E. (2006). *Community foundation handbook: What you need to know*. Washington, D.C.: Council on Foundations.

Gardner, J. W. (1990). *On Leadership*. New York: The Free Press.

Ginter, P. M., Swayne, L. E., & Duncan, W. J. (2002). *Strategic Management of Healthcare Organizations* (4th ed.). Malden, MA: Blackwell Publishing.

Goris, J. R., Vaught, B. C., & Pettit, J. D. (2000). Effects of communication direction on job performance and satisfaction: A moderated regression analysis. *The Journal of Business, 37*, 348-364.

Government-University-Industry Research Roundtable Annual Report (2002). Retrieved on April 12, 2008 from http://www7.nationalacademies.org/guirr/index.html.

Hackathorn, R. (2004). Real time to real value. Retrieved on January 1, 2008 from http://www.dmreview.com.

Hamel, G. (2000). *Leading the Revolution: How to Thrive in Turbulent Times by Making Innovation a Way of Life*. New York: Penguin Putnam.

Heesen, B. (2008). Retrieved on February 8, 2008 from www.heesenonline.de.

Hersey, P., Blanchard, K. H., & Johnson, D. E. (2001). *Management of Organizational Behavior: Leading Human Resources* (8th ed.). Upper Saddle River, NJ: Prentice Hall.

Hrebiniak, L. (2005). *Making Strategy Work: Leading Effective Execution and Change.* Upper Saddle River, NJ: Wharton School Publishing.

Industrial Research Institute (2008). Retrieved April 12, 2008 from http://www.iriinc.org.

Jue, A. (2006). *Leadership Moments: Turning Points that Changed Lives and Organizations*. Victoria, BC, Canada: Trafford Publishing.

Kaplan, R. S., & Norton, D. P. (2001). *The Strategy-Focused Organization: How Balanced Scorecard Companies Thrive in the New Business Environment.* Boston: Harvard Business School Press.

Kouzes, J. M., & Posner, B. Z. (2002). *The Leadership Challenge.* San Francisco: Jossey-Bass.

Lawler, E. E. (2006). *Built to Change.* San Francisco: Jossey-Bass.

Leininger, M. (1991, April/May). Transcultural nursing: The study and practice field. *Imprint*, pp. 55-65.

Maini, B. S., & Morrel-Samuels, P. (2006, September/October). Cascading improvements in communication: Adopting a new approach to organizational communication. *The Physician Executive, 38.*

Managing by the (open) book (1995, July). *Supervisory Management,* 1, 6.

Mehrabian, A. (1971). *Silent Messages*. Belmont, CA: Wadsworth.

Millman, D. (1993). *The Life You Were Born to Live*. Canada: New World Library.

Mills, A. J. (1988). Organizational acculturation and gender discrimination. In P. K. Kresl (Ed.), *Canadian Issues, XI—Women and the Workplace*: 1-22. Montreal: Association of Canadian Studies/International Council for Canadian Studies.

Miranda, G., & Thiel, K. (2007). Improving organizational speed and agility. *McKinsey Quarterly, 2007*(1), 14-15.

Moody, D., & Walsh, P. (1999). Measuring the value of information: An asset valuation approach. Proceedings of the 7th European Conference on Information Systems (ECIS '99). Copenhagen, Denmark, June 23-25, 1999, pp. 496-512.

Moorcroft, D. (2003, October/November). Linking communication strategy with organizational goals. *Strategic Communication Management, 7*(6), 24-27.

Mulaik, J. S., Megenity, J., Cannon, R., Chance, K. S., Cannella, K., Garland, L. M., & Gilead, M. P. (1991). Patients' perception of nurses' use of touch. *Western Journal of Nursing Research 13*(3), 306-323.

National Council of University Research Administrators (2008). Retrieved on April 12, 2008 from http://www.ncura.edu.

National Restaurant Association (NRA) (2007). Restaurant industry facts. Retrieved on December 17, 2007 from http://www.restaurant.org/research/ind_glance.cfm.

Nichols, R., & Stevens, L. (in press). Listening to people. In *Harvard Business Review on Effective Communication* (1999). Boston, MA: Harvard Business School Press.

Niven, P. R. (2002). *Balanced Scorecard Step-by-Step: Maximizing Performance*. New York: John Wiley & Sons.

Perry, P. (1998, November 30). Opening your book to profit. *Management,* 104.

Prince, C. J. (1999, July/August). Does open-book really work? *Chief Executive*, 24.

Rayburn, J. (2007). A matter of trust (and more). *Public Relations Tactics, 14*(3), 21.

Roberts, C., & Shea, L. J. (1999). Top management teams in the hotel industry. *The Journal of Applied Hospitality Management*, 2(1), 72-87.

Roberts, C., & Shea, L. J. (2003). A comparison of hotel executive teams in Singapore and the USA. *Quest*. Singapore Hotel Association: Singapore.

Robertson, P., & Matthews, S. (1997, May). Like an open book. *CA Magazine*, 33-35.

Rossouw, G. J. & van Vuuren, L. J. (2003). Modes of managing morality: A descriptive model of strategies for managing ethics. *Journal of Business Ethics, 46*(4). Retrieved November 7, 2005 from University of Phoenix eResources.

Ruesch, J. (1961). *Therapeutic Communication*. New York: Norton.

SAP (2008). Retrieved on February 11, 2008 from www.sap.com.

Scinta, J. (2007, July/August). Where more R&D dollars should go. *Harvard Business Review*, 26.

Senge, P. (1994). *The Fifth Discipline*. New York: Doubleday.

Shea, L. J., & Roberts, C. (2002). Trends in hotel industry top management team composition: A longitudinal analysis—Phase 2. *The Journal of Applied Hospitality Management*, 5(1), 116-133.

Shortell, S. M., & Kaluzny, A. D. (2000). *Healthcare Management: Organizational Design and Behavior* (4th ed.). Albany, NY: Delmar Thompson Learning.

Smoking health care workers not wanted: At Cleveland Clinic smokers could lose jobs (2005, July 5). Retrieved March 12, 2008 from http://abcnews.go.com/GMA/Health/story?id=909135.

Sonnefeld, J., & Ward, A. (2007). *Firing Back: How Great Leaders Rebound After Career Disasters.* Boston: Harvard Business School Press.

Stack, J. (1992). *The Great Game of Business.* New York: Doubleday.

Sutton, R. (2007). Como sobreviver no escritório. Manual para resistir aos chefes truculentos. *Epoca*. Ed., 469.

The Joint Commission on Accreditation of Healthcare Organizations (2007). *Standards*. Retrieved July 28, 2007 from The Joint Commission on Accreditation of Healthcare Organizations Web Site: http://www.jointcommission.org.

The need to know (1999, September). *Inc.,* 107.

The shift to open-book management (1998, May 15). *Financial Executives Institute Financial Executive*, 50.

University-Industry Demonstration Partnership (2008). Retrieved April 12, 2008 from www.uidp.org/about_uidp.

U. S. Bureau of Labor Statistics (2005). *Charting the U. S. labor market in 2005.* Chart 4.6. Electronically retrieved on October 17, 2006 from http://stats.bls.gov/cps/labor2005/chart4-6.pdf.

Ward, A. J., Lankau, M. J., Amason, A. C., Sonnenfeld, J. A., & Agle, B. R. (2007). *Improving the performance of top management teams.* MIT Sloan Management Review: Cambridge.

Watson Wyatt Worldwide (2003/2004). Connecting organizational communication to financial performance. *Communication ROI Study*. New York: Author.

Watson Wyatt Worldwide (2006/2007). Debunking the myths of employee engagement. *WorkUSA® Survey Report.* New York: Author.

Watson Wyatt Worldwide (2007/2008). Playing to win in a global economy. *Global Strategic Rewards® Report and United States Findings*. New York: Author.

Webster's Encyclopedic Unabridged Dictionary of the English Language (1996). New York, NY: Random House.

Wiersema, W. H. (1998, December). Should management open its books to employees? *Electrical Apparatus,* 47-49.

Wikipedia (2007). Retrieved on June 15, 2007 from http://de.wikipedia.org/wiki/Business_Intelligence.

Wuthnow, R. (2002). United States: Bridging the privileged and the marginalized? In R. D. Putman (Ed.), *Democracies in Flux: The Evolution of Social Capital in Contemporary Society* (pp. 59-102). New York: Oxford University Press.

Zukav, G. (1990). *The Seat of the Soul.* New York: Fireside.

AUTHOR'S BIOGRAPHY

Richard Schuttler, Ph.D.

Dr. Richard Schuttler is an international public speaker, educator, and author. He has 20 years of diversified, domestic and international management and leadership improvement expertise within academia, federal/state governments, and Fortune 1000 environments developing strategies and implementation methods. He has mentored executives, faculty, and students from around the world in a variety of professional leadership and management settings. He is the owner of Organizational Troubleshooter, LLC (www.orgtroubleshooter.org).

Dr. Schuttler served as Dean at the University of Phoenix (*Business Week*'s 2004 #3 Hot Growing Companies) where he was responsible for the Doctor of Management in Organizational Leadership and Doctor of Business Administration degree programs that experienced tremendous growth during his five-year tenure. Richard has an extensive and proven assessment background applying the Malcolm Baldrige National Quality Awards criteria. He is a Senior Member with the American Society for Quality and has served as a judge with the International Team Excellence Award program criteria.

Richard served in the U.S. Navy and retired after 23 years of honorable service. He earned his Ph.D. in Applied Management and Decision Sciences from Walden University. His research and consulting background is with quantitative and qualitative methods in multiple industries focusing on improving efficiency and effectiveness with people and process.

More information on the *Laws of Communication* and its companion *Supervisor Leadership and Communication Inventory* can be found online at www.lawsofcomm.com and www.slci.ws. Richard can be reached directly via email at DrRich@slci.ws.